ॐ

ॐ

सीताराम

ॐ ॐ ॐ ॐ ॐ ॐ ॐ ॐ ॐ

ॐ ॐ ॐ ॐ ॐ ॐ ॐ ॐ ॐ ॐ ॐ ॐ

ॐ ॐ ॐ ॐ ॐ ॐ ॐ ॐ ॐ ॐ ॐ ॐ ॐ

ॐ ॐ ॐ ॐ ॐ ॐ ॐ ॐ ॐ ॐ ॐ ॐ ॐ ॐ ॐ ॐ ॐ

ॐ ॐ ॐ ॐ ॐ ॐ ॐ ॐ ॐ ॐ ॐ ॐ ॐ ॐ ॐ ॐ ॐ ॐ ॐ ॐ

ॐ ॐ ॐ ॐ ॐ ॐ ॐ ॐ ॐ ॐ ॐ ॐ ॐ ॐ ॐ ॐ ॐ ॐ ॐ ॐ

ॐ ॐ ॐ ॐ ॐ ॐ ॐ ॐ ॐ ॐ ॐ ॐ ॐ ॐ ॐ ॐ ॐ

vivekacūḍāmaṇi

विवेकचूडामणि

Belongs to

Published by: only **RAMA** only

(an Imprint of e1i1 Corporation)

Title: **Vivekachudamani of Shankaracharya**

Sub-Title: **the Fiery Crest-Jewel of Wisdom, Pocket-sized Edition.**

Author-Translator: **Vidya Wati**

This Journal is derived from the Vivekachū□āudamani composed in Sanskrit millenniums ago by **Bhagawāna Adi Shankaracharya** of Bharat Varsha (prehistoric India)

Identifiers

ISBN: **978-1-945739-79-8** (Paperback)

—⌘—

This Book is also available in a Journal format:

The Fiery Crest-Jewel of Wisdom, Shankara's Vivekachūḍāmani:

My Self: the Ātmā Journal -- A Daily Journey of Self Discovery

ISBN: **978-1-945739-41-5** (Paperback)

(365 page Journal Book with space for taking notes and journaling your daily thoughts)

—⌘—

This Book is also available in regular book size: 6.14"x 9.21 as:

ISBN: **978-1-945739-44-6** (Paperback)

ISBN: **978-1-945739-45-3** (Hardback)

—⌘—

www.e1i1.com -- www.OnlyRama.com

Our books can be bought online, or at Amazon, or any bookstore.

If a book is not available at your neighborhood bookstore they will be happy to order it for you.

(Certain Hardcover Editions may not be immediately available—we apologize)

Some of our Current/Forthcoming Books are listed below. This is a partial list and we are continually adding new books.

- **Tulsi Ramayana—Holy Book of Hindus:** Ramcharitmanas with English Translation/Transliteration
- **Ramcharitmanas:** Ramayana of Tulsidas with Transliteration (in English)
- **Sundarakanda:** The Fifth-Ascent of Tulsi Ramayana
- **Bhagavad Gita, The Holy Book of Hindus:** Sanskrit Text, English Translation/Transliteration
- **My Bhagavad Gita Journal:** Journal for recording your everyday thoughts alongside the Gita
- **Rama Hymns:** Hanuman-Chalisa, Rāma-Raksha-Stotra, Nama-Ramayanam etc.
- **Legacy Books - Endowment of Devotion (several):** Legacy Journals for Writing the Rama Name alongside Sacred Hindu Scriptures like the Bhagavad Gita, Hanuman-Chalisa, Rāma-Raksha-Stotra, Bhushumdi-Ramayana, Nama-Ramayanam, Rama-Shata-Nama-Stotra
- **Rama Jayam - Likhita Japam Rama-Nama Mala alongside Sacred Hindu Texts (several):** Journals for Writing the Rama Name 100,000 Times alongside various Hindu Texts
- **Vivekachudamani, Fiery Crest-Jewel of Wisdom:** My Self: the Ātmā Journal -- A Daily Journey of Self Discovery
- **Ashtavakra Gītā, the Fiery Octave:** My Self: the Ātmā Journal
- **The Fiery Gem of Wisdom:** My Self: the Ātmā Journal
- **Avadhoota Gītā**

A Brief Note

Vivekachūḍāmani, the classic of Vedanta philosophy, is a blessing bestowed upon humanity by the Supreme Master Bhagwāna Adi Shankarāchārya born several hundred years ago. The exact date of Shankara's advent is lost in the depths of history but based on the records of the cardinal institutions Shankara founded, he likely lived from 509-477 BC, passing away at the age of 32.

Consolidating the highest flights of Vedic thoughts Shankara presented the doctrine of *Advaita Vedanta* through several of his Sanskrit treatises which discuss the unity of the *Jiva* (individual soul) and *Brahama* (the Supreme Reality). His works are considered the bedrock of *Advaita Vedanta* philosophy.

In his higher works like this one—aptly named Vivekachudamani (an exquisite Crest-jewel of the Highest-wisdom)—it might appear that Shankara is criticizing practices such as work and ritualistic worship because such practices would, after all, only further strengthen the notion that the Self within us is different from the Supreme-Self. This "notion-of-separation" is wrong from the Vedantic point of view because he who insists that I am 'this' here, and Brahama is 'that' there, has not really understood Brahama. However one should realize that this state of perceived-oneness is a very high state and in the beginning all the many observances of Vedic Dharma are very much necessary to lay down and build the foundations of spiritual life. As Shankara himself points out: Self-knowledge is gained when one's mind is first purified by an ethical life which observes *Yamas* such as no-violence, no-stealing etc., and *Niyamas* such as purity, contentment etc. Elsewhere Shankara has specifically emphasized the need for such ethics—especially during the *Brahamacharya* (early) phase—stating that the lack of it causes the downfall of aspirants. So despite some verses in this work where Shankara exhorts that attainment of Self-Realization can never come about through work and rituals, it is safe to conclude that such preparatory work is most certainly necessary to prepare one in one's spiritual journey; and then once having arrived at the doorsteps of Liberation, all dualistic practices must necessarily be discarded before stepping across that all important threshold. Or else, one simply fails to enter *Nirvana*, the realm of non-duality.

— ॐ —

The teachings in this book are based on the path of *Sanyasa-Yoga*—that of complete renunciation. Be warned, this is an extremely stern path, suited only for a rare few. Most everyone else would do better following the easier paths laid out in the Vedic Dharma: that of *Karma-Yoga* (the way of Action) and that of *Bhakti-Yoga* (the way of Devotion). The Bhagawada Gitā and the Ramāyana of Tulsidāsa are two excellent scriptures which guide aspirants along these paths.

Saints of the *Bhakti* genre (such as Sant Tulsidāsa) affirm that Bhakti and chanting the Rāmā Nāma in itself is enough to gain divine grace. This is no contradiction. The Vedic Dharma shows humanity several paths for deliverance from sufferings and gaining complete bliss, and it allows us freedom in choosing which path to follow—in line with our inner nature and our circumstances and station in life. Because the course of human life is winding and often goes through many twists and turns, so whatever principal path we may choose to follow in our spiritual pursuit, we will certainly benefit by traversing the other paths from time to time in order to gain a better understanding of things.

Notwithstanding the severity of the path of complete renunciation the teachings and conclusions of this work are nevertheless very much valid for all of us. To the extent that all paths merge in the end—and that Vedic Dharma exhorts us to eventually embrace renunciation, especially in the last quarter of life—the teachings given here will serve us well at some juncture in life. Finally it is well to remember that renunciation is the ultimate fate that none can escape: because one day death will forcibly take everything away from us—even this body which we so fondly cherish.

The translation given in this book is by no means verbatim; it is merely a feeble attempt to present the gist—with many superfluous words added to expound on the meaning. A scrupulous reader could do better referencing the other excellent translations and commentaries on this great classic should they so desire. We take solace in the fact that Shankara himself cautions against cherry-picking phrases and nitpicking meanings as long as the underlying theme or purport is understood.

—ॐ—

शङ्कराचार्यविरचितं
śaṅkarācāryaviracitaṁ

॥ विवेकचूडामणिः ॥

vivekacūḍāmaṇiḥ

सर्ववेदान्तसिद्धान्तगोचरं तमगोचरम् ।
sarvavedāntasiddhāntagocaraṁ tamagocaram ,
गोविन्दं परमानन्दं सद्गुरुं प्रणतोऽस्म्यहम् ॥ १ ॥
govindaṁ paramānandaṁ sadguruṁ praṇato'smyaham (1)

1. I venerate as my *Sadguru*: Govinda, of the nature of the Supreme-Bliss, beyond the reach of speech and mind, known only in the light of Vedānta.

जन्तूनां नरजन्म दुर्लभमतः पुंस्त्वं ततो विप्रता
jantūnāṁ narajanma durlabhamataḥ puṁstvaṁ tato vipratā
तस्माद्वैदिकधर्ममार्गपरता विद्वत्त्वमस्मात्परम् ।
tasmādvaidikadharmamārgaparatā vidvattvamasmātparam ,
आत्मानात्मविवेचनं स्वनुभवो ब्रह्मात्मना संस्थितिः
ātmānātmavivecanaṁ svanubhavo brahmātmanā saṁsthitiḥ
मुक्तिर्नो शतजन्मकोटिसुकृतैः पुण्यैर्विना लभ्यते ॥ २ ॥
muktirno śatajanmakoṭisukṛtaiḥ puṇyairvinā labhyate (2)

2. For all beings a human birth is difficult to obtain—even more so attaining to full manhood and getting instilled in the Sattvika ways of life; rarer still is a continued attachment to the path of Vedic Dharma; and higher still—erudition in the sacred lore. Striving, discriminating between the Self and not-Self, and gaining the actuality of Self-Realization—these come next in the order of rareness; and beyond that—continuing in that state of identity with Brahama and thereby achieve complete Liberation (Mukti)—that singular ascension is not attained except through the well-earned merits accumulated over hundreds of millions of births.

दुर्लभं त्रयमेवैतद्देवानुग्रहहेतुकम् ।
durlabhaṁ trayamevaitaddevānugrahahetukam ,
मनुष्यत्वं मुमुक्षुत्वं महापुरुषसंश्रयः ॥ ३ ॥
manuṣyatvaṁ mumukṣutvaṁ mahāpuruṣasaṁśrayaḥ (3)

3. There are three things that are utmost rare and directly owing to the grace of God, namely—a human birth, the longing for Liberation, and the protective care of a perfected master.

लब्ध्वा कथञ्चिन्नरजन्म दुर्लभं तत्रापि पुंस्त्वं श्रुतिपारदर्शनम् ।
labdhvā kathañcinnarajanma durlabhaṁ tatrāpi puṁstvaṁ śrutipāradarśanam ,
यस्त्वात्ममुक्तौ न यतेत मूढधीः स ह्यात्महा स्वं विनिहन्त्यसद्ग्रहात् ॥४॥
yastvātmamuktau na yateta mūḍhadhīḥ sa hyātmahā svaṁ vinihantyasadgrahāt (4)

4. He who, having by some means obtained this privileged human birth born a man—and furthermore having knowledge and learning and grasp of the sacred scriptures—does not exert himself for self-liberation, that fool is certainly committing suicide thereby—for he imperils himself by holding as life-support those very things which themselves are tenuous and unreal.

इतः को न्वस्ति मूढात्मा यस्तु स्वार्थे प्रमाद्यति ।
itaḥ ko nvasti mūḍhātmā yastu svārthe pramādyati ,
दुर्लभं मानुषं देहं प्राप्य तत्रापि पौरुषम् ॥५॥
durlabhaṁ mānuṣaṁ dehaṁ prāpya tatrāpi pauruṣam (5)

5. Is there a greater fool than the person who, having gotten this rare opportunity of a human existence—and with a masculine body to boot—still neglects to gain his own highest good and achieve the real purpose of human life?

वदन्तु शास्त्राणि यजन्तु देवान्कुर्वन्तु कर्माणि भजन्तु देवताः ।
vadantu śāstrāṇi yajantu devān kurvantu karmāṇi bhajantu devatāḥ ,
आत्मैक्यबोधेन विनापि मुक्तिर्न सिध्यति ब्रह्मशतान्तरेऽपि ॥६॥
ātmaikyabodhena vināpi muktirna sidhyati brahmaśatāntare'pi (6)

6. Let scholars cite all their scriptures, and let people perform all the *Yajnas* unto all the gods, and let them perform every ritual, and worship every deity—but without effecting the actualization of one's identity with *Brahama*—in an act of direct Self-Realization—there is no Liberation to be had; nay, not even in the lifetime of a hundred Creators put together.

अमृतत्त्वस्य नाशास्ति वित्तेनेत्येव हि श्रुतिः ।
amṛtattvasya nāśāsti vittenetyeva hi śrutiḥ ,
ब्रवीति कर्मणो मुक्तेरहेतुत्वं स्फुटं यतः ॥७॥
bravīti karmaṇo mukterahetutvaṁ sphuṭaṁ yataḥ (7)

7. "There is no immortality to be had by means of riches..." etc.,—such indeed is the authoritative pronouncement of the

Shrutis. It is abundantly clear that *Karma* (works/deeds/actions) is not the direct agent of Liberation.

अतो विमुक्त्यै प्रयतेत विद्वान् सन्न्यस्तबाह्यार्थसुखस्पृहः सन् ।
ato vimuktyai prayateta vidvān sannyastabāhyārthasukhaspṛhaḥ san ,
सन्तं महान्तं समुपेत्य देशिकं तेनोपदिष्टार्थसमाहितात्मा ॥८॥
santaṁ mahāntaṁ samupetya deśikaṁ tenopadiṣṭārthasamāhitātmā (8)

8. Therefore a man of learning should ceaselessly strive for Liberation having renounced his desire for pleasures from external objects. And having duly approached a good and generous preceptor; and from him having learnt and assimilated the teachings, he should live harmonized in that acquired wisdom, fixing his mind steadily upon the inculcated Truth.

उद्धरेदात्मनाऽऽत्मानं मग्नं संसारवारिधौ ।
uddharedātmanā''ātmānaṁ magnaṁ saṁsāravāridhau ,
योगारूढत्वमासाद्य सम्यग्दर्शननिष्ठया ॥९॥
yogārūḍhatvamāsādya samyagdarśananiṣṭhayā (9)

9. And thus having attained to the *Yogārūdha* state, he should strive for complete salvation—inundated as he is in this ocean of births and deaths—by means of firm devotion to right knowledge: the knowledge by which one discriminates the Real from the non-Real.

सन्न्यस्य सर्वकर्माणि भवबन्धविमुक्तये ।
sannyasya sarvakarmāṇi bhavabandhavimuktaye ,
यत्यतां पण्डितैर्धीरैरात्माभ्यास उपस्थितैः ॥१०॥
yatyatāṁ paṇḍitairdhīrairātmābhyāsa upasthitaiḥ (10)

10. And having commenced the practice of Realization of the Self (finding who 'I' am), let that wise and erudite person eventually give up all works—and thus rent asunder all the bonds of *Karmas* that have ensnared the *Jiva* in this web of births and deaths.

चित्तस्य शुद्धये कर्म न तु वस्तूपलब्धये ।
cittasya śuddhaye karma na tu vastūpalabdhaye ,
वस्तुसिद्धिर्विचारेण न किञ्चित्कर्मकोटिभिः ॥११॥
vastusiddhirvicāreṇa na kiñcitkarmakoṭibhiḥ (11)

11. On its own, work cannot impart Self-Realization (the attainment of Oneness between the Self and the Supreme-Self). Work may lead to the purification of mind but never to the direct perception of Reality. Verily the attainment of Reality (Self-Realization) is brought about only through the act of

Intellect—the discrimination of the Real from the non-Real—and not in the least by tens of millions of worldly actions.

सम्यग्विचारतः सिद्धा रज्जुतत्त्वावधारणा ।
samyagvicārataḥ siddhā rajjutattvāvadhāraṇā ,
भ्रान्तोदितमहासर्पभयदुःखविनाशिनी ॥ १२ ॥
bhrāntoditamahāsarpabhayaduḥkhavināśinī (12)

12. Fear and anxiety—caused by encountering a 'snake' (which's actually hallucination worked up in the deluded Mind upon seeing some rope in the dark)—is removed when the conviction of the reality of rope is gained through adequate reasoning (when things have been put to light). Similarly anxiety and misery within the deluded mind—conjured up due to this delusive universe—is removed only in light of the Truth of Self.

अर्थस्य निश्चयो दृष्टो विचारेण हितोक्तितः ।
arthasya niścayo dṛṣṭo vicāreṇa hitoktitaḥ ,
न स्नानेन न दानेन प्राणायमशतेन वा ॥ १३ ॥
na snānena na dānena prāṇāyamaśatena vā (13)

13. The Truth is to be realized within the Self; and by the Self—beginning with Inquiry, and Hearing the salutary counsel of the wise, and one's own Reasoning and Experiencing. Neither sacred baths nor any amount of charity nor even hundreds of daily *Prānāyāmas* can substitute for Direct Realization.

अधिकारिणमाशास्ते फलसिद्धिर्विशेषतः ।
adhikāriṇamāśāste phalasiddhirviśeṣataḥ ,
उपाया देशकालाद्याः सन्त्यस्मिन्सहकारिणः ॥ १४ ॥
upāyā deśakālādyāḥ santyasminsahakāriṇaḥ (14)

14. The success in this struggle depends essentially on the qualified aspirant—with time, place and other such means being but auxiliary in this regard.

अतो विचारः कर्तव्यो जिज्ञासोरात्मवस्तुनः ।
ato vicāraḥ kartavyo jijñāsorātmavastunaḥ ,
समासाद्य दयासिन्धुं गुरुं ब्रह्मविदुत्तमम् ॥ १५ ॥
samāsādya dayāsindhuṁ guruṁ brahmaviduttamam (15)

15. So having duly approached a Master—who should be the best of the Knowers of *Brahama,* and an ocean of mercy—the seeker of the Reality of Self should take to the path of Inquiry, Hearing, Reasoning, and direct Experiencing.

मेधावी पुरुषो विद्वानूहापोहविचक्षणः ।
medhāvī puruṣo vidvānūhāpohavicakṣaṇaḥ ,
अधिकार्यात्मविद्यायामुक्तलक्षणलक्षितः ॥ १६ ॥
adhikāryātmavidyāyāmuktalakṣaṇalakṣitaḥ (16)

16. An intelligent and learned person—skilled in arguing in favor of the scriptures and in refuting counter-arguments against them—one who has such characteristics is a fit recipient of the knowledge of the *Ātmā*.

विवेकिनो विरक्तस्य शमादिगुणशालिनः ।
vivekino viraktasya śamādiguṇaśālinaḥ ,
मुमुक्षोरेव हि ब्रह्मजिज्ञासायोग्यता मता ॥ १७ ॥
mumukṣoreva hi brahmajijñāsāyogyatā matā (17)

17. He who discriminates between the Real and the non-Real, whose mind is turned away from the non-Real, who possesses calmness and the allied virtues, who has a yearning for freedom—he alone who has these characteristics, is a fit recipient of the Knowledge of *Brahama*, the supreme Reality.

साधनान्यत्र चत्वारि कथितानि मनीषिभिः ।
sādhanānyatra catvāri kathitāni manīṣibhiḥ ,
येषु सत्स्वेव सन्निष्ठा यदभावे न सिध्यति ॥ १८ ॥
yeṣu satsveva sanniṣṭhā yadabhāve na sidhyati (18)

18. Regarding this, sages have spoken of four essential qualifications, which alone being present, the Devotion to *Brahama* succeeds; and in the absence of which, it fails.

आदौ नित्यानित्यवस्तुविवेकः परिगण्यते ।
ādau nityānityavastuvivekaḥ parigaṇyate ,
इहामुत्रफलभोगविरागस्तदनन्तरम् ।
ihāmutraphalabhogavirāgastadanantaram ,
शमादिषट्कसम्पत्तिर्मुमुक्षुत्वमिति स्फुटम् ॥ १९ ॥
śamādiṣaṭkasampattirmumukṣutvamiti sphuṭam (19)

19. The first enumerated is the Discrimination between the Real and the non-Real; next is Aversion to the enjoyment of the fruits of work—in this life or hereafter; then comes Calmness etc.,—the group of Six-Treasures; and lastly is clearly the Yearning for Liberation itself.

ब्रह्म सत्यं जगन्मिथ्येत्येवंरूपो विनिश्चयः ।
brahma satyaṁ jaganmithyetyevaṁrūpo viniścayaḥ ,
सोऽयं नित्यानित्यवस्तुविवेकः समुदाहृतः ॥ २० ॥
so'yaṁ nityānityavastuvivekaḥ samudāhṛtaḥ (20)

20. "*Brahama* alone is Real (self-existent), and the universe non-Real (not self-existent)"—the insight, discernment, and firm conviction by which one comprehends this Vedic dictum: that is designated to be *Viveka* (or Discrimination between the Real and the non-Real).

तद्वैराग्यं जिहासा या दर्शनश्रवणादिभिः ।
tadvairāgyaṁ jihāsā yā darśanaśravaṇādibhiḥ ,
देहादिब्रह्मपर्यन्ते ह्यनित्ये भोगवस्तुनि ॥ २१ ॥
dehādibrahmaparyante hyanitye bhogavastuni (21)

21. Transient as they are, the desire to give up of all ephemeral delights of sense-objects—like sight, touch etc., that have their origin in the realm of the non-Real—ranging from the enjoyments derived through the body of mortals to that of king of gods—that is designated to be *Vairāgya* (or Renunciation).

विरज्य विषयव्राताद्दोषदृष्ट्या मुहुर्मुहुः ।
virajya viṣayavrātāddoṣadṛṣṭyā muhurmuhuḥ ,
स्वलक्ष्ये नियतावस्था मनसः शम उच्यते ॥ २२ ॥
svalakṣye niyatāvasthā manasaḥ śama ucyate (22)

22. The tranquil state of the mind—where it rests steadfastly upon the avowed goal (Self-Realization), after having detached itself from the manifold sense-objects through a relentless observation of their defects—that is designated to be *Shama* (or Calmness).

विषयेभ्यः परावर्त्य स्थापनं स्वस्वगोलके ।
viṣayebhyaḥ parāvartya sthāpanaṁ svasvagolake ,
उभयेषामिन्द्रियाणां स दमः परिकीर्तितः ।
ubhayeṣāmindriyāṇāṁ sa damaḥ parikīrtitaḥ ,
बाह्यानालम्बनं वृत्तेरेषोपरतिरुत्तमा ॥ २३ ॥
bāhyānālambanaṁ vṛttereṣoparatiruttamā (23)

23. Turning both kinds of sense-organs (that of knowledge and that of action) away from their marks (sense-objects), and holding them restrained to their respective centers—that is designated to be *Dama* (or self-control). The best *Uparati* (self-withdrawal) is that state where the mind always abides in complete Quietude, gaining total freedom from the influences of external objects.

सहनं सर्वदुःखानामप्रतीकारपूर्वकम् ।
sahanaṁ sarvaduḥkhānāmapratīkārapūrvakam ,
चिन्ताविलापरहितं सा तितिक्षा निगद्यते ॥ २४ ॥
cintāvilāparahitaṁ sā titikṣā nigadyate (24)

24. The bearing of all afflictions without caring to redress them, now or in the future, remaining ever free from any feeling of anxiety, lament, or revenge on account of them—that is designated to be *Titikshā* (or forbearance).

शास्त्रस्य गुरुवाक्यस्य सत्यबुद्ध्यवधारणम् ।
śāstrasya guruvākyasya satyabuddhyavadhāraṇam ,
सा श्रद्धा कथिता सद्भिर्यया वस्तूपलभ्यते ॥२५॥
sā śraddhā kathitā sadbhiryayā vastūpalabhyate (25)

25. Accepting with a firm resolve as true—that which the Scriptures and the Gurus indoctrinate—this is designated by sages to be *Shraddhā* (or Faith), which is highly conducive to the perception of Reality.

सर्वदा स्थापनं बुद्धेः शुद्धे ब्रह्मणि सर्वदा ।
sarvadā sthāpanaṁ buddheḥ śuddhe brahmaṇi sarvadā ,
तत्समाधानमित्युक्तं न तु चित्तस्य लालनम् ॥२६॥
tatsamādhānamityuktaṁ na tu cittasya lālanam (26)

26. Not the mere indulgence of thought (out of curiosity), but complete contemplation—a constant concentration of the intellect upon the ever-pure *Brahama*—that is designated to be *Samādhāna* (or self-settledness).

अहङ्कारादिदेहान्तान् बन्धानज्ञानकल्पितान् ।
ahaṅkārādidehāntān bandhānajñānakalpitān ,
स्वस्वरूपावबोधेन मोक्तुमिच्छा मुमुक्षुता ॥२७॥
svasvarūpāvabodhena moktumicchā mumukṣutā (27)

27. An intense yearning for Freedom—to be released of all bondages, from that of egoism to that of body, to be relieved of all thralldoms superimposed by dint of Ignorance—by realizing one's Real Nature: that is designated to be *Mumukshutā* (or Longing for Liberation).

मन्दमध्यमरूपापि वैराग्येण शमादिना ।
mandamadhyamarūpāpi vairāgyeṇa śamādinā ,
प्रसादेन गुरोः सेयं प्रवृद्धा सूयते फलम् ॥२८॥
prasādena guroḥ seyaṁ pravṛddhā sūyate phalam (28)

28. Even though this *Mumukshutā* be torpid or moderate to begin with, yet it will become developed by other means like *Vairāgya*, *Shama* etc., to eventually bear fruit—with the added blessings of the guru.

वैराग्यं च मुमुक्षुत्वं तीव्रं यस्य तु विद्यते ।
vairāgyaṁ ca mumukṣutvaṁ tīvraṁ yasya tu vidyate ,
तस्मिन्नेवार्थवन्तः स्युः फलवन्तः शमादयः ॥२९॥
tasminnevārthavantaḥ syuḥ phalavantaḥ śamādayaḥ (29)

29. And if it be so that *Mumukshutā* burns quite bright in the heart even at the very outset, then those other means like *Vairāgya*, *Shama* etc., really have a meaningful impact in the yielding of desired end.

एतयोर्मन्दता यत्र विरक्तत्वमुमुक्षयोः ।
etayormandatā yatra viraktatvamumukṣayoḥ ,
मरौ सलिलवत्तत्र शमादेर्भानमात्रता ॥३०॥
marau salilavattatra śamāderbhānamātratā (30)

30. But where this *Mumukshutā* is only seeming and simply too dull and insipid, then the other means like *Vairāgya*, *Shama* etc., too are rendered decrepit and illusory—like the appearance of mirage in a desert, void of real substance.

मोक्षकारणसामग्र्यां भक्तिरेव गरीयसी ।
mokṣakāraṇasāmagryāṁ bhaktireva garīyasī ,
स्वस्वरूपानुसन्धानं भक्तिरित्यभिधीयते ॥३१॥
svasvarūpānusandhānaṁ bhaktirityabhidhīyate (31)

31. Among the means most conducive to Liberation, *Bhaktī* holds a supreme spot. A constant contemplation and seeking of one's true Self, one's Real Nature—that is designated to be *Bhaktī* (Devotion).

स्वात्मतत्त्वानुसन्धानं भक्तिरित्यपरे जगुः ।
svātmatattvānusandhānaṁ bhaktirityapare jaguḥ ,
उक्तसाधनसम्पन्नस्तत्त्वजिज्ञासुरात्मनः ।
uktasādhanasampannastattvajijñāsurātmanaḥ ,
उपसीदेद्गुरुं प्राज्ञं यस्माद्बन्धविमोक्षणम् ॥३२॥
upasīdedguruṁ prājñaṁ yasmādbandhavimokṣaṇam (32)

32. A ceaseless Inquiry into the Truth—to discover the gist of Existence, the essence of the *Ātmā*—that is maintained to be *Bhaktī* by others. One who has the above mentioned qualifications and is desirous to know the Truth of the Self, should approach an illumined Master for gaining emancipation from these worldly thralldoms.

श्रोत्रियोऽवृजिनोऽकामहतो यो ब्रह्मवित्तमः ।
śrotriyo'vṛjino'kāmahato yo brahmavittamaḥ ,
ब्रह्मण्युपरतः शान्तो निरिन्धन इवानलः ।
brahmaṇyuparataḥ śānto nirindhana ivānalaḥ ,
अहेतुकदयासिन्धुर्बन्धुरानमतां सताम् ॥ ३३ ॥
ahetukadayāsindhurbandhurānamatāṁ satām (33)

33. One who is sinless, unsmitten by desires, well-versed in the Vedas; one who is a par-excellence Knower-of-*Brahama* and continually abides in That Supreme Reailty; of a fiery calm—like the silent fire which has consumed its fuel; one who is a boundless reservoir of mercy which requires no reason to confer grace; one who is a friend to all the good people who have sought refuge in him—

तमाराध्य गुरुं भक्त्या प्रह्वप्रश्रयसेवनैः ।
tamārādhya guruṁ bhaktyā prahvapraśrayasevanaiḥ ,
प्रसन्नं तमनुप्राप्य पृच्छेज्ज्ञातव्यमात्मनः ॥ ३४ ॥
prasannaṁ tamanuprāpya pṛcchejjñātavyamātmanaḥ (34)

34. —making reverence to that Master with devotion; and approaching him when he is pleased with prostration, humility, service etc.,—the disciple should then put forth his inquiry:

शिष्य उवाच :
śiṣya uvāca :

स्वामिन्नमस्ते नतलोकबन्धो कारुण्यसिन्धो पतितं भवाब्धौ ।
svāminnamaste natalokabandho kāruṇyasindho patitaṁ bhavābdhau ,
मामुद्धरात्मीयकटाक्षदृष्ट्या ऋज्व्यातिकारुण्यसुधाभिवृष्ट्या ॥ ३५ ॥
māmuddharātmīyakaṭākṣadṛṣṭyā ṛjvyātikāruṇyasudhābhivṛṣṭyā (35)

35. The disciple says: O master, O friend of those that have come seeking refuge, O thou ocean of mercy, I bow to thee. Please save me, fallen as I am in this worldly sea of births and deaths; save me with a straightforward glance of thy eyes, which shed nectar-like grace supreme.

दुर्वारसंसारदवाग्नितप्तं दोधूयमानं दुरदृष्टवातैः ।
durvārasaṁsāradavāgnitaptaṁ dodhūyamānaṁ duradṛṣṭavātaiḥ ,
भीतं प्रपन्नं परिपाहि मृत्योः शरण्यमन्यद्यदहं न जाने ॥ ३६ ॥
bhītaṁ prapannaṁ paripāhi mṛtyoḥ śaraṇyamanyadyadahaṁ na jāne (36)

36. Save me from Death—burning as I am in this blazing inferno of worldly forest, tossed violently hither and thither by the winds of these savage storm of misfortunes. I am frightened

inside and out and have come seeking refuge—and other than thee I know of no other sanctuary.

शान्ता महान्तो निवसन्ति सन्तो वसन्तवल्लोकहितं चरन्तः ।
śāntā mahānto nivasanti santo vasantavallokahitaṁ carantaḥ ,
तीर्णाः स्वयं भीमभवार्णवं जनानहेतुनान्यानपि तारयन्तः ॥३७॥
tīrṇāḥ svayaṁ bhīmabhavārṇavaṁ janānahetunānyānapi tārayantaḥ (37)

37. There are good souls, equanimous and magnanimous, who do good to others even as does the season of spring, and who—having themselves crossed this dreadful ocean of births and deaths—help others cross the same with no selfish motive whatsoever.

अयं स्वभावः स्वत एव यत्परश्रमापनोदप्रवणं महात्मनाम् ।
ayaṁ svabhāvaḥ svata eva yatparaśramāpanodapravaṇaṁ mahātmanām ,
सुधांशुरेष स्वयमर्ककर्कशप्रभाभितप्तामवति क्षितिं किल ॥३८॥
sudhāṁśureṣa svayamarkakarkaśaprabhābhitaptāmavati kṣitiṁ kila (38)

38. Indeed it is the very nature of the generous to voluntarily remove the afflictions of others—even as the moon of its own accord cools the earth parched by the flaming sunrays.

ब्रह्मानन्दरसानुभूतिकलितैः पूतैः सुशीतैर्युतै-
brahmānandarasānubhūtikalitaiḥ pūtaiḥ suśītairyutai-
र्युष्मद्वाक्कलशोज्झितैः श्रुतिसुखैर्वाक्यामृतैः सेचय ।
ryuṣmadvākkalaśojjhitaiḥ śrutisukhairvākyāmṛtaiḥ secaya ,
संतप्तं भवतापदावदहनज्वालाभिरेनं प्रभो
saṁtaptaṁ bhavatāpadāvadahanajvālābhirenaṁ prabho
धन्यास्ते भवदीक्षणक्षणगतेः पात्रीकृताः स्वीकृताः ॥३९॥
dhanyāste bhavadīkṣaṇakṣaṇagateḥ pātrīkṛtāḥ svīkṛtāḥ (39)

39. O master, let thy ambrosial speech—sweetened by the enjoyment of the elixir-like bliss of *Brahama*, pure, cooling, issuing in streams from thy lips as though from a cool water pitcher, so pleasing to the ear—shower down like a rainfall upon me: who am being seared with these worldly afflictions as though from the flaming tongues of a forest fire. Blessed are those upon whom even a passing glance of thy eyes alights, accepting them as thine own.

कथं तरेयं भवसिन्धुमेतं का वा गतिर्मे कतमोऽस्त्युपायः ।
kathaṁ tareyaṁ bhavasindhumetaṁ kā vā gatirme katamo'styupāyaḥ ,
जाने न किञ्चित्कृपयाऽव मां प्रभो संसारदुःखक्षतिमातनुष्व ॥४०॥
jāne na kiñcitkṛpayā'va māṁ prabho saṁsāraduḥkhakṣatimātanuṣva (40)

40. How to cross this ocean of temporal existence? What is my ultimate terminus, and what my fate? What means should I

adopt to traverse through life?—of all such matters, I know absolutely naught. Please condescend to save me, O master, and describe at length how to put an end to this misery of worldly existence.

तथा वदन्तं शरणागतं स्वं संसारदावानलतापतप्तम् ।
tathā vadantaṁ śaraṇāgataṁ svaṁ saṁsāradāvānalatāpataptam ,
निरीक्ष्य कारुण्यरसार्द्रदृष्ट्या दद्यादभीतिं सहसा महात्मा ॥४१॥
nirīkṣya kāruṇyarasārdradṛṣṭyā dadyādabhītiṁ sahasā mahātmā (41)

41. Tormented by the afflictions of the world—which is like a forest on fire—as the disciple thus speaks with great anguish, earnestly beseeching his aegis, the saint—with his eyes softened with pity—casts a benign glance of grace upon him and spontaneously bids him give up all fear.

विद्वान् स तस्मा उपसत्तिमीयुषे मुमुक्षवे साधु यथोक्तकारिणे ।
vidvān sa tasmā upasattimīyuṣe mumukṣave sādhu yathoktakāriṇe ,
प्रशान्तचित्ताय शमान्विताय तत्त्वोपदेशं कृपयैव कुर्यात् ॥४२॥
praśāntacittāya śamānvitāya tattvopadeśaṁ kṛpayaiva kuryāt (42)

42. Unto him—who has thus sought shelter thirsting for Liberation, who abides obediently by the injunctions of scriptures, who is of calm demeanor and of serene mind—the sage proceeds to inculcate the highest Truth out of the utmost kindness of heart.

श्रीगुरुवाच :
śrīguruvāca :

मा भैष्ट विद्वंस्तव नास्त्यपायः संसारसिन्धोस्तरणेऽस्त्युपायः ।
mā bhaiṣṭa vidvaṁstava nāstyapāyaḥ saṁsārasindhostaraṇe'styupāyaḥ ,
येनैव याता यतयोऽस्य पारं तमेव मार्गं तव निर्दिशामि ॥४३॥
yenaiva yātā yatayo'sya pāraṁ tameva mārgaṁ tava nirdiśāmi (43)

43. The Master says: Fear not, O learned one, there is no death for thee; verily there is a sovereign means of crossing this sea of relative existence. That very supreme path, treading which our ancient sages of yore have managed to go beyond—that very way I shall now inculcate to thee.

अस्त्युपायो महान्कश्चित्संसारभयनाशनः ।
astyupāyo mahānkaścitsaṁsārabhayanāśanaḥ ,
तेन तीर्त्वा भवाम्भोधिं परमानन्दमाप्स्यसि ॥४४॥
tena tīrtvā bhavāmbhodhiṁ paramānandamāpsyasi (44)

44. Verily there is one Supreme Way which puts an end to the fear of relative existence. And through that thou shalt cross this sea of *Samsāra* and attain to Bliss-Supreme.

वेदान्तार्थविचारेण जायते ज्ञानमुत्तमम् ।
vedāntārthavicāreṇa jāyate jñānamuttamam ,
तेनात्यन्तिकसंसारदुःखनाशो भवत्यनु ॥४५॥
tenātyantikasaṁsāraduḥkhanāśo bhavatyanu (45)

45. Reasoning upon the import of Vedānta leads to Knowledge most sublime; and this Knowledge is forthwith succeeded by an immediate destruction of every misery born of relative existence.

श्रद्धाभक्तिध्यानयोगान्मुमुक्षोः मुक्तेर्हेतून्वक्ति साक्षाच्छ्रुतेर्गीः ।
śraddhābhaktidhyānayogānmumukṣoḥ mukterhetūnvakti sākṣācchrutergīḥ,
यो वा एतेष्वेव तिष्ठत्यमुष्य मोक्षोऽविद्याकल्पिताद्देहबन्धात् ॥४६॥
yo vā eteṣveva tiṣṭhatyamuṣya mokṣo'vidyākalpitāddehabandhāt (46)

46. The practices of *Shraddhā* (Faith), *Bhaktī* (Devotion) and *Dhyāna-Yoga* (Meditation)—these are declared in the scriptures to be the immediate expedients that aid the seeker in attaining to Liberation; and whosoever follows these disciplines, ensured is his freedom from these bondages that have been forged by Nescience.

अज्ञानयोगात्परमात्मनस्तव ह्यनात्मबन्धस्तत एव संसृतिः ।
ajñānayogātparamātmanastava hyanātmabandhastata eva saṁsṛtiḥ ,
तयोर्विवेकोदितबोधवह्निः अज्ञानकार्यं प्रदहेत्समूलम् ॥४७॥
tayorvivekoditabodhavahniḥ ajñānakāryaṁ pradahetsamūlam (47)

47. Verily it is through the touch of Ignorance that thou, who art the Supreme Self, find thyself under the shackles of the not-Self—and whence alone proceed these rounds of births and deaths. The Fiery Knowledge—kindled through discrimination between the Self and the not-Self—burns up the effects of Nescience entirely, right down to the very roots.

शिष्य उवाच :
śiṣya uvāca :

कृपया श्रूयतां स्वामिन्प्रश्नोऽयं क्रियते मया ।
kṛpayā śrūyatāṁ svāminpraśno'yaṁ kriyate mayā ,
यदुत्तरमहं श्रुत्वा कृतार्थः स्यां भवन्मुखात् ॥४८॥
yaduttaramahaṁ śrutvā kṛtārthaḥ syāṁ bhavanmukhāt (48)

48. The disciple says: Condescend to listen, O Master, to the questions which I now put. If I could be blessed with the answers straight from your lips, I shall feel most gratified.

को नाम बन्धः कथमेष आगतः कथं प्रतिष्ठास्य कथं विमोक्षः ।
ko nāma bandhaḥ kathameṣa āgataḥ kathaṁ pratiṣṭhāsya kathaṁ vimokṣaḥ,
कोऽसावनात्मा परमः क आत्मा तयोर्विवेकः कथमेतदुच्यताम् ॥४९॥
ko'sāvanātmā paramaḥ ka ātmā tayorvivekaḥ kathametaducyatām (49)

49. What forsooth is Bondage? How has it come upon the Self? How it continues to persist? How is one to be freed of it entirely? What is the not-Self? Who or what is the Supreme Self? And what is Discrimination—through which one differentiates between the Self and the not-Self? Do please delineate upon these subjects and expatiate in great details, O Master.

श्रीगुरुवाच :
śrīguruvāca :

धन्योऽसि कृतकृत्योऽसि पावितं ते कुलं त्वया ।
dhanyo'si kṛtakṛtyo'si pāvitaṁ te kulaṁ tvayā ,
यदविद्याबन्धमुक्त्या ब्रह्मीभवितुमिच्छसि ॥५०॥
yadavidyābandhamuktyā brahmībhavitumicchasi (50)

50. The Guru replied: Blessed are you—in that you quest after life's objective and have thusly sanctified your family and lineage—in that you wish to attain to *Brahama*, the Absolute Being, by freeing yourself from the bondages of Ignorance!

ऋणमोचनकर्तारः पितुः सन्ति सुतादयः ।
ṛṇamocanakartāraḥ pituḥ santi sutādayaḥ ,
बन्धमोचनकर्ता तु स्वस्मादन्यो न कश्चन ॥५१॥
bandhamocanakartā tu svasmādanyo na kaścana (51)

51. A father may have his sons and others to redeem him from his financial debts, but there is no one other than one's own Self to deliver one from the within bondages that are upon the Self (and which are self-imposed).

मस्तकन्यस्तभारादेर्दुःखमन्यैर्निवार्यते ।
mastakanyastabhārāderduḥkhamanyairnivāryate ,
क्षुधादिकृतदुःखं तु विना स्वेन न केनचित् ॥५२॥
kṣudhādikṛtaduḥkhaṁ tu vinā svena na kenacit (52)

52. Troubles—such as that caused by a burden upon the head—can be readily removed by an outsider, but to end the within

anguish—like hunger, pain etc.,—one oneself must endeavor to be rid of these.

पथ्यमौषधसेवा च क्रियते येन रोगिणा ।
pathyamauṣadhasevā ca kriyate yena rogiṇā ,
आरोग्यसिद्धिर्दृष्टाऽस्य नान्यानुष्ठितकर्मणा ॥५३॥
ārogyasiddhirdṛṣṭā'sya nānyānuṣṭhitakarmaṇā (53)

53. He alone is seen to recover from a malady who takes the proper food and supplements himself, through his own body—not if such restitutions are undertaken on his behalf by another.

वस्तुस्वरूपं स्फुटबोधचक्षुषा स्वेनैव वेद्यं न तु पण्डितेन ।
vastusvarūpaṁ sphuṭabodhacakṣuṣā svenaiva vedyaṁ na tu paṇḍitena ,
चन्द्रस्वरूपं निजचक्षुषैव ज्ञातव्यमन्यैरवगम्यते किम् ॥५४॥
candrasvarūpaṁ nijacakṣuṣaiva jñātavyamanyairavagamyate kim (54)

54. The true nature of Reality is to be known personally through the eyes of clear illumination, in an act of first-hand direct experience—and not through the preachings of others. The beauty of the Moon must be enjoyed in person by one's own eyes. Can one truly experience it from sermons imparted by another?

अविद्याकामकर्मादिपाशबन्धं विमोचितुम् ।
avidyākāmakarmādipāśabandhaṁ vimocitum ,
कः शक्नुयाद्विनात्मानं कल्पकोटिशतैरपि ॥५५॥
kaḥ śaknuyādvinātmānaṁ kalpakoṭiśatairapi (55)

55. Who else but one's own self can rid one of the bondages caused by the fetters of the within ignorance, desires, actions etc.? None; not even in a billion years?

न योगेन न साङ्ख्येन कर्मणा नो न विद्यया ।
na yogena na sāṅkhyena karmaṇā no na vidyayā ,
ब्रह्मात्मैकत्वबोधेन मोक्षः सिध्यति नान्यथा ॥५६॥
brahmātmaikatvabodhena mokṣaḥ sidhyati nānyathā (56)

56. Neither by Yoga, nor by Sānkhya, nor by work, nor by learning can Liberation be gained, or bestowed—the only appointed means is a direct in-person Actualization. Only by the Realization of Oneness—between the Self and the Supreme-Self—is Liberation attained, and there simply is no other way.

वीणाया रूपसौन्दर्यं तन्त्रीवादनसौष्ठवम् ।
vīṇāyā rūpasaundaryaṁ tantrīvādanasauṣṭhavam ,
प्रजारञ्जनमात्रं तन्न साम्राज्याय कल्पते ॥५७॥
prajārañjanamātraṁ tanna sāmrājyāya kalpate (57)

57. The lovely form of the *Veena* and the mastery of playing on its chords—serves only to please the others; they do nothing for the Self, they do not suffice to impart emancipation.

वाग्वैखरी शब्दझरी शास्त्रव्याख्यानकौशलम् ।
vāgvaikharī śabdajharī śāstravyākhyānakauśalam ,
वैदुष्यं विदुषां तद्वद्भुक्तये न तु मुक्तये ॥५८॥
vaiduṣyaṁ viduṣāṁ tadvadbhuktaye na tu muktaye (58)

58. A fancy speech full of mellifluent words, and the skill in expounding the scriptures, and also eruditeness and scholarship—all these may bring acclaim and some personal enjoyment to the scholar, but they are no good for bringing about his Liberation.

अविज्ञाते परे तत्त्वे शास्त्राधीतिस्तु निष्फला ।
avijñāte pare tattve śāstrādhītistu niṣphalā ,
विज्ञातेऽपि परे तत्त्वे शास्त्राधीतिस्तु निष्फला ॥५९॥
vijñāte'pi pare tattve śāstrādhītistu niṣphalā (59)

59. Study and rote learning of Scriptures is useless if the highest Truth remains unassimilated and uncomprehended; and that study is equally futile once the highest Truth has been obtained.

शब्दजालं महारण्यं चित्तभ्रमणकारणम् ।
śabdajālaṁ mahāraṇyaṁ cittabhramaṇakāraṇam ,
अतः प्रयत्नाज्ज्ञातव्यं तत्त्वज्ञैस्तत्त्वमात्मनः ॥६०॥
ataḥ prayatnājjñātavyaṁ tattvajñaistattvamātmanaḥ (60)

60. The maze of scriptural texts is a dense forest which causes the mind to ramble about wandering lost in its confounding labyrinths; instead cutting straight to the chase, a genuine seeker of Reality should forthwith find the true nature of his Self in all earnestness, without any loss of time.

अज्ञानसर्पदष्टस्य ब्रह्मज्ञानौषधं विना ।
ajñānasarpadaṣṭasya brahmajñānauṣadhaṁ vinā ,
किमु वेदैश्च शास्त्रैश्च किमु मन्त्रैः किमौषधैः ॥६१॥
kimu vedaiśca śāstraiśca kimu mantraiḥ kimauṣadhaiḥ (61)

61. For one who has been bitten by the deadly serpent of Ignorance, the only remedy is the knowledge of *Brahama*. Of what avail is the recitation of the Vedas and scriptures and mantras and similar concoctions to one who is in the terminal state of a terrible malady?

न गच्छति विना पानं व्याधिरौषधशब्दतः ।
na gacchati vinā pānaṁ vyādhirauṣadhaśabdataḥ ,

विनाऽपरोक्षानुभवं ब्रह्मशब्दैर्न मुच्यते ॥ ६२ ॥
vinā'parokṣānubhavaṁ brahmaśabdairna mucyate (62)

62. A sickness is not cured by merely repeating the name of the medication—one must actually ingest the pill; likewise, without direct Realization, one will not be Liberated merely by hearing and discoursing on *Brahama*.

अकृत्वा दृश्यविलयमज्ञात्वा तत्त्वमात्मनः ।
akṛtvā dṛśyavilayamajñātvā tattvamātmanaḥ ,
ब्रह्मशब्दैः कुतो मुक्तिरुक्तिमात्रफलैर्नृणाम् ॥ ६३ ॥
brahmaśabdaiḥ kuto muktiruktimātraphalairnṛṇām (63)

63. Without causing the objective universe to vanish, and without realizing the true nature of the Self, how can one achieve full Liberation by merely talking of *Brahama*? It would just be a wasted effort of speech.

अकृत्वा शत्रुसंहारमगत्वाखिलभूश्रियम् ।
akṛtvā śatrusaṁhāramagatvākhilabhūśriyam ,
राजाहमिति शब्दान्नो राजा भवितुमर्हति ॥ ६४ ॥
rājāhamiti śabdānno rājā bhavitumarhati (64)

64. Without eliminating his enemies and without bringing the entire region under the dominion of his sword, one cannot legitimately claim to be a king by simply proclaiming, "Listen, I am a monarch".

आप्तोक्तिं खननं तथोपरिशिलाद्युत्कर्षणं स्वीकृतिं
āptoktiṁ khananaṁ tathopariśilādyutkarṣaṇaṁ svīkṛtiṁ
निक्षेपः समपेक्षते न हि बहिःशब्दैस्तु निर्गच्छति ।
nikṣepaḥ samapekṣate na hi bahiḥśabdaistu nirgacchati ,
तद्वद्ब्रह्मविदोपदेशमननध्यानादिभिर्लभ्यते
tadvadbrahmavidopadeśa-mananadhyānādibhirlabhyate
मायाकार्यतिरोहितं स्वममलं तत्त्वं न दुर्युक्तिभिः ॥ ६५ ॥
māyākāryatirohitaṁ svamamalaṁ tattvaṁ na duryuktibhiḥ (65)

65. For it to be owned, a hidden treasure-trove requires proper identification and an exact location, and then excavation and removing of the rocks; and thereafter there is the unearthing of the treasure-chest, and finally laying hands upon the gold—and the treasure doesn't come out by merely calling out its name. Similarly the Treasure of the Self—which has been hidden deep under by *Māyā* and her forces—is to be possessed through the competent instructions of a knower of *Brahama*, followed by reflection, meditation, and so forth—and it cannot be gained merely with lengthy discourses and convoluted arguments.

तस्मात्सर्वप्रयत्नेन भवबन्धविमुक्तये ।
tasmātsarvaprayatnena bhavabandhavimuktaye ,
स्वैरेव यत्नः कर्तव्यो रोगादाविव पण्डितैः ॥६६॥
svaireva yatnaḥ kartavyo rogādāviva paṇḍitaiḥ (66)

66. Therefore—just as in the case of bodily diseases and internal maladies—the wise should strive personally and with every means in his power, to free himself from the bondages of this dreadful transmigratory disease of repeated births and deaths.

यस्त्वयाद्य कृतः प्रश्नो वरीयाञ्छास्त्रविन्मतः ।
yastvayādya kṛtaḥ praśno varīyāñchāstravinmataḥ ,
सूत्रप्रायो निगूढार्थो ज्ञातव्यश्च मुमुक्षुभिः ॥६७॥
sūtraprāyo nigūḍhārtho jñātavyaśca mumukṣubhiḥ (67)

67. The questions that you have put up today are excellent, endorsed by those versed in the sacred lore, aphoristic, pregnant with meaning, and beneficial—which all the seekers of Liberation must needs know.

शृणुष्वावहितो विद्वन्यन्मया समुदीर्यते ।
śṛṇuṣvāvahito vidvanyanmayā samudīryate ,
तदेतच्छ्रवणात्सद्यो भवबन्धाद्विमोक्ष्यसे ॥६८॥
tadetacchravaṇātsadyo bhavabandhādvimokṣyase (68)

68. So hearken with attention, O learned one, to what I am going to say; listen and follow earnestly, and forthwith you shall be freed from the bondages of *Samsāra*—this dire ocean of worldly existence.

मोक्षस्य हेतुः प्रथमो निगद्यते वैराग्यमत्यन्तमनित्यवस्तुषु ।
mokṣasya hetuḥ prathamo nigadyate vairāgyamatyantamanityavastuṣu ,
ततः शमश्चापि दमस्तितिक्षा न्यासः प्रसक्ताखिलकर्मणां भृशम् ॥६९॥
tataḥ śamaścāpi damastitikṣā nyāsaḥ prasaktākhilakarmaṇāṁ bhṛśam (69)

69. The first step towards Liberation is an extreme aversion to everything that is perishable and impermanent; then follow calmness, self-control, forbearance, and utter relinquishment of all *Karmas* impelled by selfish motive.

ततः श्रुतिस्तन्मननं सतत्त्वध्यानं चिरं नित्यनिरन्तरं मुनेः ।
tataḥ śrutistanmananaṁ satattvadhyānaṁ ciraṁ nityanirantaraṁ muneḥ ,
ततोऽविकल्पं परमेत्य विद्वान् इहैव निर्वाणसुखं समृच्छति ॥७०॥
tato'vikalpaṁ parametya vidvān ihaiva nirvāṇasukhaṁ samṛcchati (70)

70. Thereafter comes Hearing, followed by Reflection, and then a long unbroken steady Meditation upon the sublime Truth. After that, the learned seeker attains to the supreme *Nirvikalpa*

Samādhi and thereby Realizes the highest Bliss of *Nirvana* even in this life.

यद्बोद्धव्यं तवेदानीमात्मानात्मविवेचनम् ।
yadboddhavyaṁ tavedānīmātmānātmavivecanam ,
तदुच्यते मया सम्यक् श्रुत्वात्मन्यवधारय ॥७१॥
taducyate mayā samyak śrutvātmanyavadhāraya (71)

71. Now I am going to describe to you fully of that which you must needs know: the Discrimination between the Self and the not-Self. Listen to it with attention and then carefully reflect upon it in your mind.

मज्जास्थिमेदःपलरक्तचर्म त्वगाह्वयैर्धातुभिरेभिरन्वितम् ।
majjāsthimedaḥpalaraktacarma tvagāhvayairdhātubhirebhiranvitam ,
पादोरुवक्षोभुजपृष्ठमस्तकैः अङ्गैरुपाङ्गैरुपयुक्तमेतत् ॥७२॥
pādoruvakṣobhujapṛṣṭhamastakaiḥ aṅgairupāṅgairupayuktametat (72)

72. Composed of the seven ingredients—marrow, bone, fat, flesh, blood, skin, cuticle—and comprising of the following parts—legs, thighs, chest, arms, back, head—

अहम्ममेति प्रथितं शरीरं मोहास्पदं स्थूलमितीर्यते बुधैः ।
ahammameti prathitaṁ śarīraṁ mohāspadaṁ sthūlamitīryate budhaiḥ ,
नभोनभस्वद्दहनाम्बुभूमयः सूक्ष्माणि भूतानि भवन्ति तानि ॥७३॥
nabhonabhasvaddahanāmbubhūmayaḥ sūkṣmāṇi bhūtāni bhavanti tāni (73)

73. —this body—which is the seat of the delusion of 'I' and 'mine'—is designated by sages as the Gross-body. The sky, air, fire, water, earth are the subtle elements;

परस्परांशैर्मिलितानि भूत्वा स्थूलानि च स्थूलशरीरहेतवः ।
parasparāṁśairmilitāni bhūtvā sthūlāni ca sthūlaśarīrahetavaḥ ,
मात्रास्तदीया विषया भवन्ति शब्दादयः पञ्च सुखाय भोक्तुः ॥७४॥
mātrāstadīyā viṣayā bhavanti śabdādayaḥ pañca sukhāya bhoktuḥ (74)

74. These elements, uniting with portions of one another and becoming progressively complex, go on to form the Gross-body. The subtle essences of these elements constitute the sense-objects: five in number, such as sight, sound etc., which conduce to the enjoyments by the Experiencer, the individual Soul.

य एषु मूढा विषयेषु बद्धा रागोरुपाशेन सुदुर्दमेन ।
ya eṣu mūḍhā viṣayeṣu baddhā rāgorupāśena sudurdamena ,
आयान्ति निर्यान्त्यध ऊर्ध्वमुच्चैः स्वकर्मदूतेन जवेन नीताः ॥७५॥
āyānti niryāntyadha ūrdhvamuccaiḥ svakarmadūtena javena nītāḥ (75)

75. Those fools who are tied to the sense-objects with the stout rope of attachments—so very difficult to snap, alas—repeatedly come and go, rolling up and down on the ocean-waves of births and deaths, carried amain by the powerful emissary in the form of their accumulated past *Karmas*.

शब्दादिभिः पञ्चभिरेव पञ्च पञ्चत्वमापुः स्वगुणेन बद्धाः ।
śabdādibhiḥ pañcabhireva pañca pañcatvamāpuḥ svaguṇena baddhāḥ ,
कुरङ्गमातङ्गपतङ्गमीन भृङ्गा नरः पञ्चभिरञ्चितः किम् ॥ ७६ ॥
kuraṅgamātaṅgapataṅgamīna bhṛṅgā naraḥ pañcabhirañcitaḥ kim (76)

76. The deer, the elephant, the moth, the fish and the bee—these five meet their death tied to one or other of the five senses. What then is in store for man who is attached to all the five!

दोषेण तीव्रो विषयः कृष्णसर्पविषादपि ।
doṣeṇa tīvro viṣayaḥ kṛṣṇasarpaviṣādapi ,
विषं निहन्ति भोक्तारं द्रष्टारं चक्षुषाप्ययम् ॥ ७७ ॥
viṣaṁ nihanti bhoktāraṁ draṣṭāraṁ cakṣuṣāpyayam (77)

77. Sense-objects are more venomous in their deadly effect than even the poison of king cobra. Poison kills one who ingests it, but behold: the sense-objects kill even from a distance, those who merely look at them with the eyes!

विषयाशामहापाशाद्यो विमुक्तः सुदुस्त्यजात् ।
viṣayāśāmahāpāśādyo vimuktaḥ sudustyajāt ,
स एव कल्पते मुक्त्यै नान्यः षट्शास्त्रवेद्यपि ॥ ७८ ॥
sa eva kalpate muktyai nānyaḥ ṣaṭśāstravedyapi (78)

78. He who is free from the terrible snare of the hankering after sense-objects—so hard to get rid of—he alone is fit for Liberation and none else, even though he be versed in all the six schools of philosophy.

आपातवैराग्यवतो मुमुक्षून् भवाब्धिपारं प्रतियातुमुद्यतान् ।
āpātavairāgyavato mumukṣūn bhavābdhipāraṁ pratiyātumudyatān ,
आशाग्रहो मज्जयतेऽन्तराले निगृह्य कण्ठे विनिवर्त्य वेगात् ॥ ७९ ॥
āśāgraho majjayate'ntarāle nigṛhya kaṇṭhe vinivartya vegāt (79)

79. Those who seek liberation merely ostensibly—who have only an apparent dispassion in trying to cross this ocean of worldly existence—are violently grabbed by throat by the shark of hankerings and dragged and drowned mid-way.

विषयाख्यग्रहो येन सुविरक्त्यसिना हतः ।
viṣayākhyagraho yena suviraktyasinā hataḥ ,

स गच्छति भवाम्भोधेः पारं प्रत्यूहवर्जितः ॥८०॥
sa gacchati bhavāmbhodheḥ pāraṁ pratyūhavarjitaḥ (80)

80. He alone is able to get across the ocean of *Samsāra* unimpeded who has first killed this shark—known as the sense-objects—with the sharp sword of mature dispassion.

विषमविषयमार्गैर्गच्छतोऽनच्छबुद्धेः
viṣamaviṣayamārgairgacchato'nacchabuddheḥ
प्रतिपदमभियातो मृत्युरप्येष विद्धि ।
pratipadamabhiyāto mṛtyurapyeṣa viddhi ,
हितसुजनगुरूक्त्या गच्छतः स्वस्य युक्त्या
hitasujanagurūktyā gacchataḥ svasya yuktyā
प्रभवति फलसिद्धिः सत्यमित्येव विद्धि ॥८१॥
prabhavati phalasiddhiḥ satyamityeva viddhi (81)

81. Know that death quickly overtakes the foolish person who walks the perilous path of sense-pleasures. Only he who treads the rightful path—in accordance with the instructions of a well-meaning noble guru—whose directives are borne out by his own intellectual reasoning—he alone achieves the true end; aye, know that for sure.

मोक्षस्य काङ्क्षा यदि वै तवास्ति त्यजातिदूराद्विषयान्विषं यथा ।
mokṣasya kāṅkṣā yadi vai tavāsti tyajātidūrādviṣayānviṣaṁ yathā ,
पीयूषवत्तोषदयाक्षमार्जव प्रशान्तिदान्तीर्भज नित्यमादरात् ॥८२॥
pīyūṣavattoṣadayākṣamārjava praśāntidāntīrbhaja nityamādarāt (82)

82. If indeed you have a true longing for Liberation, then shun all sense-objects from a safe distance—as if they were venomous, extremely toxic; and do always religiously cultivate within you, the nectar-like virtues of contentment, compassion, pardon, tranquility, self-control and *Ārjava* (straightliness, simplicity, sincerity, harmony).

अनुक्षणं यत्परिहृत्य कृत्यं अनाद्यविद्याकृतबन्धमोक्षणम् ।
anukṣaṇaṁ yatparihṛtya kṛtyaṁ anādyavidyākṛtabandhamokṣaṇam ,
देहः परार्थोऽयममुष्य पोषणे यः सज्जते स स्वमनेन हन्ति ॥८३॥
dehaḥ parārtho'yamamuṣya poṣaṇe yaḥ sajjate sa svamanena hanti (83)

83. Freeing oneself from the bondages of Ignorance—so tenacious and seemingly beginning-less—should be an unremitting undertaking for the seeker; whosoever leaves that aside—to instead passionately pander to the body which is an object for others to enjoy—commits suicide thereby.

शरीरपोषणार्थी सन् य आत्मानं दिदृक्षति ।
śarīrapoṣaṇārthī san ya ātmānaṁ didṛkṣati ,

ग्राहं दारुधिया धृत्वा नदीं तर्तुं स गच्छति ॥८४॥
grāhaṁ dārudhiyā dhṛtvā nadīṁ tartuṁ sa gacchati (84)

84. Whosoever seeks to realize the Self by devoting himself to the gratification of the body, is alike a delirious man attempting to ford the river by holding on to a croc—mistaking it for a log.

मोह एव महामृत्युर्मुमुक्षोर्वपुरादिषु ।
moha eva mahāmṛtyurmumukṣorvapurādiṣu ,
मोहो विनिर्जितो येन स मुक्तिपदमर्हति ॥८५॥
moho vinirjito yena sa muktipadamarhati (85)

85. For a seeker of Liberation, infatuating over things like the body etc., is dire death. Verily he alone who has thoroughly conquered this, merits the State of Freedom.

मोहं जहि महामृत्युं देहदारसुतादिषु ।
mohaṁ jahi mahāmṛtyuṁ dehadārasutādiṣu ,
यं जित्वा मुनयो यान्ति तद्विष्णोः परमं पदम् ॥८६॥
yaṁ jitvā munayo yānti tadviṣṇoḥ paramaṁ padam (86)

86. Conquer this horrific death that lies before—this infatuating over body, spouse, progeny, etc., things. Conquering over these alone have the sages of yore managed to reach the Supreme Abode of Vishnu.

त्वङ्मांसरुधिरस्नायुमेदोमज्जास्थिसङ्कुलम् ।
tvaṅmāṁsarudhirasnāyumedomajjāsthisaṅkulam ,
पूर्णं मूत्रपुरीषाभ्यां स्थूलं निन्द्यमिदं वपुः ॥८७॥
pūrṇaṁ mūtrapurīṣābhyāṁ sthūlaṁ nindyamidaṁ vapuḥ (87)

87. This Gross-body—composed as it is of skin, flesh, blood, veins, arteries, fat, marrow, bones—is quite repulsive really; and to boot it's filled with urine, feces and other offensive things.

पञ्चीकृतेभ्यो भूतेभ्यः स्थूलेभ्यः पूर्वकर्मणा ।
pañcīkṛtebhyo bhūtebhyaḥ sthūlebhyaḥ pūrvakarmaṇā ,
समुत्पन्नमिदं स्थूलं भोगायतनमात्मनः ।
samutpannamidaṁ sthūlaṁ bhogāyatanamātmanaḥ ,
अवस्था जागरस्तस्य स्थूलार्थानुभवो यतः ॥८८॥
avasthā jāgarastasya sthūlārthānubhavo yataḥ (88)

88. The Gross-body is caused by one's past *Karmas* and fashioned out of the gross elements—formed of the union of the subtle elements and other gross elements; it is the medium of experiences for the soul; and that state in which it perceives the world of gross objects, that is called its Waking-State.

बाह्येन्द्रियैः स्थूलपदार्थसेवां स्रक्चन्दनस्त्र्यादिविचित्ररूपाम् ।
bāhyendriyaiḥ sthūlapadārthasevāṁ srakcandanastryādivicitrarūpām ,

करोति जीवः स्वयमेतदात्मना तस्मात्प्रशस्तिर्वपुषोऽस्य जागरे ॥८९॥
karoti jīvaḥ svayametadātmanā tasmātpraśastirvapuṣo'sya jāgare (89)

89. Although separate and distinct, the individual soul—identifying itself with it by the means of sense-organs—enjoys physical sense-objects such as garlands, sandal-paste, mate etc., with the gross-body; hence this body is said to have the greatest play in the waking-state.

सर्वोऽपि बाह्यसंसारः पुरुषस्य यदाश्रयः ।
sarvo'pi bāhyasaṁsāraḥ puruṣasya yadāśrayaḥ ,
विद्धि देहमिदं स्थूलं गृहवद्गृहमेधिनः ॥९०॥
viddhi dehamidaṁ sthūlaṁ gṛhavadgṛhamedhinaḥ (90)

90. The Gross-body—upon which rests the Soul's entire dealings with the external world—is what a House is to the indwelling Householder,

स्थूलस्य सम्भवजरामरणानि धर्माः
sthūlasya sambhavajarāmaraṇāni dharmāḥ
स्थौल्यादयो बहुविधाः शिशुताद्यवस्थाः ।
sthaulyādayo bahuvidhāḥ śiśutādyavasthāḥ ,
वर्णाश्रमादिनियमा बहुधाऽमयाः स्युः
varṇāśramādiniyamā bahudhā'mayāḥ syuḥ
पूजावमानबहुमानमुखा विशेषाः ॥९१॥
pūjāvamānabahumānamukhā viśeṣāḥ (91)

91. Birth, decay and death are the various characteristics of the Gross-body, and stoutness, childhood etc., its different conditions. It is beholden to the many rules of the social system regarding caste, order of life etc.; and it becomes subjected to assorted worldly maladies; and it meets diverse types of treatments at the hands of society such as accolades, insult, high honor etc.

बुद्धीन्द्रियाणि श्रवणं त्वगक्षि घ्राणं च जिह्वा विषयावबोधनात् ।
buddhīndriyāṇi śravaṇaṁ tvagakṣi ghrāṇaṁ ca jihvā viṣayāvabodhanāt ,
वाक्पाणिपादा गुदमप्युपस्थः कर्मेन्द्रियाणि प्रवणेन कर्मसु ॥९२॥
vākpāṇipādā gudamapyupasthaḥ karmendriyāṇi pravaṇena karmasu (92)

92. The ears, skin, eyes, nose, tongue are the organs of cognition—which serve the Soul to know of the external world; and the speech, hands, legs, etc., are the organs of action—by which the Soul interacts with the outside.

निगद्यतेऽन्तःकरणं मनोधीः अहङ्कृतिश्चित्तमिति स्ववृत्तिभिः ।
nigadyate'ntaḥkaraṇaṁ manodhīḥ ahaṅkṛtiścittamiti svavṛttibhiḥ ,
मनस्तु सङ्कल्पविकल्पनादिभिः बुद्धिः पदार्थाध्यवसायधर्मतः ॥९३॥
manastu saṅkalpavikalpanādibhiḥ buddhiḥ padārthādhyavasāyadharmataḥ (93)

अत्राभिमानादहमित्यहङ्कृतिः ।
atrābhimānādahamityahaṅkṛtiḥ ,
स्वार्थानुसन्धानगुणेन चित्तम् ॥ ९४ ॥
svārthānusandhānaguṇena cittam (94)

93-94. *Antāhkarana*, (or the inner-organ) is called severally as *Manas* (mind), *Buddhi* (intellect), *Ahankāra* (ego), and *Chitta* (consciousness)—in accordance with the respective functions. *Manas* is so called for its considering the pros and cons of things; *Buddhi* for its property of determining the truth of objects; the *Ahankāra* for its identifying with the body as one's own Self; and *Chitta*, for its function of illuminating things it is presently engaged/interested in.

प्राणापानव्यानोदानसमाना भवत्यसौ प्राणः ।
prāṇāpānavyānodānasamānā bhavatyasau prāṇaḥ ,
स्वयमेव वृत्तिभेदाद्विकृतिभेदात्सुवर्णसलिलादिवत् ॥ ९५ ॥
svayameva vṛttibhedādvikṛtibhedātsuvarṇasalilādivat (95)

95. Likewise one and the same *Prāna* proper (vital force) becomes *Prāna, Apāna, Vyāna, Udāna* and *Samāna* according to the diversity of functions and modifications it assumes—just like gold (or water) which takes on various functional occurrences like necklace, ring, (ice, frost) etc.

वागादि पञ्च श्रवणादि पञ्च प्राणादि पञ्चाभ्रमुखानि पञ्च ।
vāgādi pañca śravaṇādi pañca prāṇādi pañcābhramukhāni pañca ,
बुद्ध्याद्यविद्यापि च कामकर्मणी पुर्यष्टकं सूक्ष्मशरीरमाहुः ॥ ९६ ॥
buddhyādyavidyāpi ca kāmakarmaṇī puryaṣṭakaṁ sūkṣmaśarīramāhuḥ (96)

96. The speech etc., Action-organs that are five; and the ear etc., Knowledge-organs five; and the group of five *Prānas*; and the aether, fire etc., five Elements; along with the discriminative Intellect, and also Nescience and Desires and Actions—these Eight 'Dominions' together comprise the sheath called the Subtle-body.

इदं शरीरं शृणु सूक्ष्मसंज्ञितं लिङ्गं त्वपञ्चीकृतभूतसम्भवम् ।
idaṁ śarīraṁ śṛṇu sūkṣmasaṁjñitaṁ liṅgaṁ tvapañcīkṛtabhūtasambhavam ,
सवासनं कर्मफलानुभावकं स्वाज्ञानतोऽनादिरुपाधिरात्मनः ॥ ९७ ॥
savāsanaṁ karmaphalānubhāvakaṁ svājñānato'nādirupādhirātmanaḥ (97)

97. Now listen: this Subtle-body—also called the *Linga*-body—is produced from out of the combinations of various subtle elements subdivisions; and it is possessed of the *Vāsanās*—the accumulated latent desires and impressions that cause the soul

to experience the fruits of past *Karmas*. This is a beginningless superimposition upon the soul, with Nescience (Ignorance of the Self) as its cause.

स्वप्नो भवत्यस्य विभक्त्यवस्था स्वमात्रशेषेण विभाति यत्र ।
svapno bhavatyasya vibhaktyavasthā svamātraśeṣeṇa vibhāti yatra ,
स्वप्ने तु बुद्धिः स्वयमेव जाग्रत् कालीननानाविधवासनाभिः ॥९८॥
svapne tu buddhiḥ svayameva jāgrat kālīnanānāvidhavāsanābhiḥ (98)

98. Distinct from the waking-state, Dream is a state of the soul where it shines by itself—expressing everything on its own. In dream the *Buddhi* itself takes on the roles of the causal agency etc.,—reveling both as the Seer and Doer—drawing from the various latent impressions of the waking-state.

कर्त्रादिभावं प्रतिपद्य राजते यत्र स्वयं भाति ह्ययं परात्मा ।
kartrādibhāvaṁ pratipadya rājate yatra svayaṁ bhāti hyayaṁ parātmā ,
धीमात्रकोपाधिरशेषसाक्षी न लिप्यते तत्कृतकर्मलेशैः ।
dhīmātrakopādhiraśeṣasākṣī na lipyate tatkṛtakarmaleśaiḥ ,
यस्मादसङ्गस्तत एव कर्मभिः न लिप्यते किञ्चिदुपाधिना कृतैः ॥९९॥
yasmādasaṅgastata eva karmabhiḥ na lipyate kiñcidupādhinā kṛtaiḥ (99)

99. In Dream, the supreme *Ātmā* shines fiery in its own glory—with *Buddhi* as its only superimposition. The *Ātmā* is not touched in the least by the activities of the *Buddhi*—abiding merely as the Witness to everything. The *Ātmā* is completely unattached, wholly holy and stainless: the unalloyed Seer unsullied by any of the works which its superimpositions may perform.

सर्वव्यापृतिकरणं लिङ्गमिदं स्याच्चिदात्मनः पुंसः ।
sarvavyāpṛtikaraṇaṁ liṅgamidaṁ syāccidātmanaḥ puṁsaḥ ,
वास्यादिकमिव तक्ष्णस्तेनैवात्मा भवत्यसङ्गोऽयम् ॥१००॥
vāsyādikamiva takṣṇastenaivātmā bhavatyasaṅgo'yam (100)

100. The Subtle-body is merely the instrument—alike the adze and assorted tools of a carpenter—for all the 'actions and interactions' of the *Ātmā*: which forsooth is of the nature of pure Intelligence. The *Ātmā* abides perfectly unattached from it.

अन्धत्वमन्दत्वपटुत्वधर्माः सौगुण्यवैगुण्यवशाद्धि चक्षुषः ।
andhatvamandatvapaṭutvadharmāḥ sauguṇyavaiguṇyavaśāddhi cakṣuṣaḥ ,
बाधिर्यमूकत्वमुखास्तथैव श्रोत्रादिधर्मा न तु वेत्तुरात्मनः ॥१०१॥
bādhiryamūkatvamukhāstathaiva śrotrādidharmā na tu vetturātmanaḥ (101)

101. Blindness, weakness, sharpness of vision etc., are merely conditions due to the defectiveness or fitness of eyes; and deafness, dumbness, etc., the conditions of ears, vocal-cords,

and so forth—and none of these imputes can be said to pertain to the Self, the Knower.

उच्छ्वासनिःश्वासविजृम्भणक्षुत्प्रस्यन्दनाद्युत्क्रमणादिकाः क्रियाः ।
ucchvāsaniḥśvāsavijṛmbhaṇakṣutprasyandanādyutkramaṇādikāḥ kriyāḥ ,
प्राणादिकर्माणि वदन्ति तज्ज्ञाः प्राणस्य धर्मावशनापिपासे ॥ १०२ ॥
prāṇādikarmāṇi vadanti tajñāḥ prāṇasya dharmāvaśanāpipāse (102)

102. The experts designate: inhalation, exhalation, yawning, sneezing, secretion, leaving the body etc., as functions of *Prāna* and the rest; while hunger and thirst are called the characteristics of main *Prāna* proper.

अन्तःकरणमेतेषु चक्षुरादिषु वर्ष्मणि ।
antaḥkaraṇameteṣu cakṣurādiṣu varṣmaṇi ,
अहमित्यभिमानेन तिष्ठत्याभासतेजसा ॥ १०३ ॥
ahamityabhimānena tiṣṭhatyābhāsatejasā (103)

103. The *Antāhkaran* (the Inner-cause or the Mind stuff) has its seat in the organs such as the eye within the body; and it abides identifying with them as 'I'. It owes its existence just to the *Ātmā* reflecting at its core.

अहङ्कारः स विज्ञेयः कर्ता भोक्ताभिमान्ययम् ।
ahaṅkāraḥ sa vijñeyaḥ kartā bhoktābhimānyayam ,
सत्त्वादिगुणयोगेन चावस्थात्रयमश्नुते ॥ १०४ ॥
sattvādiguṇayogena cāvasthātrayamaśnute (104)

104. Know that it is the *Ahankāra* (ego) which—identifying itself with the body—takes on the notion of becoming the Doer and the Experiencer. In conjunction with the *Gunas* such as *Sattva* etc., the ego assumes the three states: of waking, dreaming, and deep-sleep.

विषयाणामानुकूल्ये सुखी दुःखी विपर्यये ।
viṣayāṇāmānukūlye sukhī duḥkhī viparyaye ,
सुखं दुःखं च तद्धर्मः सदानन्दस्य नात्मनः ॥ १०५ ॥
sukhaṁ duḥkhaṁ ca taddharmaḥ sadānandasya nātmanaḥ (105)

105. When sense-objects are favorable it *(*the *Ahankāra,* or 'I' sense) is happy, and when unfavorable, it becomes unhappy. Happiness and misery are the aspects merely of the ego and not of the *Ātmā:* which is at the core and which abides ever blissful.

आत्मार्थत्वेन हि प्रेयान्विषयो न स्वतः प्रियः ।
ātmārthatvena hi preyānviṣayo na svataḥ priyaḥ ,
स्वत एव हि सर्वेषामात्मा प्रियतमो यतः ।
svata eva hi sarveṣāmātmā priyatamo yataḥ ,
तत आत्मा सदानन्दो नास्य दुःखं कदाचन ॥ १०६ ॥

tata ātmā sadānando nāsya duḥkhaṁ kadācana (106)

106. Sense-objects appear pleasurable only because of the *Ātmā*—that shines and manifests through them—and not independently on their own. Only the *Ātmā*—by Its very intrinsic nature—is the most beloved of all. So know that the Self is ever blissful, without a tinge of sorrows, and It never suffers misery.

यत्सुषुप्तौ निर्विषय आत्मानन्दोऽनुभूयते ।
yatsuṣuptau nirviṣaya ātmānando'nubhūyate ,
श्रुतिः प्रत्यक्षमैतिह्यमनुमानं च जाग्रति ॥ १०७ ॥
śrutiḥ pratyakṣamaitihyamanumānaṁ ca jāgrati (107)

107. That in profound-sleep we experience the bliss of the *Ātmā*—completely independent of the sense-objects—is clearly attested in the *Shrutis*, and traditions, and also borne out by direct experience and inference.

अव्यक्तनाम्नी परमेशशक्तिः अनाद्यविद्या त्रिगुणात्मिका परा ।
avyaktanāmnī parameśaśaktiḥ anādyavidyā triguṇātmikā parā ,
कार्यानुमेया सुधियैव माया यया जगत्सर्वमिदं प्रसूयते ॥ १०८ ॥
kāryānumeyā sudhiyaiva māyā yayā jagatsarvamidaṁ prasūyate (108)

108. *Māyā*, also called the 'Unmanifest', is the power of the Lord-God. She is the beginning-less Nescience (*Avidyā*) made up of the three *Gunas*, and is inherently superior to the effects (being their cause). She is inferred by those of clear intellect from the effects she creates. It is through the powers of *Māyā* that the Lord-God projects forth this here entire Creation.

सन्नाप्यसन्नाप्युभयात्मिका नो भिन्नाप्यभिन्नाप्युभयात्मिका नो ।
sannāpyasannāpyubhayātmikā no bhinnāpyabhinnāpyubhayātmikā no ,
साङ्गाप्यनङ्गा ह्युभयात्मिका नो महाद्भुताऽनिर्वचनीयरूपा ॥ १०९ ॥
sāṅgāpyanaṅgā hyubhayātmikā no mahādbhutā'nirvacanīyarūpā (109)

109. *Māyā* is not existent, and not non-existent, and not partaking of either characteristic or both; *Māyā* is neither distinct, nor non-distinct, nor either of them or both; she's neither with parts, nor part-less, nor either or both; verily this *Māyā* is the wonderful most—and can never be described in words.

शुद्धाद्वयब्रह्मविबोधनाश्या सर्पभ्रमो रज्जुविवेकतो यथा ।
śuddhādvayabrahmavibodhanāśyā sarpabhramo rajjuvivekato yathā ,
रजस्तमःसत्त्वमिति प्रसिद्धा गुणास्तदीयाः प्रथितैः स्वकार्यैः ॥ ११० ॥
rajastamaḥsattvamiti prasiddhā guṇāstadīyāḥ prathitaiḥ svakāryaiḥ (110)

110. But by the realization of the Singular-Absolute (*Brahama*, the one without a second) *Māyā* stands decimated—just as the mistaken idea of a snake is destroyed through the discriminative knowledge of the rope. Of the *Gunas* (characteristics) of *Māyā*, there are three: *Rajas*, *Tamas* and *Sattva*, named after their respective functions.

विक्षेपशक्ती रजसः क्रियात्मिका यतः प्रवृत्तिः प्रसृता पुराणी ।
vikṣepaśaktī rajasaḥ kriyātmikā yataḥ pravṛttiḥ prasṛtā purāṇī ,
रागादयोऽस्याः प्रभवन्ति नित्यं दुःखादयो ये मनसो विकाराः ॥ १११ ॥
rāgādayo'syāḥ prabhavanti nityaṁ duḥkhādayo ye manaso vikārāḥ (111)

111. *Rajas* has its *Vikshepa-shakti* (or projecting power), the very nature of which is intense activity. From *Rajas* is the primeval flow of action and motility prevalent throughout Nature; and from *Rajas* again are the modifications of the Mind—such as attachment, pleasure, grief etc.,—that are being continually produced.

कामः क्रोधो लोभदम्भाद्यसूया अहङ्कारेर्ष्यामत्सराद्यास्तु घोराः ।
kāmaḥ krodho lobhadambhādyasūyā ahaṅkārerṣyāmatsarādyāstu ghorāḥ ,
धर्मा एते राजसाः पुम्प्रवृत्तिर्यस्मादेषा तद्रजो बन्धहेतुः ॥ ११२ ॥
dharmā ete rājasāḥ pumpravṛttiryasmādeṣā tadrajo bandhahetuḥ (112)

112. Desire, ire, avarice, arrogance, spite, egoism, jealousy, envy, etc.,—these are the dreadful attributes of *Rajas*, the very source and reason of worldly propensities which people have. Therefore *Rajas* is the prime cause of bondage.

एषाऽऽवृतिर्नाम तमोगुणस्य शक्तिर्मया वस्त्ववभासतेऽन्यथा ।
eṣā''vṛtirnāma tamoguṇasya śaktirmayā vastvavabhāsate'nyathā ,
सैषा निदानं पुरुषस्य संसृतेः विक्षेपशक्तेः प्रवणस्य हेतुः ॥ ११३ ॥
saiṣā nidānaṁ puruṣasya saṁsṛteḥ vikṣepaśakteḥ pravaṇasya hetuḥ (113)

113. *Avriti* (or the veiling power) is the power of *Tamas*, which makes things appear to be other than what they really are. It is *Tamas* which causes the soul's repeated transmigrations and initiates the actions of the projecting power (*Vikshepa-shakti*).

प्रज्ञावानपि पण्डितोऽपि चतुरोऽप्यत्यन्तसूक्ष्मात्मदृग्-
prajñāvānapi paṇḍito'pi caturo'pyatyantasūkṣmātmadṛg-
व्यालीढस्तमसा न वेत्ति बहुधा सम्बोधितोऽपि स्फुटम् ।
vyālīḍhastamasā na vetti bahudhā sambodhito'pi sphuṭam ,
भ्रान्त्यारोपितमेव साधु कलयत्यालम्बते तद्गुणान्
bhrāntyāropitameva sādhu kalayatyālambate tadguṇān
हन्तासौ प्रबला दुरन्ततमसः शक्तिर्महत्यावृतिः ॥ ११४ ॥
hantāsau prabalā durantatamasaḥ śaktirmahatyāvṛtiḥ (114)

114. Even the learned and most wise—men who are otherwise experts and clever in understanding the subtle-most nuances of scriptural texts—even they are overpowered by *Tamas* and cannot understand the exceedingly subtle *Ātmā* though clearly explained in manifold ways. That which is simply superimposed by delusion—they take it to be Real and become attached to its effects. Alas, how powerful the great *Avriti Shakti* of the dreadful *Tamas*!

अभावना वा विपरीतभावनाऽसंभावना विप्रतिपत्तिरस्याः ।
abhāvanā vā viparītabhāvanā'sambhāvanā vipratipattirasyāḥ ,
संसर्गयुक्तं न विमुञ्चति ध्रुवं विक्षेपशक्तिः क्षपयत्यजस्रम् ॥ ११५ ॥
saṁsargayuktaṁ na vimuñcati dhruvaṁ
vikṣepaśaktiḥ kṣapayatyajasram (115)

115. Absence of opinion, or contrary opinion, doubts and lack of definite belief—these never desert one who has even the remotest association with the Veiling-power; and then the Projecting-power gives endless troubles too.

अज्ञानमालस्यजडत्वनिद्रा प्रमादमूढत्वमुखास्तमोगुणाः ।
ajñānamālasyajaḍatvanidrā pramādamūḍhatvamukhāstamoguṇāḥ ,
एतैः प्रयुक्तो न हि वेत्ति किञ्चित् निद्रालुवत्स्तम्भवदेव तिष्ठति ॥ ११६ ॥
etaiḥ prayukto na hi vetti kiñcit nidrāluvatstambhavadeva tiṣṭhati (116)

116. Ignorance, languor, dullness, sleep, inadvertence, stupidity etc.,—these are the attributes of *Tamas*. One bound by them cannot correctly comprehend— remaining inert instead, alike a stump of wood or a block of stone.

सत्त्वं विशुद्धं जलवत्तथापि ताभ्यां मिलित्वा सरणाय कल्पते ।
sattvaṁ viśuddhaṁ jalavattathāpi tābhyāṁ militvā saraṇāya kalpate ,
यत्रात्मबिम्बः प्रतिबिम्बितः सन् प्रकाशयत्यर्क इवाखिलं जडम् ॥ ११७ ॥
yatrātmabimbaḥ pratibimbitaḥ san prakāśayatyarka ivākhilaṁ jaḍam (117)

117. Pure *Sattva* is like clear water; yet in conjunction with *Rajas* and *Tamas* it makes for transmigration. However, in the unmixed pure *Sattva,* the light of the Self becomes clearly reflected and the true nature of the world is revealed to its stark fullness.

मिश्रस्य सत्त्वस्य भवन्ति धर्माः त्वमानिताद्या नियमा यमाद्याः ।
miśrasya sattvasya bhavanti dharmāḥ tvamānitādyā niyamā yamādyāḥ ,
श्रद्धा च भक्तिश्च मुमुक्षुता च दैवी च सम्पत्तिरसन्निवृत्तिः ॥ ११८ ॥
śraddhā ca bhaktiśca mumukṣutā ca daivī ca sampattirasannivṛttiḥ (118)

118. Complete absence of pride etc., observing *Niyamas* (do's) and *Yamas* (don'ts) etc., and also faith, devotion, yearning for

liberation, divine propensities, and turning away from the non-Real—all these are the traits of mixed *Sattva*.

विशुद्धसत्त्वस्य गुणाः प्रसादः स्वात्मानुभूतिः परमा प्रशान्तिः ।
viśuddhasattvasya guṇāḥ prasādaḥ svātmānubhūtiḥ paramā praśāntiḥ ,
तृप्तिः प्रहर्षः परमात्मनिष्ठा यया सदानन्दरसं समृच्छति ॥ ११९ ॥
tṛptiḥ praharṣaḥ paramātmaniṣṭhā yayā sadānandarasaṁ samṛcchati (119)

119. The traits of arrantly pure *Sattva* are: cheerfulness, self-realization, supreme peace, contentment, bliss, and a steady abidance in the *Param-Ātmā*—by which the aspirant comes to enjoy bliss everlasting.

अव्यक्तमेतत्त्रिगुणैर्निरुक्तं तत्कारणं नाम शरीरमात्मनः ।
avyaktametattriguṇairniruktaṁ tatkāraṇaṁ nāma śarīramātmanaḥ ,
सुषुप्तिरेतस्य विभक्त्यवस्था प्रलीनसर्वेन्द्रियबुद्धिवृत्तिः ॥ १२० ॥
suṣuptiretasya vibhaktyavasthā pralīnasarvendriyabuddhivṛttiḥ (120)

120. This undifferentiated—the meld or coalescence of the three *Gunas*—is spoken of as the causal-body of the Soul. Profound-sleep is its special state in which the functions of the mind, together with the sense-organs, all become suspended.

सर्वप्रकारप्रमितिप्रशान्तिः बीजात्मनावस्थितिरेव बुद्धेः ।
sarvaprakārapramitipraśāntiḥ bījātmanāvasthitireva buddheḥ ,
सुषुप्तिरेतस्य किल प्रतीतिः किञ्चिन्न वेद्मीति जगत्प्रसिद्धेः ॥ १२१ ॥
suṣuptiretasya kila pratītiḥ kiñcinna vedmīti jagatprasiddheḥ (121)

121. Profound-sleep is the cessation of every kind of perception—where the Mind remains in a subtle seed-like form. The evidence of this is borne out by the universal verdict "I did not know anything" in that state.

देहेन्द्रियप्राणमनोऽहमादयः सर्वे विकारा विषयाः सुखादयः ।
dehendriyaprāṇamano'hamādayaḥ sarve vikārā viṣayāḥ sukhādayaḥ ,
व्योमादिभूतान्यखिलं च विश्वं अव्यक्तपर्यन्तमिदं ह्यनात्मा ॥ १२२ ॥
vyomādibhūtānyakhilaṁ ca viśvaṁ avyaktaparyantamidaṁ hyanātmā (122)

122. The body, sense-organs, *prānas*, *manas*, egoism, etc., and all their modifications; the sense-objects, pleasures and the rest; the gross elements such as aether etc.,—in fact, the entire universe continuing up to the Unmanifest—all this is the not-Self.

माया मायाकार्यं सर्वं महदादिदेहपर्यन्तम् ।
māyā māyākāryaṁ sarvaṁ mahadādidehaparyantam ,
असदिदमनात्मतत्त्वं विद्धि त्वं मरुमरीचिकाकल्पम् ॥ १२३ ॥
asadidamanātmatattvaṁ viddhi tvaṁ marumarīcikākalpam (123)

123. From *Mahat* down to the gross-body—everything is the effect of *Māyā*; and all these—including *Māyā* herself—know them to be the not-Self, and therefore non-Real, just like the mirage in a desert.

अथ ते सम्प्रवक्ष्यामि स्वरूपं परमात्मनः ।
atha te sampravakṣyāmi svarūpaṁ paramātmanaḥ ,
यद्विज्ञाय नरो बन्धान्मुक्तः कैवल्यमश्नुते ॥ १२४॥
yadvijñāya naro bandhānmuktaḥ kaivalyamaśnute (124)

124. Now I am going to tell you of the Real nature of the Supreme-Self—realizing which one gets freed of all bondages and thereby attains Onlyness.

अस्ति कश्चित्स्वयं नित्यमहम्प्रत्ययलम्बनः ।
asti kaścitsvayaṁ nityamahampratyayalambanaḥ ,
अवस्थात्रयसाक्षी सन्पञ्चकोशविलक्षणः ॥ १२५॥
avasthātrayasākṣī sanpañcakośavilakṣaṇaḥ (125)

यो विजानाति सकलं जाग्रत्स्वप्नसुषुप्तिषु ।
yo vijānāti sakalaṁ jāgratsvapnasuṣuptiṣu ,
बुद्धितद्वृत्तिसद्भावमभावमहमित्ययम् ॥ १२६॥
buddhitadvṛttisadbhāvamabhāvamahamityayam (126)

125-126. There exists something—a certain Causal Being, an Absolute self-existent ever-enduring Entity—which persists as the eternally abiding substratum of the consciousness of egoism: the 'I' sense. It is the enduring Witness of the three states and ever distinct from the five sheaths. It always knows everything which happens in the waking state, in dream and in profound sleep. It is always aware of the presence or absence of the mind and its functions. And that substrate of the notion of egoism: That is the *Ātmā*, the Self.

यः पश्यति स्वयं सर्वं यं न पश्यति कश्चन ।
yaḥ paśyati svayaṁ sarvaṁ yaṁ na paśyati kaścana ,
यश्चेतयति बुद्ध्यादि न तद्यं चेतयत्ययम् ॥ १२७॥
yaścetayati buddhyādi na tadyaṁ cetayatyayam (127)

127. Which itself sees all, but which none can behold, which illumines the Intellect etc., but which the Intellect etc., can never perceive or shed light upon—That is the *Ātmā*.

येन विश्वमिदं व्याप्तं यं न व्याप्नोति किञ्चन ।
yena viśvamidaṁ vyāptaṁ yaṁ na vyāpnoti kiñcana ,
आभारूपमिदं सर्वं यं भान्तमनुभात्ययम् ॥ १२८॥
ābhārūpamidaṁ sarvaṁ yaṁ bhāntamanubhātyayam (128)

128. By which this universe is pervaded, but which nothing pervades, which shining, all this creation shines as its reflection—That Fiery Tranquility is the *Ātmā*.

यस्य सन्निधिमात्रेण देहेन्द्रियमनोधियः ।
yasya sannidhimātreṇa dehendriyamanodhiyaḥ ,
विषयेषु स्वकीयेषु वर्तन्ते प्रेरिता इव ॥१२९॥
viṣayeṣu svakīyeṣu vartante preritā iva (129)

129. By whose very presence the body, the organs, the mind, the intellect all keep to their respective fields of functioning, like handmaids—That is the *Ātmā*.

अहङ्कारादिदेहान्ता विषयाश्च सुखादयः ।
ahaṅkārādidehāntā viṣayāśca sukhādayaḥ ,
वेद्यन्ते घटवद् येन नित्यबोधस्वरूपिणा ॥१३०॥
vedyante ghaṭavadyena nityabodhasvarūpiṇā (130)

130. Which is of the nature of eternal Knowledge, and by which all things—from egoism down to the body, and the sense-objects, and their experiences like pleasures etc.,—are known as palpably as a jar placed before, That is the *Ātmā*.

एषोऽन्तरात्मा पुरुषः पुराणो निरन्तराखण्डसुखानुभूतिः ।
eṣo'ntarātmā puruṣaḥ purāṇo nirantarākhaṇḍasukhānubhūtiḥ ,
सदैकरूपः प्रतिबोधमात्रो येनेषिता वागसवश्चरन्ति ॥१३१॥
sadaikarūpaḥ pratibodhamātro yeneṣitā vāgasavaścaranti (131)

131. That is the *Ātmā*—the innermost Self, the primeval *Purusha* whose very essence is the experiencing of never-ending boundless Bliss—which Entity is ever the same, and commanded by whom, the organs and *Prānas* perform their everyday functions, reflecting as the divergent modifications of That consciousness.

अत्रैव सत्त्वात्मनि धीगुहायां अव्याकृताकाश उशत्प्रकाशः ।
atraiva sattvātmani dhīguhāyāṁ avyākṛtākāśa uśatprakāśaḥ ,
आकाश उच्चै रविवत्प्रकाशते स्वतेजसा विश्वमिदं प्रकाशयन् ॥१३२॥
ākāśa uccai ravivatprakāśate svatejasā viśvamidaṁ prakāśayan (132)

132. In this very body, in the mind full of *Sattva*, in the secret chamber of the intellect, in the *Ākāsha* known as the Unmanifest, the *Ātmā*—of a charming splendor—shines fiery in all Its glory; and which, in Its brilliant self effulgence—alike the sun aloft—makes the universe to shine and become evident in all its vividness.

ज्ञाता मनोऽहङ्कृतिविक्रियाणां देहेन्द्रियप्राणकृतक्रियाणाम् ।
jñātā mano'haṅkṛtivikriyāṇāṁ dehendriyaprāṇakṛtakriyāṇām ,
अयोऽग्निवत्ताननुवर्तमानो न चेष्टते नो विकरोति किञ्चन ॥ १३३ ॥
ayo'gnivattānanuvartamāno na ceṣṭate no vikaroti kiñcana (133)

133. The Knower of the modifications of the mind and the egoism and of the activities of the body and the organs and the *Prānas*—appearing to take their forms just like a fiery ball of molten iron—and which neither acts nor is subject to changes in the least: That Final-Knower, That Ultimate Subject, That is the *Ātmā*.

न जायते नो म्रियते न वर्धते न क्षीयते नो विकरोति नित्यः ।
na jāyate no mriyate na vardhate na kṣīyate no vikaroti nityaḥ ,
विलीयमानेऽपि वपुष्यमुष्मिन्नलीयते कुम्भ इवाम्बरं स्वयम् ॥ १३४ ॥
vilīyamāne'pi vapuṣyamuṣminna līyate kumbha ivāmbaraṁ svayam (134)

134. Which is never born nor ever dies; which neither grows nor decays; which, being eternal, never undergoes any change; which does not cease to exist even when the body is destroyed; which is alike the space in a jar that endures even after the jar is destroyed; which is independently self-existent—That is my Self, the *Ātmā*.

प्रकृतिविकृतिभिन्नः शुद्धबोधस्वभावः सदसदिदमशेषं भासयन्निर्विशेषः ।
prakṛtivikṛtibhinnaḥ śuddhabodhasvabhāvaḥ
sadasadidamaśeṣaṁ bhāsayannirviśeṣaḥ ,
विलसति परमात्मा जाग्रदादिष्ववस्था स्वहमहमिति साक्षात्साक्षिरूपेण बुद्धेः ॥ १३५ ॥
vilasati paramātmā jāgradādiṣvavasthā-
svahamahamiti sākṣātsākṣirūpeṇa buddheḥ (135)

135. That Supreme Self—the Absolute of the essence of Pure Knowledge, distinct from *Prakriti* and its modifications—directly manifests this entire gross and subtle universe in the waking and other states: as the substratum of the persistent sense of egoism ('I' sense). It abides as the Witness of even the *Buddhi*, the determinative faculty.

नियमितमनसामुं त्वं स्वमात्मानमात्म न्ययमहमिति साक्षाद्विद्धि बुद्धिप्रसादात् ।
niyamitamanasāmuṁ tvaṁ svamātmānamātma nyayamahamiti sākṣādviddhi buddhiprasādāt ,
जनिमरणतरङ्गापारसंसारसिन्धुं प्रतर भव कृतार्थो ब्रह्म रूपेण संस्थः ॥ १३६ ॥
janimaraṇataraṅgāpārasaṁsārasindhuṁ pratara bhava kṛtārtho brahma rūpeṇa saṁsthaḥ (136)

136. By means of a regulated Mind and purified Intellect (*Buddhi*), directly realize thyself as the *Ātmā* within, merging thy identity with It. Firmly established within the *Ātmā* as thine own inner essence, forever cross the boundless ocean of

Samsāra, whose waves are births and deaths, and thus become liberated and ever blessed.

अत्रानात्मन्यहमिति मतिर्बन्ध एषोऽस्य पुंसः
atrānātmanyahamiti matirbandha eṣo'sya puṁsaḥ
प्राप्तोऽज्ञानाज्जननमरणक्लेशसम्पातहेतुः ।
prāpto'jñānājjananamaraṇakleśasampātahetuḥ ,
येनैवायं वपुरिदमसत्सत्यमित्यात्मबुद्ध्या
yenaivāyaṁ vapuridamasatsatyamityātmabuddhyā
पुष्यत्युक्षत्यवति विषयैस्तन्तुभिः कोशकृद्वत् ॥ १३७॥
puṣyatyukṣatyavati viṣayaistantubhiḥ kośakṛdvat (137)

137. Identifying the Self with that which is the not-Self—that is man's bondage, which has Ignorance as its roots, and which brings in its wake the miseries of births and deaths. Through this misidentification, one considers the evanescent body to be Real; and then identifying oneself with it, one nurtures, bathes, and preserves it through agreeable sense-objects; and by this way one becomes fettered—in the same way as a caterpillar becomes caught in the cocoon through the threads of its own making.

अतस्मिंस्तद्बुद्धिः प्रभवति विमूढस्य तमसा
atasmiṁstadbuddhiḥ prabhavati vimūḍhasya tamasā
विवेकाभावाद्वै स्फुरति भुजगे रज्जुधिषणा ।
vivekābhāvādvai sphurati bhujage rajjudhiṣaṇā ,
ततोऽनर्थव्रातो निपतति समादातुरधिकः
tato'narthavrāto nipatati samādāturadhikaḥ
ततो योऽसद्ग्राहः स हि भवति बन्धः श्रृणु सखे ॥ १३८॥
tato yo'sadgrāhaḥ sa hi bhavati bandhaḥ śṛṇu sakhe (138)

138. Deluded by Nescience, one mistakes a thing for what it isn't. In the absence of right discernment, one may mistake a snake for a rope; and if he grasps it with that wrong notion then great danger befalls him. So listen dear, it is the mistaking of the transitory non-Real things to be Real, which constitutes Ignorance and leads to the ensuing pitfalls and bondages.

अखण्डनित्याद्वयबोधशक्त्या स्फुरन्तमात्मानमनन्तवैभवम् ।
akhaṇḍanityādvayabodhaśaktyā sphurantamātmānamanantavaibhavam ,
समावृणोत्यावृतिशक्तिरेषा तमोमयी राहुरिवार्कबिम्बम् ॥ १३९॥
samāvṛṇotyāvṛtiśaktireṣā tamomayī rāhurivārkabimbam (139)

139. Just as the orb of Sun is obscured by *Rahu*, so too the *Ātmā*—of infinite glory that one finds fiercely glowing within as pure consciousness, which is indivisible, eternal, and non-dual,

the one without a second—is obscured by *Avriti*, the veiling power of which preponderates in *Tamas* (Ignorance).

तिरोभूते स्वात्मन्यमलतरतेजोवति पुमान्
tirobhūte svātmanyamalataratejovati pumān
अनात्मानं मोहादहमिति शरीरं कलयति ।
anātmānaṁ mohādahamiti śarīraṁ kalayati ,
ततः कामक्रोधप्रभृतिभिरमुं बन्धनगुणैः
tataḥ kāmakrodhaprabhṛtibhiramuṁ bandhanaguṇaiḥ
परं विक्षेपाख्या रजस उरुशक्तिर्व्यथयति ॥ १४० ॥
paraṁ vikṣepākhyā rajasa uruśaktirvyathayati (140)

140. Because the within *Ātmā*—endowed with the purest of splendors—is hidden from view due to Nescience, man wrongly identifies himself with the body—the not-Self. Then the merciless badgerings of the projecting powers of *Rajas*, further afflict the man through its binding fetters of lust, anger, etc.

महामोहग्राहग्रसनगलितात्मावगमनो
mahāmohagrāhagrasanagalitātmāvagamano
धियो नानावस्थां स्वयमभिनयंस्तद्गुणतया ।
dhiyo nānāvasthāṁ svayamabhinayaṁstadguṇatayā ,
अपारे संसारे विषयविषपूरे जलनिधौ
apāre saṁsāre viṣayaviṣapūre jalanidhau
निमज्योन्मज्यायं भ्रमति कुमतिः कुत्सितगतिः ॥ १४१ ॥
nimajyonmajyāyaṁ bhramati kumatiḥ kutsitagatiḥ (141)

141. The man of deluded mind—whose knowledge of the Self has been swallowed up by the shark of stark Nescience—ends up comporting as though the different states of his Mind (the superimposed attribute upon the Self) are actually the inherent qualities of his Self. And therefore he drifts up and down—now rising and now falling—upon this ever-changing worldly ocean full of the poison of sense-pleasures. Alas, what a sorry miserable fate indeed!

भानुप्रभासञ्जनिताभ्रपङ्क्तिः भानुं तिरोधाय विजृम्भते यथा ।
bhānuprabhāsañjanitābhrapaṅktiḥ bhānuṁ tirodhāya vijṛmbhate yathā ,
आत्मोदिताहङ्कृतिरात्मतत्त्वं तथा तिरोधाय विजृम्भते स्वयम् ॥ १४२ ॥
ātmoditāhaṅkṛtirātmatattvaṁ tathā tirodhāya vijṛmbhate svayam (142)

142. Formations of clouds—generated by the sun's rays—gather up and veil the very same sun which produced them, and now the clouds themselves appear clearly manifest while the sun is rendered concealed! In the same way the ego—which has arisen from the *Ātmā*—ends up covering the reality of that very *Ātmā*.

And now the ego is seen manifest in its full glory—while the *Ātmā*, the Real One, remains obscured.

कवलितदिननाथे दुर्दिने सान्द्रमेघैः व्यथयति हिमझञ्झावायुरुग्रो यथैतान् ।
kavalitadinanāthe durdine sāndrameghaiḥ vyathayati himajhañjhāvāyurugro yathaitān ,
अविरततमसाऽऽत्मन्यावृते मूढबुद्धिं क्षपयति बहुदुःखैस्तीव्रविक्षेपशक्तिः ॥ १४३ ॥
aviratatamasā''tmanyāvṛte mūḍhabuddhiṁ kṣapayati bahuduḥkhaistīvravikṣepaśaktiḥ (143)

143. On a cloudy winter day, cold shivering blasts afflict a person—when the sun becomes swallowed in thick clouds. Similarly, when the *Ātmā* becomes obscured through dense Ignorance, then the dreadful *Vikshepa Shakti* (projecting power) afflicts the foolish person with innumerous griefs.

एताभ्यामेव शक्तिभ्यां बन्धः पुंसः समागतः ।
etābhyāmeva śaktibhyāṁ bandhaḥ puṁsaḥ samāgataḥ ,
याभ्यां विमोहितो देहं मत्वाऽत्मानं भ्रमत्ययम् ॥ १४४ ॥
yābhyāṁ vimohito dehaṁ matvā'tmānaṁ bhramatyayam (144)

144. It is from these two powers that man's bondage has ensued. Bewitched by these, a man mistakes the body to be the Self, and he continues to drift from one body to another, life after life.

बीजं संसृतिभूमिजस्य तु तमो देहात्मधीरङ्कुरो
bījaṁ saṁsṛtibhūmijasya tu tamo dehātmadhīraṅkuro
रागः पल्लवमम्बु कर्म तु वपुः स्कन्धोऽसवः शाखिकाः ।
rāgaḥ pallavamambu karma tu vapuḥ skandho'savaḥ śākhikāḥ ,
अग्राणीन्द्रियसंहतिश्च विषयाः पुष्पाणि दुःखं फलं
agrāṇīndriyasaṁhatiśca viṣayāḥ puṣpāṇi duḥkhaṁ phalaṁ
नानाकर्मसमुद्भवं बहुविधं भोक्तात्र जीवः खगः ॥ १४५ ॥
nānākarmasamudbhavaṁ bahuvidhaṁ bhoktātra jīvaḥ khagaḥ (145)

145. Of this Tree of *Samsāra* (worldly existence)—Ignorance is the seed; Identification with the body is the sprout; Desires and Attachments the tender leaves; *Karmas* its water; the Body its trunk; the *Prānas* its branches; the Sense-organs its twigs; the Sense-objects its flowers. The joys and sorrows resulting from the various actions are the bitter sweet fruits of this Tree—while the individual Soul is the bird perched upon its top.

अज्ञानमूलोऽयमनात्मबन्धो नैसर्गिकोऽनादिरनन्त ईरितः ।
ajñānamūlo'yamanātmabandho naisargiko'nādirananta īritaḥ ,
जन्माप्ययव्याधिजरादिदुःखप्रवाहपातं जनयत्यमुष्य ॥ १४६ ॥
janmāpyayavyādhijarādiduḥkhapravāhapātaṁ janayatyamuṣya (146)

146. The bondage caused by the not-Self is self-caused and has its origin in Nescience; it is stated to be beginning-less and

endless, and it subjects one to the woes of birth, disease, old age, death etc.,—an endless flood of miseries.

नास्त्रैर्न शस्त्रैरनिलेन वह्निना छेत्तुं न शक्यो न च कर्मकोटिभिः ।
nāstrairna śastrairanilena vahninā chettuṁ na śakyo na ca karmakoṭibhiḥ ,
विवेकविज्ञानमहासिना विना धातुः प्रसादेन शितेन मञ्जुना ॥ १४७ ॥
vivekavijñānamahāsinā vinā dhātuḥ prasādena śitena mañjunā (147)

147. Neither by shields, nor by weapons, nor by anything made up of the air, fire, etc., physical elements, nor by millions of acts—can this bondage be destroyed. The only remedy is the fiery sword of Knowledge—born of Discrimination and sharpened further by supreme grace.

श्रुतिप्रमाणैकमतेः स्वधर्म निष्ठा तयैवात्मविशुद्धिरस्य ।
śrutipramāṇaikamateḥ svadharma niṣṭhā tayaivātmaviśuddhirasya ,
विशुद्धबुद्धेः परमात्मवेदनं तेनैव संसारसमूलनाशः ॥ १४८ ॥
viśuddhabuddheḥ paramātmavedanaṁ tenaiva saṁsārasamūlanāśaḥ (148)

148. One who is passionately devoted to the authority of the *Shrutis*, acquires deep devotion and abidance in his *Dharma;* and that *Dharma* conduces to the purity of his Mind. Gaining that pure Intellect, he comes by the Realization of the Supreme Self; and through that the Tree of *Samsāra* stands decimated—root and branch.

कोशैरन्नमयाद्यैः पञ्चभिरात्मा न संवृतो भाति ।
kośairannamayādyaiḥ pañcabhirātmā na saṁvṛto bhāti ,
निजशक्तिसमुत्पन्नैः शैवालपटलैरिवाम्बु वापीस्थम् ॥ १४९ ॥
nijaśaktisamutpannaiḥ śaivālapaṭalairivāmbu vāpīstham (149)

149. Due to the coverings of the five sheaths—the material one etc., which are the products of the its own divine potencies—the Self Itself becomes veiled and appears not to clearly shine. This is alike the underlying water in the pond rendered invisible through the accumulation of sedge—the product of water's own making.

तच्छैवालापनये सम्यक् सलिलं प्रतीयते शुद्धम् ।
tacchaivālāpanaye samyak salilaṁ pratīyate śuddham ,
तृष्णासन्तापहरं सद्यः सौख्यप्रदं परं पुंसः ॥ १५० ॥
tṛṣṇāsantāpaharaṁ sadyaḥ saukhyapradaṁ paraṁ puṁsaḥ (150)

150. Upon the removal of sedge the perfectly pristine water—which allays the pangs of thirst and gives immediate joy—appears unobstructed before the man.

पञ्चानामपि कोशानामपवादे विभात्ययं शुद्धः ।
pañcānāmapi kośānāmapavāde vibhātyayaṁ śuddhaḥ ,
नित्यानन्दैकरसः प्रत्यग्रूपः परः स्वयञ्ज्योतिः ॥ १५१ ॥
nityānandaikarasaḥ pratyagrūpaḥ paraḥ svayañjyotiḥ (151)

151. When all the five sheaths have been eliminated, the fiery Self of man shines perfect and pure, the very essence of unalloyed unending Bliss—supreme, indwelling, self-effulgent.

आत्मानात्मविवेकः कर्तव्यो बन्धमुक्तये विदुषा ।
ātmānātmavivekaḥ kartavyo bandhamuktaye viduṣā ,
तेनैवानन्दी भवति स्वं विज्ञाय सच्चिदानन्दम् ॥ १५२ ॥
tenaivānandī bhavati svaṁ vijñāya saccidānandam (152)

152. To remove his bondages, the wise should clearly discriminate between the Self and the not-Self. By that alone he comes to know of his Self as one with the Absolute—of the nature of Existence-Knowledge-Bliss; and thereby becomes he ever felicitous.

मुञ्जादिषीकामिव दृश्यवर्गात् प्रत्यञ्चमात्मानमसङ्गमक्रियम् ।
muñjādiṣīkāmiva dṛśyavargāt pratyañcamātmānamasaṅgamakriyam ,
विविच्य तत्र प्रविलाप्य सर्वं तदात्मना तिष्ठति यः स मुक्तः ॥ १५३ ॥
vivicya tatra pravilāpya sarvaṁ tadātmanā tiṣṭhati yaḥ sa muktaḥ (153)

153. Just as one would separate the enveloping sheath from the tender core of the *Munja* grass, he indeed is free who can separate all the sense-objects—perceived, felt, thought of—from the indwelling Self: which's the Subject at the core, the unattached, the actionless. And then merging his everything within the Self, the seeker should abide in a state of complete identity with That.

देहोऽयमन्नभवनोऽन्नमयस्तु कोशश्चान्नेन जीवति विनश्यति तद्विहीनः ।
deho'yamannabhavano'nnamayastu kośaścānnena jīvati vinaśyati tadvihīnaḥ ,
त्वक्चर्ममांसरुधिरास्थिपुरीषराशिर्नायं स्वयं भवितुमर्हति नित्यशुद्धः ॥ १५४ ॥
tvakcarmamāṁsarudhirāsthipurīṣarāśirnāyaṁ svayaṁ bhavitumarhati nityaśuddhaḥ (154)

154. This body of ours is the product of food and makes up the Material-sheath. It lives on food and without food it dies. It is a mass of skin, flesh, blood, bones, impurities. The body can never be the *Ātmā*—which is eternally pure and self-existent.

पूर्वं जनेरधिमृतेरपि नायमस्ति जातक्षणः क्षणगुणोऽनियतस्वभावः ।
pūrvaṁ janeradhimṛterapi nāyamasti jātakṣaṇaḥ kṣaṇaguṇo'niyatasvabhāvaḥ ,
नैको जडश्च घटवत्परिदृश्यमानः स्वात्मा कथं भवति भावविकारवेत्ता ॥ १५५ ॥
naiko jaḍaśca ghaṭavatparidṛśyamānaḥ svātmā kathaṁ bhavati bhāvavikāravettā (155)

155. The body does not exist prior to inception or posterior to dissolution—lasting but for the short intervening time; its qualities are ephemeral and it is changeful by nature; it is not a whole but full of parts; it is not self-effulgent; it is not the Seer but rather an object which is seen like a jar. How then can the body be same as the Self, which is actually the Witness of changes in all things?

पाणिपादादिमान्देहो नात्मा व्यङ्गेऽपि जीवनात् ।
pāṇipādādimāndeho nātmā vyaṅge'pi jīvanāt ,
तत्तच्छक्तेरनाशाच्च न नियम्यो नियामकः ॥ १५६ ॥
tattacchakteranāśācca na niyamyo niyāmakaḥ (156)

156. The body, made up of arms, legs, etc., cannot be the *Ātmā*, for even when the parts of body go missing, it continues to function nevertheless; and so necessarily the body must abide under the sovereign rule of an entity higher up. Therefore this body—which is subject to another's rule—cannot be the Self.

देहतद्धर्मतत्कर्मतदवस्थादिसाक्षिणः ।
dehataddharmatatkarmatadavasthādisākṣiṇaḥ ,
सत एव स्वतःसिद्धं तद्वैलक्षण्यमात्मनः ॥ १५७ ॥
sata eva svataḥsiddhaṁ tadvailakṣaṇyamātmanaḥ (157)

157. It is abundantly self-evident that the Self is the abiding enduring Reality, very much distinct from the body, and its characteristics, and its activities and its states—of all of which it is just merely the Witness.

शल्यराशिर्मांसलिप्तो मलपूर्णोऽतिकश्मलः ।
śalyarāśirmāṁsalipto malapūrṇo'tikaśmalaḥ ,
कथं भवेदयं वेत्ता स्वयमेतद्विलक्षणः ॥ १५८ ॥
kathaṁ bhavedayaṁ vettā svayametadvilakṣaṇaḥ (158)

158. How can the body—which is a bundle of bones covered with flesh, full of foul things and so impure—be the self-existent pristine *Ātmā*, the Knower, which is ever separate and distinct from the body?

त्वङ्मांसमेदोऽस्थिपुरीषराशा वहम्मतिं मूढजनः करोति ।
tvaṅmāṁsamedo'sthipurīṣarāśāvahammatiṁ mūḍhajanaḥ karoti ,
विलक्षणं वेत्ति विचारशीलो निजस्वरूपं परमार्थभूतम् ॥ १५९ ॥
vilakṣaṇaṁ vetti vicāraśīlo nijasvarūpaṁ paramārthabhūtam (159)

159. It is only the foolish man who identifies himself with the mass of skin, flesh, fat, bones, and filth; whereas the man of

discrimination always cognizes that the body is quite distinct from the Self—which is the only self-existent Reality there is.

देहोऽहमित्येव जडस्य बुद्धिः देहे च जीवे विदुषस्त्वहन्धीः ।
deho'hamityeva jaḍasya buddhiḥ dehe ca jīve viduṣastvahandhīḥ ,
विवेकविज्ञानवतो महात्मनो ब्रह्माहमित्येव मतिः सदात्मनि ॥१६०॥
vivekavijñānavato mahātmano brahmāhamityeva matiḥ sadātmani (160)

160. An ignorant person thinks of himself to be a body; a person of book-learning identifies himself as a combination of body and soul; but the sage—possessed of realization brought on by right discrimination—knows that "I am *Brahama*", and looks upon the eternal *Ātmā* alone to be his true Self.

अत्रात्मबुद्धिं त्यज मूढबुद्धे त्वङ्मांसमेदोऽस्थिपुरीषराशौ ।
atrātmabuddhiṁ tyaja mūḍhabuddhe tvaṅmāṁsamedo'sthipurīṣarāśau ,
सर्वात्मनि ब्रह्मणि निर्विकल्पे कुरुष्व शान्तिं परमां भजस्व ॥१६१॥
sarvātmani brahmaṇi nirvikalpe kuruṣva śāntiṁ paramāṁ bhajasva (161)

161. O foolish man, cease to identify yourself with this bundle of skin, flesh, fat, bones, filth; and determine that core wherefrom the 'I' truly emanates—in the Absolute *Brahama*, the Self of all—and thereby attain to Peace supreme.

देहेन्द्रियादावसति भ्रमोदितां विद्वानहन्तां न जहाति यावत् ।
dehendriyādāvasati bhramoditāṁ vidvānahantāṁ na jahāti yāvat ,
तावन्न तस्यास्ति विमुक्तिवार्ताप्यस्त्वेष वेदान्तनयान्तदर्शी ॥१६२॥
tāvanna tasyāsti vimuktivārtāpyastveṣa vedāntanayāntadarśī (162)

162. As long as the book-learned man does not give up his erroneous identification with the body, organs, etc., which are all non-Real, there cannot even be talk of emancipation for him—however erudite he may be in the highest and most sublime Vedānta philosophy.

छायाशरीरे प्रतिबिम्बगात्रे यत्स्वप्नदेहे हृदि कल्पिताङ्गे ।
chāyāśarīre pratibimbagātre yatsvapnadehe hṛdi kalpitāṅge ,
यथात्मबुद्धिस्तव नास्ति काचिज्जीवच्छरीरे च तथैव माऽस्तु ॥१६३॥
yathātmabuddhistava nāsti kācijjīvaccharīre ca tathaiva mā'stu (163)

163. Just as you do not identify yourself with your shadow-body, your reflected-body, your dream-body, or the imagined-body you have of yourself in the mind—so too you should desist from identifying with this living breathing body as well.

देहात्मधीरेव नृणामसद्धियां जन्मादिदुःखप्रभवस्य बीजम् ।
dehātmadhīreva nṛṇāmasaddhiyāṁ janmādiduḥkhaprabhavasya bījam ,
यतस्ततस्त्वं जहि तां प्रयत्नात् त्यक्ते तु चित्ते न पुनर्भवाशा ॥१६४॥
yatastatastvaṁ jahi tāṁ prayatnāt tyakte tu citte na punarbhavāśā (164)

164. Identification with the body alone is the seed from which arise attachments to the non-Reality—and the ensuing miseries of births and deaths; therefore destroy this cardinal seed with your full diligence and utmost might. When this identification is rooted out, there is no more chance of a future rebirth.

कर्मेन्द्रियैः पञ्चभिरञ्चितोऽयं प्राणो भवेत्प्राणमयस्तु कोशः ।
karmendriyaiḥ pañcabhirañcito'yaṁ prāṇo bhavetprāṇamayastu kośaḥ ,
येनात्मवानन्नमयोऽनुपूर्णः प्रवर्ततेऽसौ सकलक्रियासु ॥ १६५॥
yenātmavānannamayo'nupūrṇaḥ pravartate'sau sakalakriyāsu (165)

165. *Prānamaya-Kosha*—the Vital-sheath—is comprised of the *Prānas* and the five organs of action. Imbued with it, the Material-sheath engages itself in all activities—appearing as if it itself were living and conscious.

नैवात्मापि प्राणमयो वायुविकारो गन्ताऽऽगन्ता वायुवदन्तर्बहिरेषः ।
naivātmāpi prāṇamayo vāyuvikāro gantā''gantā vāyuvadantarbahireṣaḥ ,
यस्मात्किञ्चित्क्वापि न वेत्तीष्टमनिष्टं स्वं वान्यं वा किञ्चन नित्यं परतन्त्रः ॥ १६६॥
yasmātkiñcitkvāpi na vettīṣṭamaniṣṭaṁ svaṁ vānyaṁ vā kiñcana nityaṁ paratantraḥ (166)

166. The Vital-sheath cannot be the Self because it is a modification of *Vāyu* (wind), and like the air it enters the body and then leaves. It doesn't know even its own wellness and woes, let alone of others—being that it is fully dependent upon the Self.

ज्ञानेन्द्रियाणि च मनश्च मनोमयः स्यात्
jñānendriyāṇi ca manaśca manomayaḥ syāt
कोशो ममाहमिति वस्तुविकल्पहेतुः ।
kośo mamāhamiti vastuvikalpahetuḥ ,
संज्ञादिभेदकलनाकलितो बलीयां-
saṁjñādibhedakalanākalito balīyāṁ-
स्तत्पूर्वकोशमभिपूर्य विजृम्भते यः ॥ १६७॥
statpūrvakośamabhipūrya vijṛmbhate yaḥ (167)

167. *Manomaya-Kosha* (the Mental-sheath) is comprised of the Organs of knowledge together with the Mind; it is the cause of the notions of 'I' and 'mine' and of the diversity of things. It is very potent and endowed with the essential faculty of creating differences of names, forms etc. It manifests itself as pervading the preceding Vital-sheath.

पञ्चेन्द्रियैः पञ्चभिरेव होतृभिः प्रचीयमानो विषयाज्यधारया ।
pañcendriyaiḥ pañcabhireva hotṛbhiḥ pracīyamāno viṣayājyadhārayā ,
जाज्वल्यमानो बहुवासनेन्धनैः मनोमयाग्निर्दहति प्रपञ्चम् ॥ १६८॥
jājvalyamāno bahuvāsanendhanaiḥ manomayāgnirdahati prapañcam (168)

168. The Mental-sheath is the sacrificial fire (*Yajna*) which—fed with the fuel of numerous desires by the five sense-organs (which serve as the sacrificial priests), and set ablaze by the sense-objects (which act as the stream of oblations pouring in)—brings about and sustains this phenomenal universe.

न ह्यस्त्यविद्या मनसोऽतिरिक्ता मनो ह्यविद्या भवबन्धहेतुः ।
na hyastyavidyā manaso'tiriktā mano hyavidyā bhavabandhahetuḥ ,
तस्मिन्विनष्टे सकलं विनष्टं विजृम्भितेऽस्मिन्सकलं विजृम्भते ॥ १६९ ॥
tasminvinaṣṭe sakalaṁ vinaṣṭaṁ vijṛmbhite'sminsakalaṁ vijṛmbhate (169)

169. There is no Nescience (*Avidyā*) outside of the Mind; the Mind alone represents *Avidyā*, Ignorance, the root cause of bondages which leads to transmigration. With *Avidyā* destroyed, all else stands destroyed; and with *Avidyā* manifest, everything non-Real appears to become Real as well—in its delusional colored labyrinths.

स्वप्नेऽर्थशून्ये सृजति स्वशक्त्या भोक्त्रादिविश्वं मन एव सर्वम् ।
svapne'rthaśūnye sṛjati svaśaktyā bhoktrādiviśvaṁ mana eva sarvam ,
तथैव जाग्रत्यपि नो विशेषः तत्सर्वमेतन्मनसो विजृम्भणम् ॥ १७० ॥
tathaiva jāgratyapi no viśeṣaḥ tatsarvametanmanaso vijṛmbhaṇam (170)

170. In the Dream-state—when there is no actual contact with the external world—it is the Mind which projects the entire dream universe consisting of the seer, seen etc. The waking-state is no different; this phenomenal world is but the projection of the Mind.

सुषुप्तिकाले मनसि प्रलीने नैवास्ति किञ्चित्सकलप्रसिद्धेः ।
suṣuptikāle manasi pralīne naivāsti kiñcitsakalaprasiddheḥ ,
अतो मनःकल्पित एव पुंसः संसार एतस्य न वस्तुतोऽस्ति ॥ १७१ ॥
ato manaḥkalpita eva puṁsaḥ saṁsāra etasya na vastuto'sti (171)

171. In dreamless-sleep—where the Mind is reduced to its causal state—there exists nothing, as is evident from the universal experience of all; hence this relative existence seen in the waking state is simply the creation of the Mind, bereft of reality.

वायुनाऽऽनीयते मेघः पुनस्तेनैव नीयते ।
vāyunā''nīyate meghaḥ punastenaiva nīyate ,
मनसा कल्प्यते बन्धो मोक्षस्तेनैव कल्प्यते ॥ १७२ ॥
manasā kalpyate bandho mokṣastenaiva kalpyate (172)

172. Clouds are brought in by the wind, and it is the wind again that drives them away; so too man's Bondage is caused by the Mind, and Liberation too is caused by the same.

देहादिसर्वविषये परिकल्प्य रागं बध्नाति तेन पुरुषं पशुवद्गुणेन ।
dehādisarvaviṣaye parikalpya rāgaṁ badhnāti tena puruṣaṁ paśuvadguṇena ,
वैरस्यमत्र विषवत् सुविधाय पश्चाद् एनं विमोचयति तन्मन एव बन्धात् ॥ १७३ ॥
vairasyamatra viṣavat suvidhāya paścād enaṁ vimocayati tanmana eva bandhāt (173)

173. The Mind first creates an attachment in man for the body and sense-objects, binding him through those fetters: like a beast tied through ropes. Then learning lessons from the perniciousness and excruciations inherent in the sense-objects, the selfsame Mind creates in man an utter revulsion for them—whereby it lets go of them, thereby freed from the self-caused bondages.

तस्मान्मनः कारणमस्य जन्तोः बन्धस्य मोक्षस्य च वा विधाने ।
tasmānmanaḥ kāraṇamasya jantoḥ bandhasya mokṣasya ca vā vidhāne ,
बन्धस्य हेतुर्मलिनं रजोगुणैः मोक्षस्य शुद्धं विरजस्तमस्कम् ॥ १७४ ॥
bandhasya heturmalinaṁ rajoguṇaiḥ mokṣasya śuddhaṁ virajastamaskam (174)

174. Therefore the Mind alone is the root cause which brings about man's Bondage and Liberation. When tainted by the effects of *Rajas*, Mind leads to Bondages; and when it is pure and free of the *Rajas* and *Tamas* elements, it paves way for Liberation.

विवेकवैराग्यगुणातिरेकाच्छुद्धत्वमासाद्य मनो विमुक्त्यै ।
vivekavairāgyaguṇātirekācchuddhatvamāsādya mano vimuktyai ,
भवत्यतो बुद्धिमतो मुमुक्षोस्ताभ्यां दृढाभ्यां भवितव्यमग्रे ॥ १७५ ॥
bhavatyato buddhimato mumukṣo-stābhyāṁ dṛḍhābhyāṁ bhavitavyamagre (175)

175. By cultivating the practices of Discrimination and Renunciation, the mind attains purity and makes for Liberation; hence the wise seeker of freedom should first strengthen these two at the very outset.

मनो नाम महाव्याघ्रो विषयारण्यभूमिषु ।
mano nāma mahāvyāghro viṣayāraṇyabhūmiṣu ,
चरत्यत्र न गच्छन्तु साधवो ये मुमुक्षवः ॥ १७६ ॥
caratyatra na gacchantu sādhavo ye mumukṣavaḥ (176)

176. In the forest tracts of sense-pleasures, there prowls a mighty sinister tiger called the Mind; let the wise and virtuous who have a yearning for Liberation, never take a stroll in that place.

मनः प्रसूते विषयानशेषान् स्थूलात्मना सूक्ष्मतया च भोक्तुः ।
manaḥ prasūte viṣayānaśeṣān sthūlātmanā sūkṣmatayā ca bhoktuḥ ,
शरीरवर्णाश्रमजातिभेदान् गुणक्रियाहेतुफलानि नित्यम् ॥ १७७ ॥
śarīravarṇāśramajātibhedān guṇakriyāhetuphalāni nityam (177)

177. The Mind continually produces for the experiencer all these sense-objects—whether perceived as gross or subtle, without exception—and also the various differences stemming from body, caste, creed, and social order; and also the varieties of qualification, action, means and results; verily it's just the Mind generating all these.

असङ्गचिद्रूपममुं विमोह्य देहेन्द्रियप्राणगुणैर्निबद्ध्य ।
asaṅgacidrūpamamuṁ vimohya dehendriyaprāṇaguṇairnibaddhya ,
अहम्ममेति भ्रमयत्यजस्रं मनः स्वकृत्येषु फलोपभुक्तिषु ॥ १७८ ॥
ahammameti bhramayatyajasraṁ manaḥ svakṛtyeṣu phalopabhuktiṣu (178)

178. Deluding the *Jiva*—which is unattached pure Intelligence—and binding it through the fetters of body, organs, and *Prānas*, the Mind causes it to revels amidst the myriad enjoyments of fruits it has gathered around itself driven by the ideas of 'me' and 'mine'.

अध्यासदोषात्पुरुषस्य संसृतिः अध्यासबन्धस्त्वमुनैव कल्पितः ।
adhyāsadoṣātpuruṣasya saṁsṛtiḥ adhyāsabandhastvamunaiva kalpitaḥ ,
रजस्तमोदोषवतोऽविवेकिनो जन्मादिदुःखस्य निदानमेतत् ॥ १७९ ॥
rajastamodoṣavato'vivekino janmādiduḥkhasya nidānametat (179)

179. Man's transmigration is due to the evil of superimposition; and this bondage of superimposition is created by the Mind; therefore for the Non-discriminating Mind that has become blemished through *Rajas* and *Tamas*, it is the superimpositions which should be recognized to be the root causes of the transmigratory birth-death sufferings—and eliminated.

अतः प्राहुर्मनोऽविद्यां पण्डितास्तत्त्वदर्शिनः ।
ataḥ prāhurmano'vidyāṁ paṇḍitāstattvadarśinaḥ ,
येनैव भ्राम्यते विश्वं वायुनेवाभ्रमण्डलम् ॥ १८० ॥
yenaiva bhrāmyate viśvaṁ vāyunevābhramaṇḍalam (180)

180. The wise, who understand the secret of such things, have designated the mind to be *Avidyā* or Nescience; and in the sway of its Ignorance, this experienced universe moves about raging within the mind—like heaps of clouds in turmoil, tossed hither-thither in the gusty winds.

तन्मनःशोधनं कार्यं प्रयत्नेन मुमुक्षुणा ।
tanmanaḥśodhanaṁ kāryaṁ prayatnena mumukṣuṇā ,
विशुद्धे सति चैतस्मिन्मुक्तिः करफलायते ॥ १८१ ॥
viśuddhe sati caitasminmuktiḥ karaphalāyate (181)

181. So therefore the purification of the mind must be carried out with the greatest of diligence by the seekers of Liberation. Once the mind is purified, Liberation is as easy of access as a fruit held in one's palm.

मोक्षैकसक्त्या विषयेषु रागं निर्मूल्य सन्न्यस्य च सर्वकर्म ।
mokṣaikasaktyā viṣayeṣu rāgaṁ nirmūlya sannyasya ca sarvakarma ,
सच्छ्रद्धया यः श्रवणादिनिष्ठो रजःस्वभावं स धुनोति बुद्धेः ॥१८२॥
sacchraddhayā yaḥ śravaṇādiniṣṭho rajaḥsvabhāvaṁ sa dhunoti buddheḥ (182)

182. Through the means of a single-pointed devotion for attaining Liberation, one who roots out all the attachments for sense-objects; and renounces all actions; and regularly practices Hearing etc., with full faith in the supreme reality *Brahama*—he succeeds in Taming the Mind by purging it of its *Rājasika* nature.

मनोमयो नापि भवेत्परात्मा ह्याद्यन्तवत्त्वात्परिणामिभावात् ।
manomayo nāpi bhavetparātmā hyādyantavattvātpariṇāmibhāvāt ,
दुःखात्मकत्वाद्विषयत्वहेतोः द्रष्टा हि दृश्यात्मतया न दृष्टः ॥१८३॥
duḥkhātmakatvādviṣayatvahetoḥ draṣṭā hi dṛśyātmatayā na dṛṣṭaḥ (183)

183. Neither can the Mental-sheath be the Supreme-Self, because it has a beginning and end, and is subject to modifications, and is characterized by pain and sufferings, and importantly is itself an object of cognition—whereas the subject can never be identical with the objects of knowledge. (The Seer cannot simultaneously see itself.)

बुद्धिर्बुद्धीन्द्रियैः सार्धं सवृत्तिः कर्तृलक्षणः ।
buddhirbuddhīndriyaiḥ sārdhaṁ savṛttiḥ kartṛlakṣaṇaḥ ,
विज्ञानमयकोशः स्यात्पुंसः संसारकारणम् ॥१८४॥
vijñānamayakośaḥ syātpuṁsaḥ saṁsārakāraṇam (184)

184. The *Buddhi* and its modifications—along with the organs of perception—comprise the *Vijnānamay-Kosha* (Knowledge-sheath). It has the characteristics of being an agent, or doer, and is the cause of transmigration.

अनुव्रजच्चित्प्रतिबिम्बशक्तिः विज्ञानसंज्ञः प्रकृतेर्विकारः ।
anuvrajaccitpratibimbaśaktiḥ vijñānasaṁjñaḥ prakṛtervikāraḥ ,
ज्ञानक्रियावानहमित्यजस्रं देहेन्द्रियादिष्वभिमन्यते भृशम् ॥१८५॥
jñānakriyāvānahamityajasraṁ dehendriyādiṣvabhimanyate bhṛśam (185)

185. Accompanied by a reflection of the light of consciousness, this Knowledge-sheath is a modification of *Prakriti* (Nature); it is endowed with the functions of knowledge and action; and it

always abides completely identified with the body, sense-organs, etc.

अनादिकालोऽयमहंस्वभावो जीवः समस्तव्यवहारवोढा ।
anādikālo'yamahaṁsvabhāvo jīvaḥ samastavyavahāravoḍhā ,
करोति कर्माण्यपि पूर्ववासनः पुण्यान्यपुण्यानि च तत्फलानि ॥ १८६ ॥
karoti karmāṇyapi pūrvavāsanaḥ puṇyānyapuṇyāni ca tatphalāni (186)

186. Beginning-less in origin and of the nature of ego, it is called the *Jiva*—the embodied Self or the Soul—and it carries out all the activities on the relative plane. Through latent tendencies and desires—current and former, including from all prior lives—it performs actions good and evil, and experiences the results thereof.

भुङ्क्ते विचित्रास्वपि योनिषु व्रजन्नायाति निर्यात्यध ऊर्ध्वमेषः ।
bhuṅkte vicitrāsvapi yoniṣu vrajannāyāti niryātyadha ūrdhvameṣaḥ ,
अस्यैव विज्ञानमयस्य जाग्रत्स्वप्नाद्यवस्थाः सुखदुःखभोगः ॥ १८७ ॥
asyaiva vijñānamayasya jāgratsvapnādyavasthāḥ sukhaduḥkhabhogaḥ (187)

187. Rolling up and down on the waves of this worldly ocean, the *Jiva* comes and goes, taking births in various bodies, experiencing the variety of joys and sorrows of life as the Knowledge-sheath—which has the Waking, Dream and Deep-sleep, as its various states.

देहादिनिष्ठाश्रमधर्मकर्मगुणाभिमानः सततं ममेति ।
dehādiniṣṭhāśramadharmakarmaguṇābhimānaḥ satataṁ mameti ,
विज्ञानकोशोऽयमतिप्रकाशः प्रकृष्टसान्निध्यवशात्परात्मनः ।
vijñānakośo'yamatiprakāśaḥ prakṛṣṭasānnidhyavaśātparātmanaḥ ,
अतो भवत्येष उपाधिरस्य यदात्मधीः संसरति भ्रमेण ॥ १८८ ॥
ato bhavatyeṣa upādhirasya yadātmadhīḥ saṁsarati bhrameṇa (188)

188. It ever misidentifies the duties, functions, attributes, orders of life etc.,—which rather belong to the body—to be its very own. The Knowledge-sheath is exceedingly effulgent owing to its close proximity to the *Ātmā*. It is a superimposition on the *Ātmā* which, having identified itself with it, endures transmigration through delusion.

योऽयं विज्ञानमयः प्राणेषु हृदि स्फुरत्ययं ज्योतिः ।
yo'yaṁ vijñānamayaḥ prāṇeṣu hṛdi sphuratyayaṁ jyotiḥ ,
कूटस्थः सन्नात्मा कर्ता भोक्ता भवत्युपाधिस्थः ॥ १८९ ॥
kūṭasthaḥ sannātmā kartā bhoktā bhavatyupādhisthaḥ (189)

189. The *Ātmā*, which is self-effulgent and pure knowledge, shines in the midst of the *Prānas,* within the heart. Though immutable, the *Ātmā* seems to become the doer and the

experiencer—owing to its superimposition: the Knowledge-sheath.

स्वयं परिच्छेदमुपेत्य बुद्धेः तादात्म्यदोषेण परं मृषात्मनः ।
svayaṁ paricchedamupetya buddheḥ tādātmyadoṣeṇa paraṁ mṛṣātmanaḥ ,
सर्वात्मकः सन्नपि वीक्षते स्वयं स्वतः पृथक्त्वेन मृदो घटानिव ॥ १९० ॥
sarvātmakaḥ sannapi vīkṣate svayaṁ svataḥ pṛthaktvena mṛdo ghaṭāniva (190)

190. Although it is the Self of everything that exists the *Ātmā*, itself assuming the limitations of the *Buddhi*, and wrongly identifying itself with that non-Real entity, looks upon itself as something which it is not. This is exactly how the clay in the jar would consider itself to be distinct and different from the unmanifest clay—its substratum.

उपाधिसम्बन्धवशात्परात्मा ह्युपाधिधर्माननुभाति तद्गुणः ।
upādhisambandhavaśātparātmā hyupādhidharmānanubhāti tadguṇaḥ ,
अयोविकारानविकारिवह्निवत् सदैकरूपोऽपि परः स्वभावात् ॥ १९१ ॥
ayovikārānavikārivahnivat sadaikarūpo'pi paraḥ svabhāvāt (191)

191. The *Ātmā* is by its very nature perfect, supreme, eternal; but by dint of its identifications with its superimpositions, it assumes the characteristics of those limiting adjuncts and appears to behave as if it itself were them. This is how the pristine formless fire takes on the modifications and shapes of the molten iron objects when it turns them fiery—in the process itself becoming them.

शिष्य उवाच :
śiṣya uvāca :

भ्रमेणाप्यन्यथा वाऽस्तु जीवभावः परात्मनः ।
bhrameṇāpyanyathā vā'stu jīvabhāvaḥ parātmanaḥ ,
तदुपाधेरनादित्वान्नानादेर्नाश इष्यते ॥ १९२ ॥
tadupādheranāditvānnānādernāśa iṣyate (192)

192. The disciple now asked: Be it through delusion or otherwise, the supreme *Ātmā* has now come to consider Itself to be the *Jiva*; and this superimposition is beginning-less; and that which is beginning-less cannot be supposed to have an end either.

अतोऽस्य जीवभावोऽपि नित्या भवति संसृतिः ।
ato'sya jīvabhāvo'pi nityā bhavati saṁsṛtiḥ ,
न निवर्तेत तन्मोक्षः कथं मे श्रीगुरो वद ॥ १९३ ॥
na nivarteta tanmokṣaḥ kathaṁ me śrīguro vada (193)

193. So for the *Ātmā*, this warped sense (that of being an embodied *Jiva*) will therefore never end; and its transmigration will continue unabated unremittingly. So how can there be any Liberation for the soul, ever? Kindly enlighten me on this point, O venerable master.

श्रीगुरुरुवाच:
śrīgururuvāca :

सम्यक्पृष्टं त्वया विद्वन्सावधानेन तच्छृणु ।
samyakpṛṣṭaṁ tvayā vidvansāvadhānena tacchṛṇu ,
प्रामाणिकी न भवति भ्रान्त्या मोहितकल्पना ॥ १९४ ॥
prāmāṇikī na bhavati bhrāntyā mohitakalpanā (194)

194. The Master replied: You raise a valid point, O learned wise! Now listen with attention. Imaginations and ideations that have been conjured through Delusion, can not be accepted to be facts and realities.

भ्रान्तिं विना त्वसङ्गस्य निष्क्रियस्य निराकृतेः ।
bhrāntiṁ vinā tvasaṅgasya niṣkriyasya nirākṛteḥ ,
न घटेतार्थसम्बन्धो नभसो नीलतादिवत् ॥ १९५ ॥
na ghaṭetārthasambandho nabhaso nīlatādivat (195)

195. Apropos the *Ātmā,* which is innately actionless, formless and unattached, there can be no association with the objective world other than through Imagination and Delusion—just as on empty Space (which is truly void of attributes), the ideas of the blueness etc., of the sky have been imposed.

स्वस्य द्रष्टुर्निर्गुणस्याक्रियस्य प्रत्यग्बोधानन्दरूपस्य बुद्धेः ।
svasya draṣṭurnirguṇasyākriyasya pratyagbodhānandarūpasya buddheḥ ,
भ्रान्त्या प्राप्तो जीवभावो न सत्यो मोहापाये नास्त्यवस्तुस्वभावात् ॥ १९६ ॥
bhrāntyā prāpto jīvabhāvo na satyo mohāpāye nāstyavastusvabhāvāt (196)

196. This falsehood—that of "being an embodied *Jiva*"—which has been superimposed upon the *Ātmā* through the delusions of the *Buddhi*—is not Real; and being non-Real, it ceases to exist once the delusion has been removed; and with delusion dispelled, then what shines forth is just the Truth: that the *Ātmā* is pure, beyond attributes and qualities and beyond activities, and merely a Witness. (In *Samādhi* the *Ātmā* is directly verified within, as pristine Consciousness and Bliss).

यावद् भ्रान्तिस्तावदेवास्य सत्ता मिथ्याज्ञानोज्जृम्भितस्य प्रमादात् ।
yāvad bhrāntistāvadevāsya sattā mithyājñānojjṛmbhitasya pramādāt ,
रज्ज्वां सर्पो भ्रान्तिकालीन एव भ्रान्तेर्नाशे नैव सर्पोऽपि तद्वत् ॥ १९७ ॥
rajjvāṁ sarpo bhrāntikālīna eva bhrānternāśe naiva sarpo'pi tadvat (197)

197. This 'state' of being an embodied *Jiva* exists only so long as the delusion—caused by error and indiscrimination—persists. The rope is supposed to be a snake only so long as the false understanding lasts, and the snake disappears as soon as the confusion disappears; same is the case here.

अनादित्वमविद्यायाः कार्यस्यापि तथेष्यते ।
anāditvamavidyāyāḥ kāryasyāpi tatheṣyate ,
उत्पन्नायां तु विद्यायामाविद्यकमनाद्यपि ॥ १९८ ॥
utpannāyāṁ tu vidyāyāmāvidyakamanādyapi (198)

198. *Avidyā* (Nescience) and its effects, might appear to be beginning-less; but with the rise of *Vidyā* or Realization, the entire effects of *Avidyā*—even though ostensibly beginning-less—stand altogether eradicated, root and branch.

प्रबोधे स्वप्नवत्सर्वं सहमूलं विनश्यति ।
prabodhe svapnavatsarvaṁ sahamūlaṁ vinaśyati ,
अनाद्यपीदं नो नित्यं प्रागभाव इव स्फुटम् ॥ १९९ ॥
anādyapīdaṁ no nityaṁ prāgabhāva iva sphuṭam (199)

199. This is how the dream-world vanishes altogether upon waking up from sleep. It is clear that the phenomenal universe, even though without a beginning, is not eternal—just like the prior non-existence wasn't eternal. (Because the so called 'eternal' non-existence state ended immediately upon the birth of the universe, and therefore it wasn't really eternal).

अनादेरपि विध्वंसः प्रागभावस्य वीक्षितः ।
anāderapi vidhvaṁsaḥ prāgabhāvasya vīkṣitaḥ ,
यद्बुद्ध्युपाधिसम्बन्धात्परिकल्पितमात्मनि ॥ २०० ॥
yadbuddhyupādhisambandhātparikalpitamātmani (200)

जीवत्वं न ततोऽन्यस्तु स्वरूपेण विलक्षणः ।
jīvatvaṁ na tato'nyastu svarūpeṇa vilakṣaṇaḥ ,
सम्बन्धस्त्वात्मनो बुद्ध्या मिथ्याज्ञानपुरःसरः ॥ २०१ ॥
sambandhastvātmano buddhyā mithyājñānapuraḥsaraḥ (201)

200-201. Previous non-existence, even though beginning-less, is observed to have an end. Similarly, the embodied *Jiva*-state—which is imagined to be in the *Ātmā* through its apparent association with the superimposing adjuncts of *Buddhi* etc.—does end; being that only the *Ātmā* is Real and is moreover drastically different from its embodied states; and the perceived connections between the *Ātmā* and the *Buddhi* are completely due to error and ignorance.

विनिवृत्तिर्भवेत्तस्य सम्यग्ज्ञानेन नान्यथा ।
vinivṛttirbhavettasya samyagjñānena nānyathā ,
ब्रह्मात्मैकत्वविज्ञानं सम्यग्ज्ञानं श्रुतेर्मतम् ॥ २०२ ॥
brahmātmaikatvavijñānaṁ samyagjñānaṁ śrutermatam (202)

202. The cessation of this superimposition takes place only with the dawn of perfect understanding—and there's no other way. According to the *Shrutis*, perfect knowledge consists in the Realization of the identity of the *Jiva* with the Absolute (*Brahama*)—which alone leads to the Truth that decimates every error of misunderstanding.

तदात्मानात्मनोः सम्यग्विवेकेनैव सिध्यति ।
tadātmānātmanoḥ samyagvivekenaiva sidhyati ,
ततो विवेकः कर्तव्यः प्रत्यगात्मसदात्मनोः ॥ २०३ ॥
tato vivekaḥ kartavyaḥ pratyagātmasadātmanoḥ (203)

203. This Realization is attained only through Right Discrimination: discerning the Self from the not-Self. Therefore at all times one must be vigilantly engaged in discriminating between the Self—our inmost eternal essence, the *Ātmā*—and everything that's not the *Ātmā*.

जलं पङ्कवदत्यन्तं पङ्कापाये जलं स्फुटम् ।
jalaṁ paṅkavadatyantaṁ paṅkāpāye jalaṁ sphuṭam ,
यथा भाति तथात्मापि दोषाभावे स्फुटप्रभः ॥ २०४ ॥
yathā bhāti tathātmāpi doṣābhāve sphuṭaprabhaḥ (204)

204. Just as the muddy water appears clear and transparent once the mud has been removed, even so the Fiery *Ātmā* shines in its undimmed glorious luster when all the superimposing impurities obscuring it have disappeared.

असन्निवृत्तौ तु सदात्मना स्फुटं प्रतीतिरेतस्य भवेत्प्रतीचः ।
asannivṛttau tu sadātmanā sphuṭaṁ pratītiretasya bhavetpratīcaḥ ,
ततो निरासः करणीय एव सदात्मनः साध्वहमादिवस्तुनः ॥ २०५ ॥
tato nirāsaḥ karaṇīya eva sadātmanaḥ sādhvahamādivastunaḥ (205)

205. When the non-Real ceases to exist, then this very individual soul (the *Jiva*) is realized to be the eternal Self, the *Ātmā*, clearly and for sure. Therefore one must strive to fully remove all non-Realities like egoism etc., that veil the *Ātmā*.

अतो नायं परात्मा स्याद्विज्ञानमयशब्दभाक् ।
ato nāyaṁ parātmā syādvijñānamayaśabdabhāk ,
विकारित्वाज्जडत्वाच्च परिच्छिन्नत्वहेतुतः ।
vikāritvājjaḍatvācca paricchinnatvahetutaḥ ,
दृश्यत्वाद्व्यभिचारित्वान्नानित्यो नित्य इष्यते ॥२०६॥
dṛśyatvādvyabhicāritvānnānityo nitya iṣyate (206)

206. This Knowledge-sheath (*Vijnānamaya Kosha*) which we have been speaking of, cannot be the Supreme Self for the following reasons: because it is subject to changes and is inert and confined and is an object for the senses and is not constantly present. A something non-Real like that cannot be considered to be eternal—which the *Ātmā* is.

आनन्दप्रतिबिम्बचुम्बिततनुर्वृत्तिस्तमोजृम्भिता
ānandapratibimbacumbitatanurvṛttistamojṛmbhitā
स्यादानन्दमयः प्रियादिगुणकः स्वेष्टार्थलाभोदयः ।
syādānandamayaḥ priyādiguṇakaḥ sveṣṭārthalābhodayaḥ ,
पुण्यस्यानुभवे विभाति कृतिनामानन्दरूपः स्वयं
puṇyasyānubhave vibhāti kṛtināmānandarūpaḥ svayaṁ
सर्वो नन्दति यत्र साधु तनुभृन्मात्रः प्रयत्नं विना ॥२०७॥
sarvo nandati yatra sādhu tanubhṛnmātraḥ prayatnaṁ vinā (207)

207. The Bliss-sheath (*Ānandamaya Kosha*) is that modification of Nescience which manifests itself catching a reflection of the Blissful-One (*Ātmā*). Its attributes are pleasure etc.; it takes shape when agreeable sense objects present themselves. It also makes itself spontaneously felt by the fortunate during the fruition of their virtuous deeds. From it, every corporeal being is transported to the realm of amorous joy without the least bit of effort.

आनन्दमयकोशस्य सुषुप्तौ स्फूर्तिरुत्कटा ।
ānandamayakośasya suṣuptau sphūrtirutkaṭā ,
स्वप्नजागरयोरीषदिष्टसन्दर्शनादिना ॥२०८॥
svapnajāgarayorīṣadiṣṭasandarśanādinā (208)

208. The Bliss-sheath has its fullest play during the state of profound sleep—with only part manifestation in the dreaming and waking states: occasioned by the sight of agreeable sense-objects and so forth.

नैवायमानन्दमयः परात्मा सोपाधिकत्वात्प्रकृतेर्विकारात् ।
naivāyamānandamayaḥ parātmā sopādhikatvātprakṛtervikārāt ,
कार्यत्वहेतोः सुकृतक्रियाया विकारसङ्घातसमाहितत्वात् ॥२०९॥
kāryatvahetoḥ sukṛtakriyāyā vikārasaṅghātasamāhitatvāt (209)

209. Nor is the Bliss-sheath the supreme *Ātmā*—being that it is endowed with changeful characteristics, and it is a modification of the *Prakriti* (Nature), and is an effect of past good deeds; and being that is imbedded in the other sheaths which themselves are modifications.

पञ्चानामपि कोशानां निषेधे युक्तितः श्रुतेः ।
pañcānāmapi kośānāṁ niṣedhe yuktitaḥ śruteḥ ,
तन्निषेधावधि साक्षी बोधरूपोऽवशिष्यते ॥२१०॥
tanniṣedhāvadhi sākṣī bodharūpo'vaśiṣyate (210)

210. When all the five sheaths have been eliminated through reasoning on the Truths of Vedānta, then what remains—at the culmination of the phenomenon—is just the backdrop, the substratum, the witness: the Eternal *Ātmā* of the nature of pristine consciousness.

योऽयमात्मा स्वयञ्ज्योतिः पञ्चकोशविलक्षणः ।
yo'yamātmā svayañjyotiḥ pañcakośavilakṣaṇaḥ ,
अवस्थात्रयसाक्षी सन्निर्विकारो निरञ्जनः ।
avasthātrayasākṣī sannirvikāro nirañjanaḥ ,
सदानन्दः स विज्ञेयः स्वात्मत्वेन विपश्चिता ॥२११॥
sadānandaḥ sa vijñeyaḥ svātmatvena vipaścitā (211)

211. This *Ātmā*—which is Self-effulgent, Distinct from the five sheaths, the Witness of the three states, the Real, the Changeless, the Untainted, and of the nature of everlasting Bliss—is to be realized by the adept and wise as one's very own Self.

शिष्य उवाच :
śiṣya uvāca :

मिथ्यात्वेन निषिद्धेषु कोशेष्वेतेषु पञ्चसु ।
mithyātvena niṣiddheṣu kośeṣveteṣu pañcasu ,
सर्वाभावं विना किञ्चिन्न पश्याम्यत्र हे गुरो ।
sarvābhāvaṁ vinā kiñcinna paśyāmyatra he guro ,
विज्ञेयं किमु वस्त्वस्ति स्वात्मनाऽऽत्मविपश्चिता ॥२१२॥
vijñeyaṁ kimu vastvasti svātmanā''tmavipaścitā (212)

212. The disciple questions: After all the five sheaths have been eliminated as non-Real, then what is left remaining is simply zero, O master; and I find nothing in the universe but a Void, the absence of everything. What entity is left anymore with which the wise seeker would realize his identity?

श्रीगुरुरुवाच:
śrīgururuvāca :

सत्यमुक्तं त्वया विद्वन्निपुणोऽसि विचारणे ।
satyamuktaṁ tvayā vidvannipuṇo'si vicāraṇe ,
अहमादिविकारास्ते तदभावोऽयमप्यनु ॥२१३॥
ahamādivikārāste tadabhāvo'yamapyanu (213)

सर्वे येनानुभूयन्ते यः स्वयं नानुभूयते ।
sarve yenānubhūyante yaḥ svayaṁ nānubhūyate ,
तमात्मानं वेदितारं विद्धि बुद्ध्या सुसूक्ष्मया ॥२१४॥
tamātmānaṁ veditāraṁ viddhi buddhyā susūkṣmayā (214)

213-214. The Master answers: Well spoken, O learned man, you are clever indeed in your perceptiveness. So now listen with care. That by which all these modifications such as egoism etc., (or their absence) are known—but which itself is never comprehended or perceived (only felt or realized as the Self)—thou must discover that *Ātmā*, the Ultimate-Knower, through the sharpest, finest intellect.

तत्साक्षिकं भवेत्तत्तद्यद्यद्येनानुभूयते ।
tatsākṣikaṁ bhavettattadyadyadyenānubhūyate ,
कस्याप्यननुभूतार्थे साक्षित्वं नोपयुज्यते ॥२१५॥
kasyāpyananubhūtārthe sākṣitvaṁ nopayujyate (215)

215. That which is perceived by something else, has for its witness the latter. But when there's that something existent which can never be known to anyone, then, to witness or perceive That, that is not in the realm of possibilities.

असौ स्वसाक्षिको भावो यतः स्वेनानुभूयते ।
asau svasākṣiko bhāvo yataḥ svenānubhūyate ,
अतः परं स्वयं साक्षात्प्रत्यगात्मा न चेतरः ॥२१६॥
ataḥ paraṁ svayaṁ sākṣātpratyagātmā na cetaraḥ (216)

216. This *Ātmā* is a self-cognized Entity because It can only be cognized By Itself, and As Itself. The *Ātmā* Itself is the Supreme *Brahama*, and there's nothing else besides It that can perceive It.

जाग्रत्स्वप्नसुषुप्तिषु स्फुटतरं योऽसौ समुज्जृम्भते
jāgratsvapnasuṣuptiṣu sphuṭataraṁ yo'sau samujjṛmbhate
प्रत्यग्रूपतया सदाहमहमित्यन्तः स्फुरन्नैकधा ।
pratyagrūpatayā sadāhamahamityantaḥ sphurannaikadhā ,
नानाकारविकारभागिन इमान् पश्यन्नहन्धीमुखान्
nānākāravikārabhāgina imān paśyannahandhīmukhān
नित्यानन्दचिदात्मना स्फुरति तं विद्धि स्वमेतं हृदि ॥२१७॥
nityānandacidātmanā sphurati taṁ viddhi svametaṁ hṛdi (217)

217. That, which clearly manifests itself in the waking, dream and deep-sleep states—which is inwardly perceived in various forms as an unbroken continuity of egoistic impression 'I'—which is the Witness of the egoism and intellect that have taken on diverse forms and modifications—which makes itself felt as Existence-Consciousness-Bliss Absolute—know thou of That *Ātmā* within thy core, as thy very own Self—having nothing else as the witness.

घटोदके बिम्बितमर्कबिम्बमालोक्य मूढो रविमेव मन्यते ।
ghaṭodake bimbitamarkabimbamālokya mūḍho ravimeva manyate ,
तथा चिदाभासमुपाधिसंस्थं भ्रान्त्याहमित्येव जडोऽभिमन्यते ॥२१८॥
tathā cidābhāsamupādhisaṁsthaṁ bhrāntyāhamityeva jaḍo'bhimanyate (218)

218. On seeing the reflection of sun mirrored in the water-jar, a simpleton may think it to be some autonomous sun itself. Likewise driven by delusion, an ignorant man ends up identifying himself with the reflection of consciousness as the Real thing, his own Self. He does not realize that reflecting as the ego and intellect within the body—it is the fiery glow of the *Ātmā* which is imparting shine to those.

घटं जलं तद्गतमर्कबिम्बंविहाय सर्वं विनिरीक्ष्यतेऽर्कः ।
ghaṭaṁ jalaṁ tadgatamarkabimbaṁvihāya sarvaṁ vinirīkṣyate'rkaḥ ,
तटस्थ एतत्त्रितयावभासकः स्वयंप्रकाशो विदुषा यथा तथा ॥२१९॥
taṭastha etattritayāvabhāsakaḥ svayaṁprakāśo viduṣā yathā tathā (219)

219. The wise man eliminates all the three—the jar, the water and the reflection of the sun in it—and discerns the real truth: namely that it is some Real sun—a separate, distinct, self-luminous, self-existent entity—which is illuminating those three dependent entities.

देहं धियं चित्प्रतिबिम्बमेवं विसृज्य बुद्धौ निहितं गुहायाम् ।
dehaṁ dhiyaṁ citpratibimbamevaṁ visṛjya buddhau nihitaṁ guhāyām ,
द्रष्टारमात्मानमखण्डबोधं सर्वप्रकाशं सदसद्विलक्षणम् ॥२२०॥
draṣṭāramātmānamakhaṇḍabodhaṁ sarvaprakāśaṁ sadasadvilakṣaṇam (220)
नित्यं विभुं सर्वगतं सुसूक्ष्मं अन्तर्बहिःशून्यमनन्यमात्मनः ।
nityaṁ vibhuṁ sarvagataṁ susūkṣmaṁ antarbahiḥśūnyamananyamātmanaḥ ,
विज्ञाय सम्यङ्निजरूपमेतत् पुमान् विपाप्मा विरजो विमृत्युः ॥२२१॥
vijñāya samyaṅnijarūpametat pumān vipāpmā virajo vimṛtyuḥ (221)

220-221. Similarly, discarding the body and the intellect etc.,—which are the reflections of consciousness shining within; and realizing That Self which is the Witness, the Real, the Knowledge Absolute, the Cause of manifestation of everything –

which is hidden deep in the recesses of the *Buddhi* – which is Distinct from the gross and the subtle – which is eternal and Omnipresent – which is supremely Subtle and all-Pervading – which is without exterior or interior—and fully realizing that the true natures of one's self is not different from That Self, one reaches the state that is free from sin, free from blemishes, free from death, and becomes the very embodiment of Bliss.

विशोक आनन्दघनो विपश्चित् स्वयं कुतश्चिन्न बिभेति कश्चित् ।
viśoka ānandaghano vipaścit svayaṁ kutaścinna bibheti kaścit ,
नान्योऽस्ति पन्था भवबन्धमुक्तेः विना स्वतत्त्वावगमं मुमुक्षोः ॥२२२॥
nānyo'sti panthā bhavabandhamukteḥ
vinā svatattvāvagamaṁ mumukṣoḥ (222)

222. Verily that Realized one becomes fully illumined, fearless, sorrowless and the very personification of Bliss. For one seeking liberation, there is no other means of breaking free from the bonds of transmigration other than realizing one's Oneness within the *Ātmā*.

ब्रह्माभिन्नत्वविज्ञानं भवमोक्षस्य कारणम् ।
brahmābhinnatvavijñānaṁ bhavamokṣasya kāraṇam ,
येनाद्वितीयमानन्दं ब्रह्म सम्पद्यते बुधैः ॥२२३॥
yenādvitīyamānandaṁ brahma sampadyate budhaiḥ (223)

223. This Realization of one's identity with *Brahama* is the direct cause of Liberation from the bonds of *Samsāra*; only by that means, the wise attain Him—the singular One without a second, the Bliss Absolute.

ब्रह्मभूतस्तु संसृत्यै विद्वान्नावर्तते पुनः ।
brahmabhūtastu saṁsṛtyai vidvānnāvartate punaḥ ,
विज्ञातव्यमतः सम्यग्ब्रह्माभिन्नत्वमात्मनः ॥२२४॥
vijñātavyamataḥ samyagbrahmābhinnatvamātmanaḥ (224)

224. Once having realized *Brahama*, one no longer returns to the realm of transmigration; therefore one must strive to the fullest to fully Realize one's identity within *Brahama*.

सत्यं ज्ञानमनन्तं ब्रह्म विशुद्धं परं स्वतःसिद्धम् ।
satyaṁ jñānamanantaṁ brahma viśuddhaṁ paraṁ svataḥsiddham ,
नित्यानन्दैकरसं प्रत्यगभिन्नं निरन्तरं जयति ॥२२५॥
nityānandaikarasaṁ pratyagabhinnaṁ nirantaraṁ jayati (225)

225. *Brahama* is Existence-Knowledge-Absolute, infinite, vestal, supreme, self-existent, eternal and indivisible Bliss, devoid of interior exterior or parts, and not different from one's self at the essence. It is ever triumphant.

सदिदं परमाद्वैतं स्वस्मादन्यस्य वस्तुनोऽभावात् ।
sadidaṁ paramādvaitaṁ svasmādanyasya vastuno'bhāvāt ,
न ह्यन्यदस्ति किञ्चित् सम्यक् परमार्थतत्त्वबोधदशायाम् ॥ २२६ ॥
na hyanyadasti kiñcit samyak paramārthatattvabodhadaśāyām (226)

226. It is this supreme Singular entity *Brahama* which alone is Real. There is nothing else but That Being anywhere in existence. And in the state of direct Realization of Oneness in *Brahama*, one finds that there remains no other independent entity except *Brahama*.

यदिदं सकलं विश्वं नानारूपं प्रतीतमज्ञानात् ।
yadidaṁ sakalaṁ viśvaṁ nānārūpaṁ pratītamajñānāt ,
तत्सर्वं ब्रह्मैव प्रत्यस्ताशेषभावनादोषम् ॥ २२७ ॥
tatsarvaṁ brahmaiva pratyastāśeṣabhāvanādoṣam (227)

227. This here entire universe—which through Ignorance appears to be of diverse forms—is nothing but *Brahama*, absolutely free of any limitations which the human thoughts can conceive.

मृत्कार्यभूतोऽपि मृदो न भिन्नः कुम्भोऽस्ति सर्वत्र तु मृत्स्वरूपात् ।
mṛtkāryabhūto'pi mṛdo na bhinnaḥ kumbho'sti sarvatra tu mṛtsvarūpāt ,
न कुम्भरूपं पृथगस्ति कुम्भः कुतो मृषा कल्पितनाममात्रः ॥ २२८ ॥
na kumbharūpaṁ pṛthagasti kumbhaḥ kuto mṛṣā kalpitanāmamātraḥ (228)

228. A jar, though a modification of the clay, is not different from the clay. Throughout the jar, only the clay is present. Why then call it a jar? It is just a fancy name imposed upon the clay—an imagined fictional play of words.

केनापि मृद्भिन्नतया स्वरूपं घटस्य सन्दर्शयितुं न शक्यते ।
kenāpi mṛdbhinnatayā svarūpaṁ ghaṭasya sandarśayituṁ na śakyate ,
अतो घटः कल्पित एव मोहान्मृदेव सत्यं परमार्थभूतम् ॥ २२९ ॥
ato ghaṭaḥ kalpita eva mohānmṛdeva satyaṁ paramārthabhūtam (229)

229. None can demonstrate that the essence of a jar is something other than the clay of which it is made. The jar is merely imagined to be a separate and distinct entity due to the delusion imposed by dint of 'name and form'. Verily the component clay alone is the abiding reality in respect of the jar—and into which it eventually must return one day.

सद्ब्रह्मकार्यं सकलं सदेवं तन्मात्रमेतन्न ततोऽन्यदस्ति ।
sadbrahmakāryaṁ sakalaṁ sadevaṁ tanmātrametanna tato'nyadasti ,
अस्तीति यो वक्ति न तस्य मोहोविनिर्गतो निद्रितवत्प्रजल्पः ॥ २३० ॥
astīti yo vakti na tasya mohovinirgato nidritavatprajalpaḥ (230)

230. So too, the entire universe, being just the effect of *Brahama*, is in reality nothing but *Brahama*. At its core, it is just That Reality. It does not exist apart from That Reality. And whosoever speaks otherwise is alike a person babbling in dense sleep—fully delusional.

ब्रह्मैवेदं विश्वमित्येव वाणी श्रौती ब्रूतेऽथर्वनिष्ठा वरिष्ठा ।
brahmaivedaṁ viśvamityeva vāṇī śrautī brūte'tharvaniṣṭhā variṣṭhā ,
तस्मादेतद्ब्रह्ममात्रं हि विश्वं नाधिष्ठानाद्भिन्नताऽऽरोपितस्य ॥२३१॥
tasmādetadbrahmamātraṁ hi viśvaṁ nādhiṣṭhānādbhinnatā''ropitasya (231)

231. This universe is nothing but *Brahama*—that is the august pronouncement of the *Atharva Veda*. Verily the universe is *Brahama* and nothing but *Brahama*—because a superimposition cannot have a distinct existence separate from its substratum.

सत्यं यदि स्याज्जगदेतदात्मनोऽनन्तत्त्वहानिर्निगमाप्रमाणता ।
satyaṁ yadi syājjagadetadātmano'nantattvahānirnigamāpramāṇatā ,
असत्यवादित्वमपीशितुः स्यान्नैतत्त्रयं साधु हितं महात्मनाम् ॥२३२॥
asatyavāditvamapīśituḥ syānnaitattrayaṁ sādhu hitaṁ mahātmanām (232)

232. If the universe be Real in its manifest diverse appearances, then of the Self there would be infinite elements, and there will be no dearth of duality, and therefore the scriptures would stand falsified, and the Lord Himself would be guilty of untruth. None of these three is considered suitable or satisfying to the noble-minded.

ईश्वरो वस्तुतत्त्वज्ञो न चाहं तेष्ववस्थितः ।
īśvaro vastutattvajño na cāhaṁ teṣvavasthitaḥ ,
न च मत्स्थानि भूतानीत्येवमेव व्यचीक्लृपत् ॥२३३॥
na ca matsthāni bhūtānītyevameva vyacīklṛpat (233)

233. The Lord, who knows the secret of all things, has supported this view in the words, "I am not in them... nor are the beings in Me..." etc.

यदि सत्यं भवेद्विश्वं सुषुप्तावुपलभ्यताम् ।
yadi satyaṁ bhavedviśvaṁ suṣuptāvupalabhyatām ,
यन्नोपलभ्यते किञ्चिदतोऽसत्स्वप्नवन्मृषा ॥२३४॥
yannopalabhyate kiñcidato'satsvapnavanmṛṣā (234)

234. If this diverse universe be true, let it then be perceived in the state of profound-sleep too; but since it is not at all perceived then, therefore its manifoldness must be non-Real and false, just like a dream.

अतः पृथङ्नास्ति जगत्परात्मनः पृथक्प्रतीतिस्तु मृषा गुणादिवत् ।
ataḥ pṛthaṅnāsti jagatparātmanaḥ pṛthakpratītistu mṛṣā guṇādivat ,
आरोपितस्यास्ति किमर्थवत्ताऽधिष्ठानमाभाति तथा भ्रमेण ॥२३५॥
āropitasyāsti kimarthavattā'dhiṣṭhānamābhāti tathā bhrameṇa (235)

235. So therefore, the manifold universe has no existence aside from the singular Supreme-Self; and the perception of distinctness and separateness which appears in it is illusory—like the appearance of snake in a rope. Does a superimposed attribute have any existence separate from its substratum? It is the substrate which appears to be like the superimposed attribute due to delusion (—like 'blue' is superimposed upon the pristine Space during the day and the 'black' during the night).

भ्रान्तस्य यद्यद्भ्रमतः प्रतीतं ब्रह्मैव तत्तद्रजतं हि शुक्तिः ।
bhrāntasya yadyadbhramataḥ pratītaṁ brahmaiva tattadrajataṁ hi śuktiḥ ,
इदन्तया ब्रह्म सदैव रूप्यते त्वारोपितं ब्रह्मणि नाममात्रम् ॥२३६॥
idantayā brahma sadaiva rūpyate tvāropitaṁ brahmaṇi nāmamātram (236)

236. Through errors and delusions of Nescience, whatever the deluded beings perceive to be a distinct something in the universe—all that is just *Brahama* and *Brahama* alone; all that silvery sheen is indeed only the mother-of-pearl. *Brahama* is ever present as it is, and that which has been superimposed on *Brahama*—the 'Universe'—is merely the diversity of names and forms.

अतः परं ब्रह्म सदद्वितीयं विशुद्धविज्ञानघनं निरञ्जनम् ।
ataḥ paraṁ brahma sadadvitīyaṁ viśuddhavijñānaghanaṁ nirañjanam ,
प्रशान्तमाद्यन्तविहीनमक्रियं निरन्तरानन्दरसस्वरूपम् ॥२३७॥
praśāntamādyantavihīnamakriyaṁ nirantarānandarasasvarūpam (237)

237. So in essence, whatever appears to be manifested is nothing but the Supreme *Brahama* Itself—the Real, non-dual, arrantly pure, taintless, supremely serene, without a beginning, without an end, beyond activity, and ever of the essence of absolute Knowledge and Bliss.

निरस्तमायाकृतसर्वभेदं नित्यं सुखं निष्कलमप्रमेयम् ।
nirastamāyākṛtasarvabhedaṁ nityaṁ sukhaṁ niṣkalamaprameyam ,
अरूपमव्यक्तमनाख्यमव्ययं ज्योतिः स्वयं किञ्चिदिदं चकास्ति ॥२३८॥
arūpamavyaktamanākhyamavyayaṁ jyotiḥ svayaṁ kiñcididaṁ cakāsti (238)

238. Transcending all distinctions and diversities brought on by *Māyā*, the Supreme *Brahama* is self-effulgent, eternal,

indivisible, immeasurable, formless, unmanifest, undifferentiated, nameless, immutable, and the very essence of Bliss.

ज्ञातृज्ञेयज्ञानशून्यमनन्तं निर्विकल्पकम् ।
jñātṛjñeyajñānaśūnyamanantaṁ nirvikalpakam ,
केवलाखण्डचिन्मात्रं परं तत्त्वं विदुर्बुधाः ॥ २३९ ॥
kevalākhaṇḍacinmātraṁ paraṁ tattvaṁ vidurbudhāḥ (239)

239. That supreme Being *Brahama*—in which there are no differentiations such as knower, knowledge and known; which is infinite, transcendent, and the essence of Knowledge Absolute—is directly realized within as the very own Self by the sage.

अहेयमनुपादेयं मनोवाचामगोचरम् ।
aheyamanupādeyaṁ manovācāmagocaram ,
अप्रमेयमनाद्यन्तं ब्रह्म पूर्णमहं महः ॥ २४० ॥
aprameyamanādyantaṁ brahma pūrṇamahaṁ mahaḥ (240)

240. Which can be neither be thrown away nor taken up, which is beyond the reach of mind and speech, which is immeasurable, without a beginning and end, and replete with fullness—That is the *Ātmā*, of surpassing glory, one's very own Self.

तत्त्वम्पदाभ्यामभिधीयमानयोः ब्रह्मात्मनोः शोधितयोर्यदीत्थम् ।
tattvampadābhyāmabhidhīyamānayoḥ brahmātmanoḥ śodhitayoryadīttham ,
श्रुत्या तयोस्तत्त्वमसीति सम्यग् एकत्वमेव प्रतिपाद्यते मुहुः ॥ २४१ ॥
śrutyā tayostattvamasīti samyag ekatvameva pratipādyate muhuḥ (241)

ऐक्यं तयोर्लक्षितयोर्न वाच्ययोः निगद्यतेऽन्योन्यविरुद्धधर्मिणोः ।
aikyaṁ tayorlakṣitayorna vācyayoḥ nigadyate'nyonyaviruddhadharmiṇoḥ ,
खद्योतभान्वोरिव राजभृत्ययोः कूपाम्बुराश्योः परमाणुमेर्वोः ॥ २४२ ॥
khadyotabhānvoriva rājabhṛtyayoḥ kūpāmburāśyoḥ paramāṇumervoḥ (242)

241-242. If in the dictum "That Thou art" (*Tat-Tvam-Asi*), the *Shrutis* repeatedly establish the absolute identity of *Brahama* (*Param-Ātmā*) and the Soul (*Jīva*)—denoted by the terms *Tat* (That) and *Tvam* (Thou) respectively—then divesting these terms of their relative associations, it is their implied identity—as opposed to a literal identity—which is to be understood here. Because they are as different as two ends when it comes to a literal comparison—like the sun and a glow-worm, the king and a servant, the ocean and pond, the mount *Meru* and an atom—although they may be established to be alike in their implied identity.

तयोर्विरोधोऽयमुपाधिकल्पितो न वास्तवः कश्चिदुपाधिरेषः ।
tayorvirodho'yamupādhikalpito na vāstavaḥ kaścidupādhireṣaḥ ,
ईशस्य माया महदादिकारणं जीवस्य कार्यं शृणु पञ्चकोशम् ॥ २४३ ॥
Iśasya māyā mahadādikāraṇaṁ jīvasya kāryaṁ śṛṇu pañcakośam (243)

243. This difference is by dint of superimposition and not something innate, or real. The superimposition—in the case of *Ishwara* (the Lord-God)—is *Māyā* or Nescience, the cause of *Mahat* and the rest. And listen, this superimposition—in the case of the *Jiva* (the individual soul)—is the group of five sheaths: all, the effects of Ignorance.

एतावुपाधी परजीवयोस्तयोः सम्यङ्निरासे न परो न जीवः ।
etāvupādhī parajīvayostayoḥ samyaṅnirāse na paro na jīvaḥ ,
राज्यं नरेन्द्रस्य भटस्य खेटकस्तयोरपोहे न भटो न राजा ॥ २४४ ॥
rājyaṁ narendrasya bhaṭasya kheṭakstayorapohe na bhaṭo na rājā (244)

244. These two are superimpositions on the *Ishwara* (Lord-God) and the *Jiva* (individual soul) respectively, and when completely eliminated, there is neither the *Ishwara*, nor the *Jiva*—just only *Brahama*. A kingdom and a uniform, vested on a person, make him a king and soldier respectively, and when these superimpositions are taken away, there is neither the king, nor the soldier—just only the person as is.

अथात आदेश इति श्रुतिः स्वयं निषेधति ब्रह्मणि कल्पितं द्वयम् ।
athāta ādeśa iti śrutiḥ svayaṁ niṣedhati brahmaṇi kalpitaṁ dvayam ,
श्रुतिप्रमाणानुगृहीतबोधा त्तयोर्निरासः करणीय एव ॥ २४५ ॥
śrutipramāṇānugṛhītabodhā ttayornirāsaḥ karaṇīya eva (245)

245. The Vedas themselves in the words "Now then is the injunction..." etc., reject the imagined duality in *Brahama*. So one must needs root out these superimpositions by means of direct Realization supported by the authority of the *Shrutis*.

नेदं नेदं कल्पितत्वान्न सत्यं रज्जुदृष्टव्यालवत्स्वप्नवच्च ।
nedaṁ nedaṁ kalpitatvānna satyaṁ rajjudṛṣṭavyālavatsvapnavacca ,
इत्थं दृश्यं साधुयुक्त्या व्यपोह्य ज्ञेयः पश्चादेकभावस्तयोर्यः ॥ २४६ ॥
itthaṁ dṛśyaṁ sādhuyuktyā vyapohya jñeyaḥ paścādekabhāvastayoryaḥ (246)

246. The *Ātmā* is neither the gross things nor the subtle—which all are merely non-Real and the fancies of delusions and dreams: like a snake imagined in the rope in dark. In this way, thoroughly eliminating the manifold universe by means of reasoning supported by *Shrutis*, one should Realize that

Oneness which underlies *Ishwara* (Lord-God) and the *Jiva* (the individual soul).

ततस्तु तौ लक्षणया सुलक्ष्यौ तयोरखण्डैकरसत्वसिद्धये ।
tatastu tau lakṣaṇayā sulakṣyau tayorakhaṇḍaikarasatvasiddhaye ,
नालं जहत्या न तथाऽजहत्या किन्तूभयार्थात्मिकयैव भाव्यम् ॥ २४७ ॥
nālaṁ jahatyā na tathā'jahatyā kintūbhayārthātmikayaiva bhāvyam (247)

247. Therefore verily these two must be carefully considered through their indicative meanings in order that their absolute identity is established. Neither the method of total rejection nor that of complete retention will do; instead one must take recourse to a reasoning that synthesizes the two.

स देवदत्तोऽयमितीह चैकता विरुद्धधर्मांशमपास्य कथ्यते ।
sa devadatto'yamitīha caikatā viruddhadharmāṁśamapāsya kathyate ,
यथा तथा तत्त्वमसीतिवाक्ये विरुद्धधर्मानुभयत्र हित्वा ॥ २४८ ॥
yathā tathā tattvamasītivākye viruddhadharmānubhayatra hitvā (248)

संलक्ष्य चिन्मात्रतया सदात्मनोः अखण्डभावः परिचीयते बुधैः ।
saṁlakṣya cinmātratayā sadātmanoḥ akhaṇḍabhāvaḥ paricīyate budhaiḥ ,
एवं महावाक्यशतेन कथ्यते ब्रह्मात्मनोरैक्यमखण्डभावः ॥ २४९ ॥
evaṁ mahāvākyaśatena kathyate brahmātmanoraikyamakhaṇḍabhāvaḥ (249)

248-249. Just as in the sentence, "This is that Devadatta", the identity is emphasized, eliminating the contradictory part; similarly in the dictum "*Tat Tvam Asi*" ("That Thou art"), the wise should give up the conflicting elements on both sides so as to recognize the identity implied, noticing carefully the common mutual innate essence of both—which is *Chitta*, or Absolute Consciousness. In that way, hundreds of our scriptural texts have imparted instructions on the Oneness of *Brahama*(God) and *Jiva* (soul).

अस्थूलमित्येतदसन्निरस्य सिद्धं स्वतो व्योमवदप्रतर्क्यम् ।
asthūlamityetadasannirasya siddhaṁ svato vyomavadapratarkyam ,
अतो मृषामात्रमिदं प्रतीतं जहीहि यत्स्वात्मतया गृहीतम् ।
ato mṛṣāmātramidaṁ pratītaṁ jahīhi yatsvātmatayā gṛhītam ,
ब्रह्माहमित्येव विशुद्धबुद्ध्या विद्धि स्वमात्मानमखण्डबोधम् ॥ २५० ॥
brahmāhamityeva viśuddhabuddhyā viddhi svamātmānamakhaṇḍabodham (250)

250. Eliminating the not-Self in the light of such passages as "It is not gross..." etc., one realizes that Self: which is self-constituted, unattached like the space, and beyond the ambit of thought. Therefore reject this specter of a body—which you perceive and have accepted to be your self; and by means of the purified understanding: "I am *Brahama*", realize your true Self: which is pristine Consciousness.

मृत्कार्यं सकलं घटादि सततं मृन्मात्रमेवाहितं
mṛtkāryaṁ sakalaṁ ghaṭādi satataṁ mṛnmātramevāhitaṁ
तद्वत्सज्जनितं सदात्मकमिदं सन्मात्रमेवाखिलम् ।
tadvatsajjanitaṁ sadātmakamidaṁ sanmātramevākhilam ,
यस्मान्नास्ति सतः परं किमपि तत्सत्यं स आत्मा स्वयं
yasmānnāsti sataḥ paraṁ kimapi tatsatyaṁ sa ātmā svayaṁ
तस्मात्तत्त्वमसि प्रशान्तममलं ब्रह्माद्वयं यत्परम् ॥ २५१ ॥
tasmāttattvamasi praśāntamamalaṁ brahmādvayaṁ yatparam (251)

251. All modifications of the clay—such as pots etc., which are always accepted by the mind to be real—are in fact nothing but clay; similarly this here entire universe, which is produced from *Brahama*, is *Brahama* Itself and nothing but *Brahama*. Being that there exists nothing else whatsoever besides *Brahama*, the only self-existent Reality, which is our very own Self. So then verily thou too art That—the serene, the pure, the supreme *Brahama*, the One without a second.

निद्राकल्पितदेशकालविषयज्ञात्रादि सर्वं यथा
nidrākalpitadeśakālaviṣayajñātrādi sarvaṁ yathā
मिथ्या तद्वदिहापि जाग्रति जगत्स्वाज्ञानकार्यत्वतः ।
mithyā tadvadihāpi jāgrati jagatsvājñānakāryatvataḥ ,
यस्मादेवमिदं शरीरकरणप्राणाहमाद्यप्यसत्
yasmādevamidaṁ śarīrakaraṇaprāṇāhamādyapyasat
तस्मात्तत्त्वमसि प्रशान्तममलं ब्रह्माद्वयं यत्परम् ॥ २५२ ॥
tasmāttattvamasi praśāntamamalaṁ brahmādvayaṁ yatparam (252)

252. As the place, time, objects, knower etc., called up in a dream are all non-Real, so also is the case with the world experienced in the Waking-state: it is all the projected effects of Nescience. With the body, organs, *Prānas*, egoism, etc., all thus reasoned out to be non-Real, thereafter what remains is That: the supreme *Brahama*, the One without a second, serene and pure—which you are.

यत्र भ्रान्त्या कल्पितं तद्विवेके तत्तन्मात्रं नैव तस्माद्विभिन्नम् ।
yatra bhrāntyā kalpitaṁ tadviveke tattanmātraṁ naiva tasmādvibhinnam ,
स्वप्ने नष्टं स्वप्नविश्वं विचित्रं स्वस्माद्भिन्नं किन्नु दृष्टं प्रबोधे ॥ २५३ ॥
svapne naṣṭaṁ svapnaviśvaṁ vicitraṁ svasmādbhinnaṁ kinnu dṛṣṭaṁ prabodhe (253)

253. When covered, a thing may appear to be just like the veil itself, but when the truth of it becomes known, then it is clearly recognized to be just the underlying substrate—which it always was and not at all anything different from the original. The heterogeneous dream universe emerges, and then also submerges, in the dream state itself. Upon waking, does it still

persist as a something Real?...as something other than the imagination it was?

जातिनीतिकुलगोत्रदूरगं नामरूपगुणदोषवर्जितम् ।
jātinītikulagotradūragaṁ nāmarūpaguṇadoṣavarjitam ,
देशकालविषयातिवर्ति यद् ब्रह्म तत्त्वमसि भावयात्मनि ॥ २५४ ॥
deśakālaviṣayātivarti yad brahma tattvamasi bhāvayātmani (254)

254. That which is beyond caste and creed, family and lineage, without names and forms, merits and demerits, transcending space, time, and matter—Thou art That *Brahama*, meditate on this in thy mind.

यत्परं सकलवागगोचरं गोचरं विमलबोधचक्षुषः ।
yatparaṁ sakalavāgagocaraṁ gocaraṁ vimalabodhacakṣuṣaḥ ,
शुद्धचिद्घनमनादि वस्तु यद् ब्रह्म तत्त्वमसि भावयात्मनि ॥ २५५ ॥
śuddhacidghanamanādi vastu yad brahma tattvamasi bhāvayātmani (255)

255. That Supreme *Brahama* which is beyond the range of speech and accessible only through the eyes of pure illumination; which is the pristine totality of consciousness, the beginning-less Being—Thou art That *Brahama*, meditate on this in thy mind.

षड्भिरूर्मिभिरयोगि योगिहृद्भावितं न करणैर्विभावितम् ।
ṣaḍbhirūrmibhirayogi yogihṛdbhāvitaṁ na karaṇairvibhāvitam ,
बुद्ध्यवेद्यमनवद्यमस्ति यद् ब्रह्म तत्त्वमसि भावयात्मनि ॥ २५६ ॥
buddhyavedyamanavadyamasti yad brahma tattvamasi bhāvayātmani (256)

256. That—which is untouched by any of the sixfold sorrows—which is meditated upon within the Yogi's heart but never grasped by any sense-organ—which the *Buddhi* cannot know—which is of flawless excellence—Thou art That *Brahama*, meditate on this in thy mind.

भ्रान्तिकल्पितजगत्कलाश्रयं स्वाश्रयं च सदसद्विलक्षणम् ।
bhrāntikalpitajagatkalāśrayaṁ svāśrayaṁ ca sadasadvilakṣaṇam ,
निष्कलं निरुपमानवद्धि यद् ब्रह्म तत्त्वमसि भावयात्मनि ॥ २५७ ॥
niṣkalaṁ nirupamānavaddhi yad brahma tattvamasi bhāvayātmani (257)

257. That—which is the substratum of the universe with all its subdivisions that are all creations of delusion—which itself is its own support—which is distinct from the subtle and gross—which has no parts and has verily no exemplar—Thou art That *Brahama*: meditate on this in thy mind.

जन्मवृद्धिपरिणत्यपक्षयव्याधिनाशनविहीनमव्ययम् ।
janmavṛddhipariṇatyapakṣayavyādhināśanavihīnamavyayam ,

विश्वसृष्ट्यवविघातकारणं ब्रह्म तत्त्वमसि भावयात्मनि ॥२५८॥
viśvasṛṣṭyavavighātakāraṇaṁ brahma tattvamasi bhāvayātmani (258)

258. That—which is free from birth, growth, aging, waste, disease, death - which is indestructible - which is the cause of the projection, maintenance and dissolution of the universe—That *Brahama* thou art: meditate on this in thy mind.

अस्तभेदमनपास्तलक्षणं निस्तरङ्गजलराशिनिश्चलम् ।
astabhedamanapāstalakṣaṇaṁ nistaraṅgajalarāśiniścalam ,
नित्यमुक्तमविभक्तमूर्ति यद् ब्रह्म तत्त्वमसि भावयात्मनि ॥२५९॥
nityamuktamavibhaktamūrti yad brahma tattvamasi bhāvayātmani (259)

259. That, which is free from any differentiations; which endures ever existent; which is calm like the waveless ocean; which is ever-free; which is partless, of indivisible form—Thou art That *Brahama*, meditate on this in thy mind.

एकमेव सदनेककारणं कारणान्तरनिरास्यकारणम् ।
ekameva sadanekakāraṇaṁ kāraṇāntaranirāsyakāraṇam ,
कार्यकारणविलक्षणं स्वयं ब्रह्म तत्त्वमसि भावयात्मनि ॥२६०॥
kāryakāraṇavilakṣaṇaṁ svayaṁ brahma tattvamasi bhāvayātmani (260)

260. Which, though One and the only Reality, is the cause of the many; which refutes all causes—being itself causeless; which is beyond *Māyā* and the notions of cause and effects—Thou art That self-existent *Brahama*: meditate on this in thy mind.

निर्विकल्पकमनल्पमक्षरं यत्क्षराक्षरविलक्षणं परम् ।
nirvikalpakamanalpamakṣaraṁ yatkṣarākṣaravilakṣaṇaṁ param ,
नित्यमव्ययसुखं निरञ्जनं ब्रह्म तत्त्वमसि भावयात्मनि ॥२६१॥
nityamavyayasukhaṁ nirañjanaṁ brahma tattvamasi bhāvayātmani (261)

261. That—which is free from duality - which is infinite and indestructible - which is indefinable and distinct from the perishable and the imperishable - which is undying Bliss - which is taintless and sinless—Thou art That *Brahama*, Supreme and Eternal: meditate on this in thy mind.

यद्विभाति सदनेकधा भ्रमान्नामरूपगुणविक्रियात्मना ।
yadvibhāti sadanekadhā bhramānnāmarūpaguṇavikriyātmanā ,
हेमवत्स्वयमविक्रियं सदा ब्रह्म तत्त्वमसि भावयात्मनि ॥२६२॥
hemavatsvayamavikriyaṁ sadā brahma tattvamasi bhāvayātmani (262)

262. That Reality which although One appears to be many owing to *Māyā*; which—though taking on names and forms, attributes and changes—at the core always persists changeless,

like gold in its modifications: Thou art That *Brahama*, meditate on this in thy mind.

यच्चकास्त्यनपरं परात्परं प्रत्यगेकरसमात्मलक्षणम् ।
yaccakāstyanaparaṁ parātparaṁ pratyagekarasamātmalakṣaṇam ,
सत्यचित्सुखमनन्तमव्ययं ब्रह्म तत्त्वमसि भावयात्मनि ॥२६३॥
satyacitsukhamanantamavyayaṁ brahma tattvamasi bhāvayātmani (263)

263. That beyond which there is nothing - which shines even beyond *Māyā*, which itself is superior to its effect, the universe - which is the inmost Self of all, free from differentiations - which is the Real Self, the Existence-Knowledge-Bliss Absolute - which is infinite and immutable: Thou art That Absolute *Brahama*, meditate on this in thy mind.

उक्तमर्थमिममात्मनि स्वयं भावयेत्प्रथितयुक्तिभिर्धिया ।
uktamarthamimamātmani svayaṁ bhāvayetprathitayuktibhirdhiyā ,
संशयादिरहितं कराम्बुवत् तेन तत्त्वनिगमो भविष्यति ॥२६४॥
saṁśayādirahitaṁ karāmbuvat tena tattvanigamo bhaviṣyati (264)

264. On the Truth inculcated above by means of recognized arguments, one must meditate within, with a Purified Intellect. By that means one will realize—as palpably and easy as water gathered in one's palm—the Supreme Truth, freed of all doubts.

सम्बोधमात्रं परिशुद्धतत्त्वं विज्ञाय सङ्घे नृपवच्च सैन्ये ।
sambodhamātraṁ pariśuddhatattvaṁ vijñāya saṅghe nṛpavacca sainye ,
तदाश्रयः स्वात्मनि सर्वदा स्थितो विलापय ब्रह्मणि विश्वजातम् ॥२६५॥
tadāśrayaḥ svātmani sarvadā sthito vilāpaya brahmaṇi viśvajātam (265)

265. Altogether free of Nescience and its effects, and reigning mightily like the king of an army, and Realizing within of your supreme pure essence, and being ever established in that inner Self, let this manifold universe forever merge in *Brahama*.

बुद्धौ गुहायां सदसद्विलक्षणं ब्रह्मास्ति सत्यं परमद्वितीयम् ।
buddhau guhāyāṁ sadasadvilakṣaṇaṁ brahmāsti satyaṁ paramadvitīyam ,
तदात्मना योऽत्र वसेद्गुहायां पुनर्न तस्याङ्गगुहाप्रवेशः ॥२६६॥
tadātmanā yo'tra vasedguhāyāṁ punarna tasyāṅgaguhāpraveśaḥ (266)

266. In the cave of the *Buddhi* abides *Brahama*—the Supreme non-dual Reality, the One without a second, distinct from the gross and subtle. For one who abides in this cave in complete identity with *Brahama*, there is no more the pain, horror, sorrow of abiding in a mother's womb in future.

ज्ञाते वस्तुन्यपि बलवती वासनाऽनादिरेषा
jñāte vastunyapi balavatī vāsanā'nādireṣā
कर्ता भोक्ताप्यहमिति दृढा याऽस्य संसारहेतुः ।
kartā bhoktāpyahamiti dṛḍhā yā'sya saṁsārahetuḥ ,
प्रत्यग्दृष्ट्याऽऽत्मनि निवसता सापनेया प्रयत्ना-
pratyagdṛṣṭyā''tmani nivasatā sāpaneyā prayatnā-
न्मुक्तिं प्राहुस्तदिह मुनयो वासनातानवं यत् ॥ २६७॥
nmuktiṁ prāhustadiha munayo vāsanātānavaṁ yat (267)

267. Even after the Truth has been realized, there still persists that perverse, tenacious, residual impression—"I am the doer and seer"—which is the cause of the transmigratory cycle of births-deaths continuing unabated. Therefore this impression has to be carefully weeded out by living in a state of continual identification with the Supreme Self. The attenuation of all *Vāsanās* (impressions), here and now, is designated by the sages as Living-Liberation.

अहं ममेति यो भावो देहाक्षादावनात्मनि ।
ahaṁ mameti yo bhāvo dehākṣādāvanātmani ,
अध्यासोऽयं निरस्तव्यो विदुषा स्वात्मनिष्ठया ॥ २६८॥
adhyāso'yaṁ nirastavyo viduṣā svātmaniṣṭhayā (268)

268. The persistent notion of 'me' and 'mine' with respect to the body and organs, etc.,—which are the not-Self—must be firmly rooted out; put an end to this false identification, by being always firmly established in complete identity with *Brahama*.

ज्ञात्वा स्वं प्रत्यगात्मानं बुद्धितद्वृत्तिसाक्षिणम् ।
jñātvā svaṁ pratyagātmānaṁ buddhitadvṛttisākṣiṇam ,
सोऽहमित्येव सद्वृत्त्याऽनात्मन्यात्ममतिं जहि ॥ २६९॥
so'hamityeva sadvṛttyā'nātmanyātmamatiṁ jahi (269)

269. Realizing thy innermost Self—as the Witness of the *Buddhi* and its modifications—and ever maintaining, "I am *Brahama*", conquer over Ignorance which insists on identifying the Self with the not-Self.

लोकानुवर्तनं त्यक्त्वा त्यक्त्वा देहानुवर्तनम् ।
lokānuvartanaṁ tyaktvā tyaktvā dehānuvartanam ,
शास्त्रानुवर्तनं त्यक्त्वा स्वाध्यासापनयं कुरु ॥ २७०॥
śāstrānuvartanaṁ tyaktvā svādhyāsāpanayaṁ kuru (270)

270. Relinquishing the observance of social formalities, dispensing away with the worldly ways; foreswearing preoccupations related to the body; and without being overly

obsessed with the scriptural texts—do thou carefully wean away all superimpositions that have crept up upon the Self.

लोकवासनया जन्तोः शास्त्रवासनयापि च ।
lokavāsanayā jantoḥ śāstravāsanayāpi ca ,
देहवासनया ज्ञानं यथावन्नैव जायते ॥ २७१ ॥
dehavāsanayā jñānaṁ yathāvannaiva jāyate (271)

271. The passion to run after Society; and an excessive obsessing over Scriptural pursuits; and being overly engrossed with the Body—these Three Fixations are impediments in the path of Realization.

संसारकारागृहमोक्षमिच्छोरयोमयं पादनिबन्धशृङ्खलम् ।
saṁsārakārāgṛhamokṣamicchorayomayaṁ pādanibandhaśṛṅkhalam ,
वदन्ति तज्ज्ञाः पटु वासनात्रयं योऽस्माद्विमुक्तः समुपैति मुक्तिम् ॥ २७२ ॥
vadanti tajjñāḥ paṭu vāsanātrayaṁ yo'smādvimuktaḥ samupaiti muktim (272)

272. The wise regard these Three to be like the Iron Shackles chained to the feet of those seeking emancipation from the prison-house of the world. Only one who is free from all these will attain Liberation.

जलादिसंसर्गवशात्प्रभूतदुर्गन्धधूताऽगरुदिव्यवासना ।
jalādisaṁsargavaśātprabhūtadurgandhadhūtā'garudivyavāsanā ,
सङ्घर्षणेनैव विभाति सम्यग्विधूयमाने सति बाह्यगन्धे ॥ २७३ ॥
saṅgharṣaṇenaiva vibhāti samyagvidhūyamāne sati bāhyagandhe (273)

273. The lovely odor of the sandalwood—which had become obscured by the powerful stench of mold through contact with water—becomes re-manifest as soon as the adulterant has been fully removed by scrubbing.

अन्तःश्रितानन्तदुरन्तवासनाधूलीविलिप्ता परमात्मवासना ।
antaḥśritānantadurantavāsanādhūlīviliptā paramātmavāsanā ,
प्रज्ञातिसङ्घर्षणतो विशुद्धा प्रतीयते चन्दनगन्धवत् स्फुटम् ॥ २७४ ॥
prajñātisaṅgharṣaṇato viśuddhā pratīyate candanagandhavat sphuṭam (274)

274. The essence of the Supreme Self too—which had become covered by the fetor of the filth of endless evil impressions embedded in the mind—becomes re-manifest when purified through a constant scouring of Knowledge, becoming abundantly evident again.

अनात्मवासनाजालैस्तिरोभूतात्मवासना ।
anātmavāsanājālaistirobhūtātmavāsanā ,
नित्यात्मनिष्ठया तेषां नाशे भाति स्वयं स्फुटम् ॥ २७५ ॥
nityātmaniṣṭhayā teṣāṁ nāśe bhāti svayaṁ sphuṭam (275)

275. The desire for Self-realization is obscured by innumerable desires for things other than the Self; and when all these have been purged by a constant devotion to the Self, then the all-glorious *Ātmā* manifests itself spontaneously—all by itself.

यथा यथा प्रत्यगवस्थितं मनः तथा तथा मुञ्चति बाह्यवासनाम् ।
yathā yathā pratyagavasthitaṁ manaḥ tathā tathā muñcati bāhyavāsanām ,
निःशेषमोक्षे सति वासनानां आत्मानुभूतिः प्रतिबन्धशून्या ॥ २७६ ॥
niḥśeṣamokṣe sati vāsanānāṁ ātmānubhūtiḥ pratibandhaśūnyā (276)

276. As the Mind becomes gradually established in the inmost Self, it proportionally gives up its cravings for external things; and when all such desires have been perfectly rooted out, there is a clear, unobstructed realization of the *Ātmā*.

स्वात्मन्येव सदा स्थित्वा मनो नश्यति योगिनः ।
svātmanyeva sadā sthitvā mano naśyati yoginaḥ ,
वासनानां क्षयश्चातः स्वाध्यासापनयं कुरु ॥ २७७ ॥
vāsanānāṁ kṣayaścātaḥ svādhyāsāpanayaṁ kuru (277)

277. Being ever established within his own Self, the Yogi's mind dies; and cessation of all desires is the natural outcome of that. Therefore carefully wean away all superimpositions which are upon the Self.

तमो द्वाभ्यां रजः सत्त्वात्सत्त्वं शुद्धेन नश्यति ।
tamo dvābhyāṁ rajaḥ sattvātsattvaṁ śuddhena naśyati ,
तस्मात्सत्त्वमवष्टभ्य स्वाध्यासापनयं कुरु ॥ २७८ ॥
tasmātsattvamavaṣṭabhya svādhyāsāpanayaṁ kuru (278)

278. *Tamas* is destroyed by both *Sattva* and *Rajas*; and *Rajas* is purged out by *Sattva*; and finally *Sattva* too withers away through purification; therefore diligently eliminate all your superimpositions taking recourse to *Sattva*.

प्रारब्धं पुष्यति वपुरिति निश्चित्य निश्चलः ।
prārabdhaṁ puṣyati vapuriti niścitya niścalaḥ ,
धैर्यमालम्ब्य यत्नेन स्वाध्यासापनयं कुरु ॥ २७९ ॥
dhairyamālambya yatnena svādhyāsāpanayaṁ kuru (279)

279. Assured in the certainty that this body will be sustained through *Prārabdha*, remain steady and quiet; and tenaciously and with patience, carefully weed out all the superimpositions which are upon the Self.

नाहं जीवः परं ब्रह्मेत्यतद्व्यावृत्तिपूर्वकम् ।
nāhaṁ jīvaḥ paraṁ brahmetyatadvyāvṛttipūrvakam ,
वासनावेगतः प्राप्तस्वाध्यासापनयं कुरु ॥ २८० ॥
vāsanāvegataḥ prāptasvādhyāsāpanayaṁ kuru (280)

280. "I am not the *Jiva* (individual soul), but the Supreme *Brahama*"—thus eliminating all that is the not-Self, diligently put to an end all superimpositions which have come upon you through the momentum of past impressions.

श्रुत्या युक्त्या स्वानुभूत्या ज्ञात्वा सार्वात्म्यमात्मनः ।
śrutyā yuktyā svānubhūtyā jñātvā sārvātmyamātmanaḥ ,
क्वचिदाभासतः प्राप्तस्वाध्यासापनयं कुरु ॥२८१॥
kvacidābhāsataḥ prāptasvādhyāsāpanayaṁ kuru (281)

281. Having realized your Self to be the Universal Self, the Self-of-all—by means of scriptures, reasoning, and your own direct experiences—remain diligent; and continue to weed out the last bit of superimposition—even when the slightest trace of it raises its ugly head.

अनादानविसर्गाभ्यामीषन्नास्ति क्रिया मुनेः ।
anādānavisargābhyāmīṣannāsti kriyā muneḥ ,
तदेकनिष्ठया नित्यं स्वाध्यासापनयं कुरु ॥२८२॥
tadekaniṣṭhayā nityaṁ svādhyāsāpanayaṁ kuru (282)

282. The sage has no connection with actions—being unconcerned with the ideas of accepting, releasing etc.—which may be occurring in the body. Therefore by constant absorption and contemplation on *Brahama*, continue to do away with all superimpositions with the utmost vigilance.

तत्त्वमस्यादिवाक्योत्थब्रह्मात्मैकत्वबोधतः ।
tattvamasyādivākyotthabrahmātmaikatvabodhataḥ ,
ब्रह्मण्यात्मत्वदार्ढ्याय स्वाध्यासापनयं कुरु ॥२८३॥
brahmaṇyātmatvadārḍhyāya svādhyāsāpanayaṁ kuru (283)

283. Aye, through the Realization of the identity of Brahama and the self—resorting to such great Vedic maxims such as "That Thou art"— diligently do away with all superimpositions and strengthen your identification in *Brahama*.

अहम्भावस्य देहेऽस्मिन्निःशेषविलयावधि ।
ahambhāvasya dehe'sminniḥśeṣavilayāvadhi ,
सावधानेन युक्तात्मा स्वाध्यासापनयं कुरु ॥२८४॥
sāvadhānena yuktātmā svādhyāsāpanayaṁ kuru (284)

284. Until the identification with this body is completely rooted out, do away with your superimpositions with great care and concentrated mind, striving assiduously all the time, O sage.

प्रतीतिर्जीवजगतोः स्वप्नवद्भाति यावता ।
pratītirjīvajagatoḥ svapnavadbhāti yāvatā ,

तावन्निरन्तरं विद्वन्स्वाध्यासापनयं कुरु ॥२८५॥
tāvannirantaraṁ vidvansvādhyāsāpanayaṁ kuru (285)

285. Aye, as long as even a dream-like perception of the universe and the ego persists, do away with your superimposition diligently, O learned wise, without the least bit of break.

निद्राया लोकवार्तायाः शब्दादेरपि विस्मृतेः ।
nidrāyā lokavārtāyāḥ śabdāderapi vismṛteḥ ,
क्वचिन्नावसरं दत्त्वा चिन्तयात्मानमात्मनि ॥२८६॥
kvacinnāvasaraṁ dattvā cintayātmānamātmani (286)

286. Be not oblivious; without giving the slightest chance to forgetfulness towards the Self—on account of sleep or concern in secular matters or towards the sense-objects—continually meditate upon the *Ātmā* at thy core.

मातापित्रोर्मलोद्भूतं मलमांसमयं वपुः ।
mātāpitrormalodbhūtaṁ malamāṁsamayaṁ vapuḥ ,
त्यक्त्वा चाण्डालवद्दूरं ब्रह्मीभूय कृती भव ॥२८७॥
tyaktvā cāṇḍālavaddūraṁ brahmībhūya kṛtī bhava (287)

287. And as one does unto an outcast, shun from a safe distance this body—issued from the taints of parents and itself comprised of flesh and other impure things—and ever remain as *Brahama*, attaining the consummation of your life.

घटाकाशं महाकाश इवात्मानं परात्मनि ।
ghaṭākāśaṁ mahākāśa ivātmānaṁ parātmani ,
विलाप्याखण्डभावेन तूष्णी भव सदा मुने ॥२८८॥
vilāpyākhaṇḍabhāvena tūṣṇī bhava sadā mune (288)

288. Just as how the Space-Time enclosed within a jar is truly one with the infinite Space-Time, merge your finite soul in the Infinite Self by Meditating on their Oneness—and ever abide in peace and quietude, O sage.

स्वप्रकाशमधिष्ठानं स्वयम्भूय सदात्मना ।
svaprakāśamadhiṣṭhānaṁ svayambhūya sadātmanā ,
ब्रह्माण्डमपि पिण्डाण्डं त्यज्यतां मलभाण्डवत् ॥२८९॥
brahmāṇḍamapi piṇḍāṇḍaṁ tyajyatāṁ malabhāṇḍavat (289)

289. Becoming yourself that self-luminous *Brahama*—the sole substrate of all phenomena, beings, things—give up both the macrocosm and the microcosm, like they were two commodes full of filth.

चिदात्मनि सदानन्दे देहारूढामहन्धियम् ।
cidātmani sadānande dehārūḍhāmahandhiyam ,
निवेश्य लिङ्गमुत्सृज्य केवलो भव सर्वदा ॥२९०॥
niveśya liṅgamutsṛjya kevalo bhava sarvadā (290)

290. Shifting your identification—which is now rooted to body—to the *Ātmā*, which is Existence-Knowledge-Bliss Absolute; and discarding the subtle sheath, do thou abide ever pure, ever free.

यत्रैष जगदाभासो दर्पणान्तः पुरं यथा ।
yatraiṣa jagadābhāso darpaṇāntaḥ puraṁ yathā ,
तद्ब्रह्माहमिति ज्ञात्वा कृतकृत्यो भविष्यसि ॥२९१॥
tadbrahmāhamiti jñātvā kṛtakṛtyo bhaviṣyasi (291)

291. In Whom is found reflecting this dream-like illusory world—just as a city shining in a mirror—thou are That *Brahama*. Know this in an act of direct realization and attain the fulfillment of thy life.

यत्सत्यभूतं निजरूपमाद्यं चिदद्वयानन्दमरूपमक्रियम् ।
yatsatyabhūtaṁ nijarūpamādyaṁ cidadvayānandamarūpamakriyam ,
तदेत्य मिथ्यावपुरुत्सृजेत शैलूषवद्वेषमुपात्तमात्मनः ॥२९२॥
tadetya mithyāvapurutsṛjeta śailūṣavadveṣamupāttamātmanaḥ (292)

292. Attain to oneness in *Brahama*—the only Reality, one's innate primordial essence, absolute Knowledge and Bliss, the One without a second, the One beyond forms and activities—and forever cease identifying the self with this false body, just like an actor casts away the dress and mask he had assumed for a role.

सर्वात्मना दृश्यमिदं मृषैव नैवाहमर्थः क्षणिकत्वदर्शनात् ।
sarvātmanā dṛśyamidaṁ mṛṣaiva naivāhamarthaḥ kṣaṇikatvadarśanāt ,
जानाम्यहं सर्वमिति प्रतीतिः कुतोऽहमादेः क्षणिकस्य सिध्येत् ॥२९३॥
jānāmyahaṁ sarvamiti pratītiḥ kuto'hamādeḥ kṣaṇikasya sidhyet (293)

293. This manifold universe of names and forms is wholly non-Real. Neither is egoism Real—because it is observed to be ever changing. How can the notion, "I am all knowing", be true with regards to ego etc., which are observed to be all so transient and evanescent?

अहम्पदार्थस्त्वहमादिसाक्षी नित्यं सुषुप्तावपि भावदर्शनात् ।
ahampadārthastvahamādisākṣī nityaṁ suṣuptāvapi bhāvadarśanāt ,
ब्रूते ह्यजो नित्य इति श्रुतिः स्वयं तत्प्रत्यगात्मा सदसद्विलक्षणः ॥२९४॥
brūte hyajo nitya iti śrutiḥ svayaṁ tatpratyagātmā sadasadvilakṣaṇaḥ (294)

294. The real 'I' is that which is the Witness of the ego etc. It is ever persistent and always abides—even in state of deep-sleep. The *Shrutis* declare, "It is birthless, eternal..." etc. So the inmost Self is something totally separate and distinct from everything else having the characteristics of duality.

विकारिणां सर्वविकारवेत्ता नित्याविकारो भवितुं समर्हति ।
vikāriṇāṁ sarvavikāravettā nityāvikāro bhavituṁ samarhati ,
मनोरथस्वप्नसुषुप्तिषु स्फुटं पुनः पुनर्दृष्टमसत्त्वमेतयोः ॥२९५॥
manorathasvapnasuṣuptiṣu sphuṭaṁ punaḥ punardṛṣṭamasattvametayoḥ (295)

295. The Knower of all changes in things that undergo a change, must necessarily be constant and changeless itself. The non-Real characteristics of the gross and subtle sheaths is clearly and repeatedly observed in the states of imagination, dream and deep-sleep.

अतोऽभिमानं त्यज मांसपिण्डे पिण्डाभिमानिन्यपि बुद्धिकल्पिते ।
ato'bhimānaṁ tyaja māṁsapiṇḍe piṇḍābhimāninyapi buddhikalpite ,
कालत्रयाबाध्यमखण्डबोधं ज्ञात्वा स्वमात्मानमुपैहि शान्तिम् ॥२९६॥
kālatrayābādhyamakhaṇḍabodhaṁ jñātvā svamātmānamupaihi śāntim (296)

296. So therefore giving up your identification with this lump of flesh, and also with the ego and the subtle-body—all imagined by the *Buddhi*. Realizing your Real Self—which is the Absolute Consciousness that cannot be belied in any period of time: past, present or future—attain to serenity everlasting.

त्यजाभिमानं कुलगोत्रनामरूपाश्रमेष्वार्द्रशवाश्रितेषु ।
tyajābhimānaṁ kulagotranāmarūpāśrameṣvārdraśavāśriteṣu ,
लिङ्गस्य धर्मानपि कर्तृतादींस्त्यक्त्वा भवाखण्डसुखस्वरूपः ॥२९७॥
liṅgasya dharmānapi kartṛtādīṁstyaktvā bhavākhaṇḍasukhasvarūpaḥ (297)

297. Cease to identify yourself with your family, lineage, name, form and social order—attributes which pertain to the cruddy gross-body that is corpse-like (once bereft of the Self). So too renounce all attributes—ideas like being a doer etc.,—pertaining to the subtle-body; and just only be the Ātmā, the essence of Absolute Bliss.

सन्त्यन्ये प्रतिबन्धाः पुंसः संसारहेतवो दृष्टाः ।
santyanye pratibandhāḥ puṁsaḥ saṁsārahetavo dṛṣṭāḥ ,
तेषामेवं मूलं प्रथमविकारो भवत्यहङ्कारः ॥२९८॥
teṣāmevaṁ mūlaṁ prathamavikāro bhavatyahaṅkāraḥ (298)

298. Many obstacles are observed to exist that repeatedly hurl the individual into the whirls of birth-death waves; and as said

afore, the root of them all is the very first modification of Nescience: called the Ego.

यावत्स्यात्स्वस्य सम्बन्धोऽहङ्कारेण दुरात्मना ।
yāvatsyātsvasya sambandho'haṅkāreṇa durātmanā ,
तावन्न लेशमात्रापि मुक्तिवार्ता विलक्षणा ॥२९९॥
tāvanna leśamātrāpi muktivārtā vilakṣaṇā (299)

299. So long as one has any connection with this vile Ego—wicked, wily and most foul—there can be no talk of Emancipation—because that is the unworldly dominion which is unique and without exemplars.

अहङ्कारग्रहान्मुक्तः स्वरूपमुपपद्यते ।
ahaṅkāragrahānmuktaḥ svarūpamupapadyate ,
चन्द्रवद्विमलः पूर्णः सदानन्दः स्वयंप्रभः ॥३००॥
candravadvimalaḥ pūrṇaḥ sadānandaḥ svayamprabhaḥ (300)

300. Freed from the shackles of egoism—as the Moon from the *Rahu's*—man attains to his Real nature; and attains he his pure, infinite, ever blissful, self-effulgent, self-existent abode.

यो वा पुरे सोऽहमिति प्रतीतो बुद्ध्या प्रक्लृप्तस्तमसाऽतिमूढया ।
yo vā pure so'hamiti pratīto buddhyā praklṛptastamasā'timūḍhayā ,
तस्यैव निःशेषतया विनाशे ब्रह्मात्मभावः प्रतिबन्धशून्यः ॥३०१॥
tasyaiva niḥśeṣatayā vināśe brahmātmabhāvaḥ pratibandhaśūnyaḥ (301)

301. That which has been created by the *Buddhi*—which's thoroughly deluded by Nescience—and is perceived in the body as the persistent sense of "I am such and so"—when that Ego-sense has been completely expunged, then one attains unobstructed Oneness with *Brahama*.

ब्रह्मानन्दनिधिर्महाबलवताऽहङ्कारघोराहिना
brahmānandanidhirmahābalavatā'haṅkāraghorāhinā
संवेष्ट्यात्मनि रक्ष्यते गुणमयैश्चण्डेस्त्रिभिर्मस्तकैः
saṁveṣṭyātmani rakṣyate guṇamayaiścaṇḍestribhirmastakaiḥ
विज्ञानाख्यमहासिना श्रुतिमता विच्छिद्य शीर्षत्रयं
vijñānākhyamahāsinā śrutimatā vicchidya śīrṣatrayaṁ
निर्मूल्याहिमिमं निधिं सुखकरं धीरोऽनुभोक्तुंक्षमः ॥३०२॥
nirmūlyāhimimaṁ nidhiṁ sukhakaraṁ dhīro'nubhoktuṅkṣamaḥ (302)

302. The Treasure of the Bliss of *Brahama* is zealously guarded by the dreadful serpent of Ego coiled around it—preciously protecting it for its own use through the means of its three fierce hoods: the three *Gunas* of *Tamas, Rajas* and *Sattva*. Only a wise person who has destroyed the serpent by shearing away those three hoods through the shining sword of Realization—in

accordance with the teachings of *Shrutis*—gets to enjoy the ethereal Treasure that confers complete Bliss.

यावद्वा यत्किञ्चिद्विषदोषस्फूर्तिरस्ति चेद्देहे ।
yāvadvā yatkiñcidviṣadoṣasphūrtirasti ceddehe ,
कथमारोग्याय भवेत्तद्वदहन्तापि योगिनो मुक्त्यै ॥ ३०३ ॥
kathamārogyāya bhavettadvadahantāpi yogino muktyai (303)

303. So long as there is even a trace of poison left in the body, can there be any hope of complete recovery? Similar is the effect of the toxicity of Egoism upon a yogi's Liberation.

अहमोऽत्यन्तनिवृत्त्या तत्कृतनानाविकल्पसंहृत्या ।
ahamo'tyantanivṛttyā tatkṛtanānāvikalpasaṁhṛtyā ,
प्रत्यक्तत्त्वविवेकादिदमहमस्मीति विन्दते तत्त्वम् ॥ ३०४ ॥
pratyaktattvavivekādidamahamasmīti vindate tattvam (304)

304. By completely rooting out the ego-sense—through the stoppage of the diverse mental waves generated and spurred up by the ego—and through a steady discrimination upon the Inner Reality, one eventually discovers that Reality in an act of direct Realization, "I am *Brahama*".

अहङ्कारे कर्तर्यहमिति मतिं मुञ्च सहसा
ahaṅkāre kartaryahamiti matiṁ muñca sahasā
विकारात्मन्यात्मप्रतिफलजुषि स्वस्थितिमुषि ।
vikārātmanyātmapratiphalajuṣi svasthitimuṣi ,
यदध्यासात्प्राप्ता जनिमृतिजरादुःखबहुला
yadadhyāsātprāptā janimṛtijarāduḥkhabahulā
प्रतीचश्चिन्मूर्तेस्तव सुखतनोः संसृतिरियम् ॥ ३०५ ॥
pratīcaścinmūrtestava sukhatanoḥ saṁsṛtiriyam (305)

305. So forthwith give up your identification with the Ego—the sense of being the agent or doer - which impression is merely a modification, a reflection of the Self - which sense diverts one from being established in the Self - and identifying yourself with which, you have come by this pathetic state of embodied existence replete with the sorrows of birth, decay and death—and Realize the Truth that you are merely a Witness of all this, that you are truly the embodiment of Absolute Consciousness and Bliss.

सदैकरूपस्य चिदात्मनो विभोरानन्दमूर्तेरनवद्यकीर्तेः ।
sadaikarūpasya cidātmano vibhorānandamūrteranavadyakīrteḥ ,
नैवान्यथा क्वाप्यविकारिणस्ते विनाहमध्यासममुष्य संसृतिः ॥ ३०६ ॥
naivānyathā kvāpyavikāriṇaste vināhamadhyāsamamuṣya saṁsṛtiḥ (306)

306. But for the identification of the self with the ego-sense, there will not be this repeated birth-death cycle for you—for you are truly immutable and eternally the same: Consciousness-Absolute, Bliss-Absolute, the Omnipresent Being of untarnished glory.

तस्मादहङ्कारमिमं स्वशत्रुं भोक्तुर्गले कण्टकवत्प्रतीतम् ।
tasmādahaṅkāramimaṁ svaśatruṁ bhokturgale kaṇṭakavatpratītam ,
विच्छिद्य विज्ञानमहासिना स्फुटं भुङ्क्ष्वात्मसाम्राज्यसुखं यथेष्टम् ॥ ३०७॥
vicchidya vijñānamahāsinā sphuṭaṁ bhuṅkṣvātmasāmrājyasukhaṁ yatheṣṭam (307)

307. Therefore destroying the ego—this veritable foe which is like a thorn sticking in the throat of a man eating food—by the shining sword of Realization, enjoy directly and freely the infinite bliss of your sovereign Self, your very own empire: the Majesty of the *Ātmā*.

ततोऽहमादेर्विनिवर्त्य वृत्तिं सन्त्यक्तरागः परमार्थलाभात् ।
tato'hamādervinivartya vṛttiṁ santyaktarāgaḥ paramārthalābhāt ,
तूष्णीं समास्स्वात्मसुखानुभूत्या पूर्णात्मना ब्रह्मणि निर्विकल्पः ॥ ३०८॥
tūṣṇīṁ samāssvātmasukhānubhūtyā pūrṇātmanā brahmaṇi nirvikalpaḥ (308)

308. Checking the activities of the ego-sense and relinquishing all attachments through the experiencing of the Supreme Reality, be freed of dualities by always partaking of the infinite Bliss of the Self. And thereafter abide serene and at peace in *Brahama*—for now you have attained your infinite nature.

समूलकृत्तोऽपि महानहं पुनः व्युल्लेखितः स्याद्यदि चेतसा क्षणम् ।
samūlakṛtto'pi mahānahaṁ punaḥ vyullekhitaḥ syādyadi cetasā kṣaṇam ,
सञ्जीव्य विक्षेपशतं करोति नभस्वता प्रावृषि वारिदो यथा ॥ ३०९॥
sañjīvya vikṣepaśataṁ karoti nabhasvatā prāvṛṣi vārido yathā (309)

309. Even though completely obliterated, this terrible egoism—if allowed to be revivified in the mind even for a moment—returns to life with full vengeance to create mischief by the hundreds—like the cloud ushered in by the winds during rainy season.

निगृह्य शत्रोरहमोऽवकाशः क्वचिन्न देयो विषयानुचिन्तया ।
nigṛhya śatrorahamo'vakāśaḥ kvacinna deyo viṣayānucintayā ,
स एव सञ्जीवनहेतुरस्य प्रक्षीणजम्बीरतरोरिवाम्बु ॥ ३१०॥
sa eva sañjīvanaheturasya prakṣīṇajambīratarorivāmbu (310)

310. Overpowering this dire foe called egoism, not a moment's respite should be allowed for it to ruminate over sense-objects; because that's what will cause it to spring back to life—alike

how a citron tree which has almost dried and died becomes resurrected again in the presence of water.

देहात्मना संस्थित एव कामी विलक्षणः कामयिता कथं स्यात् ।
dehātmanā saṁsthita eva kāmī vilakṣaṇaḥ kāmayitā kathaṁ syāt ,
अतोऽर्थसन्धानपरत्वमेव भेदप्रसक्त्या भवबन्धहेतुः ॥ ३११ ॥
ato'rthasandhānaparatvameva bhedaprasaktyā bhavabandhahetuḥ (311)

311. Only he who identifies himself with the body is driven with the desires for sense-pleasures thereby. How can one who is bereft of the body-idea be covetous? The tendency to muse and mull over sense-objects strengthens the trammeling ideas of dualities, the root cause of worldly bondages.

कार्यप्रवर्धनाद्बीजप्रवृद्धिः परिदृश्यते ।
kāryapravardhanādbījapravṛddhiḥ paridṛśyate ,
कार्यनाशाद्बीजनाशस्तस्मात्कार्यं निरोधयेत् ॥ ३१२ ॥
kāryanāśādbījanāśastasmātkāryaṁ nirodhayet (312)

312. When actions flourish, their future seeds too are observed to mushroom rampantly, and when activities wane, so too do the seeds; therefore one must subdue Activity.

वासनावृद्धितः कार्यं कार्यवृद्ध्या च वासना ।
vāsanāvṛddhitaḥ kāryaṁ kāryavṛddhyā ca vāsanā ,
वर्धते सर्वथा पुंसः संसारो न निवर्तते ॥ ३१३ ॥
vardhate sarvathā puṁsaḥ saṁsāro na nivartate (313)

313. Through the increase of desires, selfish Activity increases; and when there is an increase of selfish activity, there is even more increase of Desires; and thus in this vicious cycle, man's transmigration is never at an end.

संसारबन्धविच्छित्त्यै तद् द्वयं प्रदहेद्यतिः ।
saṁsārabandhavicchittyai tad dvayaṁ pradahedyatiḥ ,
वासनावृद्धिरेताभ्यां चिन्तया क्रियया बहिः ॥ ३१४ ॥
vāsanāvṛddhiretābhyāṁ cintayā kriyayā bahiḥ (314)

314. So therefore, for the sake of breaking the chain of transmigration, the *Sanyāsin* should burn to ashes these two. Verily dwelling upon the sense-objects with Desire, and doing Selfish Activity—together lead to an incremental interminable increase of Desires.

ताभ्यां प्रवर्धमाना सा सूते संसृतिमात्मनः ।
tābhyāṁ pravardhamānā sā sūte saṁsṛtimātmanaḥ ,
त्रयाणां च क्षयोपायः सर्वावस्थासु सर्वदा ॥ ३१५ ॥
trayāṇāṁ ca kṣayopāyaḥ sarvāvasthāsu sarvadā (315)

सर्वत्र सर्वतः सर्वब्रह्ममात्रावलोकनैः ।
sarvatra sarvataḥ sarvabrahmamātrāvalokanaiḥ ,
सद्भाववासनादार्ढ्यात्तत्त्रयं लयमश्नुते ॥ ३१६ ॥
sadbhāvavāsanādārḍhyāttattrayaṁ layamaśnute (316)

315-316. Pulled in the vicious circle of Activity and Desire, the soul revolves in unending Transmigration—a perpetual cycle of births, deaths, sorrows. The way to destroy this tricycle lies in looking upon everything as *Brahama* and *Brahama* alone—throughout, under all circumstance, ever and in every respect. With the strengthening of the longing to be One in *Brahama*, these three are thereby destroyed.

क्रियानाशे भवेच्चिन्तानाशोऽस्माद्वासनाक्षयः ।
kriyānāśe bhaveccintānāśo'smādvāsanākṣayaḥ ,
वासनाप्रक्षयो मोक्षः सा जीवन्मुक्तिरिष्यते ॥ ३१७ ॥
vāsanāprakṣayo mokṣaḥ sā jīvanmuktiriṣyate (317)

317. With the ceasing of selfish action, brooding on the sense-objects ends, and this is followed by the destruction of desires; and the death of last desire is called Liberation—and is in this case considered to be Liberation-while-alive.

सद्वासनास्फूर्तिविजृम्भणे सति ह्यसौ विलीनाप्यहमादिवासना ।
sadvāsanāsphūrtivijṛmbhaṇe sati hyasau vilīnāpyahamādivāsanā ,
अतिप्रकृष्टाप्यरुणप्रभायां विलीयते साधु यथा तमिस्रा ॥ ३१८ ॥
atiprakṛṣṭāpyaruṇaprabhāyāṁ vilīyate sādhu yathā tamisrā (318)

318. When the yearning to be One in *Brahama* becomes markedly manifest, vivid and bright, the desires born of ego proportionally fade away forthwith: in the same way as the most intense darkness disappears in the rising glow of the ascending sun.

तमस्तमःकार्यमनर्थजालं न दृश्यते सत्युदिते दिनेशे ।
tamastamaḥkāryamanarthajālaṁ na dṛśyate satyudite dineśe ,
तथाऽद्वयानन्दरसानुभूतौ नैवास्ति बन्धो न च दुःखगन्धः ॥ ३१९ ॥
tathā'dvayānandarasānubhūtau naivāsti bandho na ca duḥkhagandhaḥ (319)

319. Darkness and the numerous evils of the night are nowhere seen once the sun has completely arisen; similarly upon the Realization of *Brahama*, the Bliss Absolute, there is nowhere bondages nor the least trace of misery.

दृश्यं प्रतीतं प्रविलापयन्सन् सन्मात्रमानन्दघनं विभावयन् ।
dṛśyaṁ pratītaṁ pravilāpayansan sanmātramānandaghanaṁ vibhāvayan ,
समाहितः सन्बहिरन्तरं वा कालं नयेथाः सति कर्मबन्धे ॥ ३२० ॥
samāhitaḥ sanbahirantaraṁ vā kālaṁ nayethāḥ sati karmabandhe (320)

320. Causing the perceptible world, both external and internal, to disappear; and meditating upon the Reality of *Brahama*, the Embodied-Bliss, one should pass one's time vigilantly, ever watchful of any residual *Prārabdha* that may still be left unspent.

प्रमादो ब्रह्मनिष्ठायां न कर्तव्यः कदाचन ।
pramādo Brahamaiṣṭhāyāṁ na kartavyaḥ kadācana ,
प्रमादो मृत्युरित्याह भगवान्ब्रह्मणः सुतः ॥३२१॥
pramādo mṛtyurityāha bhagavānbrahmaṇaḥ sutaḥ (321)

321. One should never be negligent in one's steadfastness in *Brahama*. Bhagawān Sanatkumāra—who is the divine son of the Creator—has called Inadvertence to be Death itself.

न प्रमादादनर्थोऽन्यो ज्ञानिनः स्वस्वरूपतः ।
na pramādādanartho'nyo jñāninaḥ svasvarūpataḥ ,
ततो मोहस्ततोऽहन्धीस्ततो बन्धस्ततो व्यथा ॥३२२॥
tato mohastato'handhīstato bandhastato vyathā (322)

322. For a wise person, there is no greater danger than being unmindful of one's Real nature; because from such inadvertence emerges Delusion; and with that, Egoism raises its ugly head; and from that ensue Bondages, which bring the whole flood of Miseries in their wake.

विषयाभिमुखं दृष्ट्वा विद्वांसमपि विस्मृतिः ।
viṣayābhimukhaṁ dṛṣṭvā vidvāṁsamapi vismṛtiḥ ,
विक्षेपयति धीदोषैर्योषा जारमिव प्रियम् ॥३२३॥
vikṣepayati dhīdoṣairyoṣā jāramiva priyam (323)

323. Finding even the wise hankering after sense-objects, this Inadvertence (towards the Self) torments through the evil propensities of the *Buddhi*, just as a woman does her doting paramour.

यथापकृष्टं शैवालं क्षणमात्रं न तिष्ठति ।
yathāpakṛṣṭaṁ śaivālaṁ kṣaṇamātraṁ na tiṣṭhati ,
आवृणोति तथा माया प्राज्ञं वापि पराङ्मुखम् ॥३२४॥
āvṛṇoti tathā māyā prājñaṁ vāpi parāṅmukham (324)

324. Just as the moss, even though pushed away, does not stay away but immediately closes up to cover the water again; even so *Māyā* (Nescience) too clouds the mind of the man—even of the most wise—if he were to turn away from the inner Self and become extrovertive.

लक्ष्यच्युतं चेद्यदि चित्तमीषद् बहिर्मुखं सन्निपतेत्ततस्ततः ।
lakṣyacyutaṁ cedyadi cittamīṣad bahirmukhaṁ sannipatettatastataḥ ,
प्रमादतः प्रच्युतकेलिकन्दुकः सोपानपङ्क्तौ पतितो यथा तथा ॥३२५॥
pramādataḥ pracyutakelikandukaḥ sopānapaṅktau patito yathā tathā (325)

325. If the mind ever so slightly strays away from the ideal and becomes outgoing, then it goes down and down and down—just how a ball inadvertently dropped on the staircase keeps bouncing down from step to step below.

विषयेष्वाविशच्चेतः सङ्कल्पयति तद्गुणान् ।
viṣayeṣvāviśaccetaḥ saṅkalpayati tadguṇān ,
सम्यक्सङ्कल्पनात्कामः कामात्पुंसः प्रवर्तनम् ॥३२६॥
samyaksaṅkalpanātkāmaḥ kāmātpuṁsaḥ pravartanam (326)

326. The mind that is attached to the sense-objects, reflects upon their qualities; and from mature reflection arises desire; and after desiring, one goes about acquiring those objects.

अतः प्रमादान्न परोऽस्ति मृत्युः विवेकिनो ब्रह्मविदः समाधौ ।
ataḥ pramādānna paro'sti mṛtyuḥ vivekino brahmavidaḥ samādhau ,
समाहितः सिद्धिमुपैति सम्यक् समाहितात्मा भव सावधानः ॥३२७॥
samāhitaḥ siddhimupaiti samyak samāhitātmā bhava sāvadhānaḥ (327)

327. Therefore unto the discriminating knower of *Brahama*, there is no worse death than Inadvertence with regards to meditation. Only the person who practices concentration on the Self regularly attains total success. So always, and with great diligence, meditate on the *Brahama* within.

ततः स्वरूपविभ्रंशो विभ्रष्टस्तु पतत्यधः ।
tataḥ svarūpavibhraṁśo vibhraṣṭastu patatyadhaḥ ,
पतितस्य विना नाशं पुनर्नारोह ईक्ष्यते ॥३२८॥
patitasya vinā nāśaṁ punarnāroha īkṣyate (328)

328. Through Inadvertence, the seeker deviates from his Real Nature. He who has thus deviated, degenerates; and that fallen man comes by complete Ruin; and he is scarcely seen to ever rise again.

सङ्कल्पं वर्जयेत्तस्मात्सर्वानर्थस्य कारणम् ।
saṅkalpaṁ varjayettasmātsarvānarthasya kāraṇam ,
जीवतो यस्य कैवल्यं विदेहे स च केवलः ।
jīvato yasya kaivalyaṁ videhe sa ca kevalaḥ ,
यत्किञ्चित् पश्यतो भेदं भयं ब्रूते यजुःश्रुतिः ॥३२९॥
yatkiñcit paśyato bhedaṁ bhayaṁ brūte yajuḥśrutiḥ (329)

329. Therefore cease this fixation and rumination and obsession over the sense-objects—which are the very cause of your

ruination. He who attains complete Onlyness even while living and breathing, he alone abides in that Oneness upon the body's dissolution. The *Yajur-Veda* has declared that one who sees the least bit of distinction anywhere, becomes overtaken with fear by that 'other'.

यदा कदा वापि विपश्चिदेष ब्रह्मण्यनन्तेऽप्यणुमात्रभेदम् ।
yadā kadā vāpi vipaścideṣa brahmaṇyanante'pyaṇumātrabhedam ,
पश्यत्यथामुष्य भयं तदैव यद्वीक्षितं भिन्नतया प्रमादात् ॥ ३३० ॥
paśyatyathāmuṣya bhayaṁ tadaiva yadvīkṣitaṁ bhinnatayā pramādāt (330)

330. In the infinite continuity of *Brahama*, whenever the wise sees even the least bit of difference, then that very thing—which through error he sees to be distinct, separate, different—becomes a source of terror for him.

श्रुतिस्मृतिन्यायशतैर्निषिद्धे दृश्येऽत्र यः स्वात्ममतिं करोति ।
śrutismṛtinyāyaśatairniṣiddhe dṛśye'tra yaḥ svātmamatiṁ karoti ,
उपैति दुःखोपरि दुःखजातं निषिद्धकर्ता स मलिम्लुचो यथा ॥ ३३१ ॥
upaiti duḥkhopari duḥkhajātaṁ niṣiddhakartā sa malimluco yathā (331)

331. He who identifies himself with the manifold universe—which has been negated by the hundreds of *Shrutis*, *Smritis* and reasoned arguments—experiences misery after misery, alike a culprit who commits something forbidden.

सत्याभिसन्धानरतो विमुक्तो महत्त्वमात्मीयमुपैति नित्यम् ।
satyābhisandhānarato vimukto mahattvamātmīyamupaiti nityam ,
मिथ्याभिसन्धानरतस्तु नश्येद् दृष्टं तदेतद्यदचौरचौरयोः ॥ ३३२ ॥
mithyābhisandhānaratastu naśyed dṛṣṭaṁ tadetadyadacauracaurayoḥ (332)

332. He who has totally devoted himself to meditation on the Reality and is free from the effects of Nescience—he forthwith attains to the eternal glory of the *Ātmā*; but he who is devoted to this non-Real universe, is seen to get destroyed—as is evident from the fate of one who is a culprit and one who is not.

यतिरसदनुसन्धिं बन्धहेतुं विहाय स्वयमयमहमस्मीत्यात्मदृष्ट्यैव तिष्ठेत्
yatirasadanusandhiṁ bandhahetuṁ vihāya svayamayamahamasmītyātmadṛṣṭyaiva tiṣṭhet
सुखयति ननु निष्ठा ब्रह्मणि स्वानुभूत्या हरति परमविद्याकार्यदुःखं प्रतीतम् ॥ ३३३ ॥
sukhayati nanu niṣṭhā brahmaṇi svānubhūtyā harati paramavidyākāryaduḥkhaṁ pratītam (333)

333. The spiritual seeker should give up dwelling on the non-Real, which causes bondage; and instead should abide fixing his thoughts upon the *Ātmā* affirming, "Verily That I am". Steadfastness in *Brahama*—gained through the Realization of one's Oneness in *Brahama*—gives rise to Bliss while thoroughly

removing the misery born of Nescience experienced in the state of Ignorance.

बाह्यानुसन्धिः परिवर्धयेत्फलं दुर्वासनामेव ततस्ततोऽधिकाम् ।
bāhyānusandhiḥ parivardhayetphalaṁ durvāsanāmeva tatastato'dhikām ,
ज्ञात्वा विवेकैः परिहृत्य बाह्यं स्वात्मानुसन्धिं विदधीत नित्यम् ॥ ३३४॥
jñātvā vivekaiḥ parihṛtya bāhyaṁ svātmānusandhiṁ vidadhīta nityam (334)

334. The dwelling on external objects only compounds their ill effects in the form of evil propensities which grow from bad to worse. Realizing this through Discrimination, one should abandon brooding over external objects and constantly apply oneself to the meditation upon the *Ātmā*.

बाह्ये निरुद्धे मनसः प्रसन्नता मनःप्रसादे परमात्मदर्शनम् ।
bāhye niruddhe manasaḥ prasannatā manaḥprasāde paramātmadarśanam ,
तस्मिन्सुदृष्टे भवबन्धनाशो बहिर्निरोधः पदवी विमुक्तेः ॥ ३३५॥
tasminsudṛṣṭe bhavabandhanāśo bahirnirodhaḥ padavī vimukteḥ (335)

335. When the external world is shut out, the mind becomes cheerful; and cheerfulness of the mind brings about the vision of the *Param-Ātmā*; and when that is perfectly Realized, the chain of births and deaths becomes forever broken. Hence the shutting out of the external world is the starting step on the path to Liberation.

कः पण्डितः सन्सदसद्विवेकी श्रुतिप्रमाणः परमार्थदर्शी ।
kaḥ paṇḍitaḥ sansadasadvivekī śrutipramāṇaḥ paramārthadarśī ,
जानन्हि कुर्यादसतोऽवलम्बं स्वपातहेतोः शिशुवन्मुमुक्षुः ॥ ३३६॥
jānanhi kuryādasato'valambaṁ svapātahetoḥ śiśuvanmumukṣuḥ (336)

336. Where is the man who is able to discriminate the Real from the non-Real, who is learned and believes in the Vedas as the authority, who in his quest for freedom is fully devoted to the Supreme-Reality *Ātmā*—and yet, like a child, who chooses to run after the non-Real external world that will surely be the cause of his ruin?

देहादिसंसक्तिमतो न मुक्तिः मुक्तस्य देहाद्यभिमत्यभावः ।
dehādisaṁsaktimato na muktiḥ muktasya dehādyabhimatyabhāvaḥ ,
सुप्तस्य नो जागरणं न जाग्रतः स्वप्नस्तयोर्भिन्नगुणाश्रयत्वात् ॥ ३३७॥
suptasya no jāgaraṇaṁ na jāgrataḥ svapnastayorbhinnaguṇāśrayatvāt (337)

337. For one who has attachments to the body, there is no Liberation; and the Liberated man has no identification with the body. The sleeping man is not awake, and the waking man is not asleep. Two contradictory states cannot be identical.

अन्तर्बहिः स्वं स्थिरजङ्गमेषु ज्ञात्वाऽऽत्मनाधारतया विलोक्य ।
antarbahiḥ svaṁ sthirajaṅgameṣu jñātvā''tmanādhāratayā vilokya ,
त्यक्ताखिलोपाधिरखण्डरूपः पूर्णात्मना यः स्थित एष मुक्तः ॥ ३३८॥
tyaktākhilopādhirakhaṇḍarūpaḥ pūrṇātmanā yaḥ sthita eṣa muktaḥ (338)

338. He alone is free who knows his Self to be within all the moving and unmoving entities and observes only the Self to be the substratum of everything. He alone is Liberated who abandons all superimpositions of names and forms and abides as the Absolute Infinite Self.

सर्वात्मना बन्धविमुक्तिहेतुः सर्वात्मभावान्न परोऽस्ति कश्चित् ।
sarvātmanā bandhavimuktihetuḥ sarvātmabhāvānna paro'sti kaścit ,
दृश्याग्रहे सत्युपपद्यतेऽसौ सर्वात्मभावोऽस्य सदात्मनिष्ठया ॥ ३३९॥
dṛśyāgrahe satyupapadyate'sau sarvātmabhāvo'sya sadātmaniṣṭhayā (339)

339. To Realize that the whole universe is just only the Self—that is the means of complete Liberation from bondages. There is nothing higher than identifying the universe with the Self. One reaches that state by excluding the external crust of names and forms, and becoming established exclusively in the essence of things: the substratum, the eternal *Ātmā*.

दृश्यस्याग्रहणं कथं नु घटते देहात्मना तिष्ठतो
dṛśyasyāgrahaṇaṁ kathaṁ nu ghaṭate dehātmanā tiṣṭhato
बाह्यार्थानुभवप्रसक्तमनसस्तत्तत्क्रियां कुर्वतः ।
bāhyārthānubhavaprasaktamanasastattatkriyāṁ kurvataḥ ,
सन्न्यस्ताखिलधर्मकर्मविषयैर्नित्यात्मनिष्ठापरैः
sannyastākhiladharmakarma-viṣayairnityātmaniṣṭhāparaiḥ
तत्त्वज्ञैः करणीयमात्मनि सदानन्देच्छुभिर्यत्नतः ॥ ३४०॥
tattvajñaiḥ karaṇīyamātmani sadānandecchubhiryatnataḥ (340)

340. But is this exclusion of the objective world even possible unto the person who lives identified with the body? – whose mind is attached to the perception of external objects? – who performs various acts towards that end? No. This practice of excluding out the objective world is carefully cultivated only by those blessed sages who are passionately devoted to the *Ātmā*, who have renounced every kind of duty and action and sense-object—and who only wish to possess Undying Bliss.

सर्वात्मसिद्धये भिक्षोः कृतश्रवणकर्मणः ।
sarvātmasiddhaye bhikṣoḥ kṛtaśravaṇakarmaṇaḥ ,
समाधिं विदधात्येषा शान्तो दान्त इति श्रुतिः ॥ ३४१॥
samādhiṁ vidadhātyeṣā śānto dānta iti śrutiḥ (341)

341. To the renunciant who has gone through the acts of hearing, and has become established in the appointed means of 'calmness, self-control... ' etc., the *Shrutis* thereafter prescribe *Samādhi*—for directly realizing that the universe is nothing but the unmanifest Supreme-Self become manifest.

आरूढशक्तेरहमो विनाशः कर्तुन्न शक्य सहसापि पण्डितैः ।
ārūḍhaśakterahamo vināśaḥ kartunna śakya sahasāpi paṇḍitaiḥ ,
ये निर्विकल्पाख्यसमाधिनिश्चलाः तानन्तराऽनन्तभवा हि वासनाः ॥ ३४२ ॥
ye nirvikalpākhyasamādhiniścalāḥ tānantarā'nantabhavā hi vāsanāḥ (342)

342. Even the most-wise cannot abruptly destroy egoism after it has become strengthened over a lifetime—indeed *Vāsanās* (desires) that bind the ego are the effect of myriads of lifetimes. Verily this dissolution occurs only upon experiencing the *Nirvikalpa Samādhi*—absorption in the Complete Tranquility of Perfect Non-duality.

अहम्बुद्ध्यैव मोहिन्या योजयित्वाऽऽवृतेर्बलात् ।
ahambuddhyaiva mohinyā yojayitvā''vṛterbalāt ,
विक्षेपशक्तिः पुरुषं विक्षेपयति तद्गुणैः ॥ ३४३ ॥
vikṣepaśaktiḥ puruṣaṁ vikṣepayati tadguṇaiḥ (343)

343. The projecting-power, along with the connected veiling-power, deludes a man with the siren of an egoistic idea and distracts him with the ballast of her agitations.

विक्षेपशक्तिविजयो विषमो विधातुं निःशेषमावरणशक्तिनिवृत्त्यभावे ।
vikṣepaśaktivijayo viṣamo vidhātuṁ niḥśeṣamāvaraṇaśaktinivṛttyabhāve ,
दृग्दृश्ययोः स्फुटपयोजलवद्विभागे नश्येत्तदावरणमात्मनि च स्वभावात् ।
dṛgdṛśyayoḥ sphuṭapayojalavadvibhāge naśyettadāvaraṇamātmani ca svabhāvāt ,
निःसंशयेन भवति प्रतिबन्धशून्यो विक्षेपणं न हि तदा यदि चेन्मृषार्थे ॥ ३४४ ॥
niḥsaṁśayena bhavati pratibandhaśūnyo vikṣepaṇaṁ na hi tadā yadi cenmṛṣārthe (344)

344. Exceedingly difficult it is to conquer the projecting-power unless the veiling-power is rooted out as well. That covering over the *Ātmā* vanishes spontaneously when the Seer and the Seen are discerned individually and as clearly as milk and water—with the victory held fully accomplished and free of obstructions when there is no more oscillations in the mind arising from the non-Real.

सम्यग्विवेकः स्फुटबोधजन्यो विभज्य दृग्दृश्यपदार्थतत्त्वम् ।
samyagvivekaḥ sphuṭabodhajanyo vibhajya dṛgdṛśyapadārthatattvam ,
छिनत्ति मायाकृतमोहबन्धं यस्माद्विमुक्तस्तु पुनर्न संसृतिः ॥ ३४५ ॥
chinatti māyākṛtamohabandhaṁ yasmādvimuktastu punarna saṁsṛtiḥ (345)

345. Through perfect discrimination—brought on by direct Realization—one clearly distinguishes the Subject from the Object at their very essence. This breaks the fetters of Delusion created by *Māyā*; and for one who has been freed from *Māyā*, there is no more transmigration.

परावरैकत्वविवेकवह्निः दहत्यविद्यागहनं ह्यशेषम् ।
parāvaraikatvavivekavahniḥ dahatyavidyāgahanaṁ hyaśeṣam ,
किं स्यात्पुनः संसरणस्य बीजं अद्वैतभावं समुपेयुषोऽस्य ॥ ३४६ ॥
kiṁ syātpunaḥ saṁsaraṇasya bījaṁ advaitabhāvaṁ samupeyuṣo'sya (346)

346. The impenetrable dense forest of *Avidyā* (Nescience), becomes entirely consumed in the Fiery Knowledge kindled with direct Realization: the Realization of the Oneness of *Jiva* and *Brahama*. For one who has Realized this state of Oneness, is there any seed left for future transmigration?

आवरणस्य निवृत्तिर्भवति हि सम्यक्पदार्थ दर्शनतः ।
āvaraṇasya nivṛttirbhavati hi samyakpadārtha darśanataḥ ,
मिथ्याज्ञानविनाशस्तद्विक्षेपजनितदुःखनिवृत्तिः ॥ ३४७ ॥
mithyājñānavināśastadvikṣepajanitaduḥkhanivṛttiḥ (347)

347. Veils which obscure the Truth are indeed lifted once the Reality is fully experienced. The ending of illusory knowledge, deluding ideas, and the cessation of every kind of misery and sorrow—which had ensued from *Māyā*'s distracting influences to begin with—follow as a matter of course.

एतत्त्रितयं दृष्टं सम्यग्रज्जुस्वरूपविज्ञानात् ।
etattritayaṁ dṛṣṭaṁ samyagrajjusvarūpavijñānāt ,
तस्माद्वस्तुसतत्त्वं ज्ञातव्यं बन्धमुक्तये विदुषा ॥ ३४८ ॥
tasmādvastusatattvaṁ jñātavyaṁ bandhamuktaye viduṣā (348)

348. The aforementioned transition is observed in the case of rope when its real nature (that of it not being a snake) becomes fully realized (thus ending the ensuing fear of snake). Therefore the wise man should know the real nature of things—for the breaking of his worldly bondages.

अयोऽग्नियोगादिव सत्समन्वयान् मात्रादिरूपेण विजृम्भते धीः ।
ayo'gniyogādiva satsamanvayān mātrādirūpeṇa vijṛmbhate dhīḥ ,
तत्कार्यमेतद्द्वितयं यतो मृषा दृष्टं भ्रमस्वप्नमनोरथेषु ॥ ३४९ ॥
tatkāryametaddvitayaṁ yato mṛṣā dṛṣṭaṁ bhramasvapnamanoratheṣu (349)

ततो विकाराः प्रकृतेरहम्मुखा देहावसाना विषयाश्च सर्वे ।
tato vikārāḥ prakṛterahammukhā dehāvasānā viṣayāśca sarve ,
क्षणेऽन्यथाभावितया ह्यमीषा मसत्त्वमात्मा तु कदापि नान्यथा ॥ ३५० ॥
kṣaṇe'nyathābhāvitayā hyamīṣā masattvamātmā tu kadāpi nānyathā (350)

349-350. Through its contact with fire, just as a piece of iron becomes visible as a fiery iron, the *Buddhi* too, through the inherence of *Brahama*, manifests itself as the Knower and the Known—which are the effects of *Buddhi*. And these two (Knower/Known) are discovered to be non-Real—as is found in the case of delusion, dream, and imagination. And therefore, the effects of *Prakriti* too—from egoism down to the body and the sense-objects—are all non-Real. Their non-Reality is owing to them being subject to changes with time; whereas the Real (the *Ātmā*) never changes.

नित्याद्वयाखण्डचिदेकरूपो बुद्ध्यादिसाक्षी सदसद्विलक्षणः ।
nityādvayākhaṇḍacidekarūpo buddhyādisākṣī sadasadvilakṣaṇaḥ ,
अहम्पदप्रत्ययलक्षितार्थः प्रत्यक् सदानन्दघनः परात्मा ॥ ३५१ ॥
ahampadapratyayalakṣitārthaḥ pratyak sadānandaghanaḥ parātmā (351)

351. The Supreme Self is ever eternal, indivisible, pure consciousness, non-dual, the one without a second, the witness of the *Buddhi* etc., distinct from the gross and subtle, the gist of the notion and sense of 'I', and the essence of innate eternal Bliss.

इत्थं विपश्चित्सदसद्विभज्य निश्चित्य तत्त्वं निजबोधदृष्ट्या ।
ittharh vipaścitsadasadvibhajya niścitya tattvarh nijabodhadṛṣṭyā ,
ज्ञात्वा स्वमात्मानमखण्डबोधं तेभ्यो विमुक्तः स्वयमेव शाम्यति ॥ ३५२ ॥
jñātvā svamātmānamakhaṇḍabodharh tebhyo vimuktaḥ svayameva śāmyati (352)

352. A wise person, discriminating thus the Real from the non-Real, and ascertaining the Truth through his illuminative insight, and realizing his own Self which is Knowledge-Absolute—becomes rid of all obstructing impediments and gets to partake directly of the infinite inner Bliss.

अज्ञानहृदयग्रन्थेर्निःशेषविलयस्तदा ।
ajñānahṛdayagranthernihśeṣavilayastadā ,
समाधिनाऽविकल्पेन यदाऽद्वैतात्मदर्शनम् ॥ ३५३ ॥
samādhinā'vikalpena yadā'dvaitātmadarśanam (353)

353. When the *Ātmā*, the One without a second, is realized through the means of *Nirvikalpa Samādhi*, then the heart's knot of Ignorance becomes completely obliterated.

त्वमहमिदमितीयं कल्पना बुद्धिदोषात् प्रभवति परमात्मन्यद्वये निर्विशेषे ।
tvamahamidamitīyarh kalpanā buddhidoṣāt prabhavati paramātmanyadvaye nirviśeṣe ,
प्रविलसति समाधावस्य सर्वो विकल्पो विलयनमुपगच्छेद्वस्तुतत्त्वावधृत्या ॥ ३५४ ॥
pravilasati samādhāvasya sarvo vikalpo vilayanamupagacchedvastutattvāvadhṛtyā (354)

354. Such imaginations as 'you', 'I', 'this' occur through the errors of the *Buddhi*; but when the *Param-Ātmā*, the Absolute *Brahama*, the One without a second, becomes manifest in *Samādhi* in direct Realization, then all such errors, delusions, imaginations stand destroyed for the aspirant.

शान्तो दान्तः परमुपरतः क्षान्तियुक्तः समाधिं
śānto dāntaḥ paramuparataḥ kṣāntiyuktaḥ samādhiṁ
कुर्वन्नित्यं कलयति यतिः स्वस्य सर्वात्मभावम् ।
kurvannityaṁ kalayati yatiḥ svasya sarvātmabhāvam ,
तेनाविद्यातिमिरजनितान्साधु दग्ध्वा विकल्पान्
tenāvidyātimirajanitānsādhu dagdhvā vikalpān
ब्रह्माकृत्या निवसति सुखं निष्क्रियो निर्विकल्पः ॥ ३५५ ॥
brahmākṛtyā nivasati sukhaṁ niṣkriyo nirvikalpaḥ (355)

355. Serene, self-controlled, perfectly withdrawn from the sense-world, steadfast in forbearance, and devoting himself to the practice of *Samādhi*, the *Sanyāsin* directly experiences his own Self to be the Universal-Self of everything in existence. Destroying completely by this means every imagination which was due to the darkness of Ignorance, he lives blissfully as *Brahama*—freed from actions and oscillations of the mind.

समाहिता ये प्रविलाप्य बाह्यं श्रोत्रादि चेतः स्वमहं चिदात्मनि ।
samāhitā ye pravilāpya bāhyaṁ śrotrādi cetaḥ svamahaṁ cidātmani ,
त एव मुक्ता भवपाशबन्धैः नान्ये तु पारोक्ष्यकथाभिधायिनः ॥ ३५६ ॥
ta eva muktā bhavapāśabandhaiḥ nānye tu pārokṣyakathābhidhāyinaḥ (356)

356. Such alone are free from the bondages of transmigration who have merged the objective world, the sense-organs, the mind—nay, their very ego—in the *Ātmā*, the Consciousness Absolute, in an act of *Samādhi*. Aye, such alone and none else—who are merely found cackling like some word-repeating parrot.

उपाधिभेदात्स्वयमेव भिद्यते चोपाध्यपोहे स्वयमेव केवलः ।
upādhibhedātsvayameva bhidyate copādhyapohe svayameva kevalaḥ ,
तस्मादुपाधेर्विलयाय विद्वान् वसेत्सदाऽकल्पसमाधिनिष्ठया ॥ ३५७ ॥
tasmādupādhervilayāya vidvān vasetsadā'kalpasamādhiniṣṭhayā (357)

357. Due to association with the diversity of the supervening adjuncts (*Upādhis*), a man is apt to think of himself as full of diverseness as well; but with the removal of all such associations, he is rendered his own Self—the immutable, the non-dual. So until the eradication of all *Upādhis* has come to pass, let the wise person remain steadily engaged in attaining the highest state of *Nirvikalpa*.

सति सक्तो नरो याति सद्भावं ह्येकनिष्ठया ।
sati sakto naro yāti sadbhāvaṁ hyekaniṣṭhayā ,
कीटको भ्रमरं ध्यायन् भ्रमरत्वाय कल्पते ॥३५८॥
kīṭako bhramaraṁ dhyāyan bhramaratvāya kalpate (358)

358. Through the practice of single-pointed devotion, attached to the Real, one really becomes the Real: in just the same way as the roach—thinking exclusively of the wasp (*Bhramara*)—becomes the wasp itself.

क्रियान्तरासक्तिमपास्य कीटको ध्यायन्नलित्वं ह्यलिभावमृच्छति ।
kriyāntarāsaktimapāsya kīṭako dhyāyannalitvaṁ hyalibhāvamṛcchati ,
तथैव योगी परमात्मतत्त्वं ध्यात्वा समायाति तदेकनिष्ठया ॥३५९॥
tathaiva yogī paramātmatattvaṁ dhyātvā samāyāti tadekaniṣṭhayā (359)

359. Just as the roach, giving up every other activity and thinking intently upon the *Bhramara*, ends up metamorphosed into that, exactly in the same way the Yogi, meditating on the truth of the *Param-Ātmā*, becomes the *Param-Ātmā* through his single-pointed devotion.

अतीव सूक्ष्मं परमात्मतत्त्वं न स्थूलदृष्ट्या प्रतिपत्तुमर्हति ।
atīva sūkṣmaṁ paramātmatattvaṁ na sthūladṛṣṭyā pratipattumarhati ,
समाधिनात्यन्तसुसूक्ष्मवृत्त्या ज्ञातव्यमार्यैरतिशुद्धबुद्धिभिः ॥३६०॥
samādhinātyantasusūkṣmavṛttyā jñātavyamāryairatiśuddhabuddhibhiḥ (360)

360. The truth of the *Param-Ātmā* is extremely subtle and cannot be reached by the gross outgoing tendencies of the mind; it is accessible only to a noble soul of perfectly pure mind—gained by the means of *Samādhi,* brought on by the extraordinary fineness of mental state.

यथा सुवर्णं पुटपाकशोधितं त्यक्त्वा मलं स्वात्मगुणं समृच्छति ।
yathā suvarṇaṁ puṭapākaśodhitaṁ tyaktvā malaṁ svātmaguṇaṁ samṛcchati ,
तथा मनः सत्त्वरजस्तमोमलं ध्यानेन सन्त्यज्य समेति तत्त्वम् ॥३६१॥
tathā manaḥ sattvarajastamomalaṁ dhyānena santyajya sameti tattvam (361)

361. Just as gold—by a thorough heating in the fire—gives up all impurities and attains to its own luster, so too does the mind. The mind becomes stainless and attains to the nature of *Brahama* by giving up the impurities of *Sattva*, *Rajas* and *Tamas* in the Fiery state of Meditation.

निरन्तराभ्यासवशात्तदित्थं पक्वं मनो ब्रह्मणि लीयते यदा ।
nirantarābhyāsavaśāttaditthaṁ pakvaṁ mano brahmaṇi līyate yadā ,
तदा समाधिः सविकल्पवर्जितः स्वतोऽद्वयानन्दरसानुभावकः ॥३६२॥
tadā samādhiḥ savikalpavarjitaḥ svato'dvayānandarasānubhāvakaḥ (362)

362. Purified thusly through constant practice, when the mind becomes merged in *Brahama*, then *Samādhi* has passed from the *Savikalpa* to the *Nirvikalpa* stage; and this directly leads to the Realization of the highest Bliss: the Bliss of *Brahama*, the One without a second.

समाधिनाऽनेन समस्तवासनाग्रन्थेर्विनाशोऽखिलकर्मनाशः ।
samādhinā'nena samastavāsanāgranthervināśo'khilakarmanāśaḥ ,
अन्तर्बहिः सर्वत एव सर्वदा स्वरूपविस्फूर्तिरयत्नतः स्यात् ॥३६३॥
antarbahiḥ sarvata eva sarvadā svarūpavisphūrtirayatnataḥ syāt (363)

363. By this *Nirvikalpa Samādhi* stand destroyed all knots (like desires etc.,) of the mind, and all work is now at end. And then there takes place—inside and out and everywhere and forever—a spontaneous manifestation of one's Real nature, blazing forth in all its glory.

श्रुतेः शतगुणं विद्यान्मननं मननादपि ।
śruteḥ śataguṇaṁ vidyānmananaṁ mananādapi ,
निदिध्यासं लक्षगुणमनन्तं निर्विकल्पकम् ॥३६४॥
nididhyāsaṁ lakṣaguṇamanantaṁ nirvikalpakam (364)

364. Reflection should be considered a hundred times superior to Hearing; and Meditation a hundred-thousand times superior to Reflection; but the *Nirvikalpa Samādhi* is infinite in its results.

निर्विकल्पकसमाधिना स्फुटं ब्रह्मतत्त्वमवगम्यते ध्रुवम् ।
nirvikalpakasamādhinā sphuṭaṁ brahmatattvamavagamyate dhruvam ,
नान्यथा चलतया मनोगतेः प्रत्ययान्तरविमिश्रितं भवेत् ॥३६५॥
nānyathā calatayā manogateḥ pratyayāntaravimiśritaṁ bhavet (365)

365. By the *Nirvikalpa Samādhi* alone is the truth of *Brahama* clearly, decidedly, and intimately Realized—and in no other way; for otherwise the mind—being precarious by nature—is apt to get mixed with some or other modification.

अतः समाधत्स्व यतेन्द्रियः सन् निरन्तरं शान्तमनाः प्रतीचि ।
ataḥ samādhatsva yatendriyaḥ san nirantaraṁ śāntamanāḥ pratīci ,
विध्वंसय ध्वान्तमनाद्यविद्यया कृतं सदेकत्वविलोकनेन ॥३६६॥
vidhvaṁsaya dhvāntamanādyavidyayā kṛtaṁ sadekatvavilokanena (366)

366. Therefore with a serene mind, and the senses well controlled, and ever concentrating upon the Self abiding within, and realizing your identity with That Supreme Reality—destroy forever the darkness of Nescience which seems to be beginning-less.

योगस्य प्रथमद्वारं वाङ्निरोधोऽपरिग्रहः ।
yogasya prathamadvāraṁ vāṅnirodho'parigrahaḥ ,
निराशा च निरीहा च नित्यमेकान्तशीलता ॥ ३६७॥
nirāśā ca nirīhā ca nityamekāntaśīlatā (367)

367. The first steps to Yoga are: the control of speech; non-accumulation and non-receiving of things; entertaining no expectations; freedom from activity; and a love for solitude.

एकान्तस्थितिरिन्द्रियोपरमणे हेतुर्दमश्चेतसः
ekāntasthitirindriyoparamaṇe heturdamaścetasaḥ
संरोधे करणं शमेन विलयं यायादहंवासना ।
saṁrodhe karaṇaṁ śamena vilayaṁ yāyādahaṁvāsanā ,
तेनानन्दरसानुभूतिरचला ब्राह्मी सदा योगिनः
tenānandarasānubhūtiracalā brāhmī sadā yoginaḥ
तस्माच्चित्तनिरोध एव सततं कार्यः प्रयत्नो मुनेः ॥ ३६८॥
tasmāccittanirodha eva satataṁ kāryaḥ prayatno muneḥ (368)

368. Living in a retired place serves to control the sense-organs; and the control of sense-organs serves to control the mind; and control of the mind leads to destruction of egoism; and this gives the Yogi an unbroken realization of the Bliss of *Brahama*. Therefore the seeker should always strive to control the mind with great diligence.

वाचं नियच्छात्मनि तं नियच्छ बुद्धौ धियं यच्छ च बुद्धिसाक्षिणि ।
vācaṁ niyacchātmani taṁ niyaccha buddhau dhiyaṁ yaccha ca buddhisākṣiṇi ,
तं चापि पूर्णात्मनि निर्विकल्पे विलाप्य शान्तिं परमां भजस्व ॥ ३६९॥
taṁ cāpi pūrṇātmani nirvikalpe vilāpya śāntiṁ paramāṁ bhajasva (369)

369. Restraining the speech in the *Manas* (Mind); and restraining the *Manas* in the *Buddhi*; and restraining the *Buddhi* in the Witness of the *Buddhi*; and having even that Witness merge into the Infinite Absolute Self—be ushered into the realm of Supreme-Tranquility.

देहप्राणेन्द्रियमनोबुद्ध्यादिभिरुपाधिभिः ।
dehaprāṇendriyamanobuddhyādibhirupādhibhiḥ ,
यैर्यैर्वृत्तेःसमायोगस्तत्तद्भावोऽस्य योगिनः ॥ ३७०॥
yairyairvṛtteḥsamāyogastattadbhāvo'sya yoginaḥ (370)

370. The body, *Prānas*, organs, *Manas*, *Buddhi* etc.,—with whichever of these supervening adjuncts the Mind is associated with, the yogi is metamorphosed, as it were, verily into that.

तन्निवृत्त्या मुनेः सम्यक् सर्वोपरमणं सुखम् ।
tannivṛttyā muneḥ samyak sarvoparamaṇaṁ sukham ,
सन्दृश्यते सदानन्दरसानुभवविप्लवः ॥ ३७१॥
sandṛśyate sadānandarasānubhavaviplavaḥ (371)

371. When this outgoing association of the mind becomes well controlled and restrained, then the man of reflection is found to become easily detached from everything—and he thereby experiences overabundant everlasting Bliss.

अन्तस्त्यागो बहिस्त्यागो विरक्तस्यैव युज्यते ।
antastyāgo bahistyāgo viraktasyaiva yujyate ,
त्यजत्यन्तर्बहिःसङ्गं विरक्तस्तु मुमुक्षया ॥ ३७२ ॥
tyajatyantarbahiḥsaṅgaṁ viraktastu mumukṣayā (372)

372. Only a within-detached person (*Virakta*) is befitting to such internal and external relinquishment. An exceedingly dispassionate man alone—out of desire to be Free—forgoes every internal and external tie without a thought.

बहिस्तु विषयैः सङ्गं तथान्तरहमादिभिः ।
bahistu viṣayaiḥ saṅgaṁ tathāntarahamādibhiḥ ,
विरक्त एव शक्नोति त्यक्तुं ब्रह्मणि निष्ठितः ॥ ३७३ ॥
virakta eva śaknoti tyaktuṁ brahmaṇi niṣṭhitaḥ (373)

373. Only one who is a *Virakta* (thoroughly dispassionate), and a *Bhakta* (exceedingly passionate to be One with the Absolute *Brahama*), can give up the external attachment towards sense-objects, and the internal attachments for the ego etc.

वैराग्यबोधौ पुरुषस्य पक्षिवत् पक्षौ विजानीहि विचक्षण त्वम् ।
vairāgyabodhau puruṣasya pakṣivat pakṣau vijānīhi vicakṣaṇa tvam ,
विमुक्तिसौधाग्रलताधिरोहणं ताभ्यां विना नान्यतरेण सिध्यति ॥ ३७४ ॥
vimuktisaudhāgralatādhirohaṇaṁ tābhyāṁ vinā nānyatareṇa sidhyati (374)

374. O learned sage, know Dispassion and Discrimination to be like the two wings of a bird in the case of an seeker aspiring to fly to the Land of Freedom; unless both are present, none can, with the help of just one wing, reach the crowning branch of Liberation which grows, as it were, at the very top of the edifice there.

अत्यन्तवैराग्यवतः समाधिः समाहितस्यैव दृढप्रबोधः ।
atyantavairāgyavataḥ samādhiḥ samāhitasyaiva dṛḍhaprabodhaḥ ,
प्रबुद्धतत्त्वस्य हि बन्धमुक्तिः मुक्तात्मनो नित्यसुखानुभूतिः ॥ ३७५ ॥
prabuddhatattvasya hi bandhamuktiḥ muktātmano nityasukhānubhūtiḥ (375)

375. The extremely dispassionate man alone experiences *Samādhi*; and the man of *Samādhi* alone gets steady Realization; and the man of steady Realization alone is forever freed of bondages; and it is only the Free Soul who gets to experience Eternal Bliss.

वैराग्यान्न परं सुखस्य जनकं पश्यामि वश्यात्मनः
vairāgyānna paraṁ sukhasya janakaṁ paśyāmi vaśyātmanaḥ
तच्चेच्छुद्धतरात्मबोधसहितं स्वाराज्यसाम्राज्यधुक् ।
taccecchuddhatarātmabodhasahitaṁ svārājyasāmrājyadhuk ,
एतद्द्वारमजस्रमुक्तियुवतेर्यस्मात्त्वमस्मात्परं
etaddvāramajasramukti-yuvateryasmāttvamasmātparaṁ
सर्वत्रास्पृहया सदात्मनि सदा प्रज्ञां कुरु श्रेयसे ॥ ३७६ ॥
sarvatrāspṛhayā sadātmani sadā prajñāṁ kuru śreyase (376)

376. For the man of self-control there is no better begetter of happiness than Dispassion; and if that be coupled with a clear Realization of the Self, one becomes vested with the sovereign reign over the inner and outer worlds—and that, O dear, is the doorway to the Diva of eternal Liberation. Therefore for thy own well-being, do thou take to the path of arrant Dispassion—both within and without—and always abide with thy concentration fixed upon the eternal *Ātmā*.

आशां छिन्द्धि विषोपमेषु विषयेष्वेषैव मृत्योः कृति
āśāṁ chinddhi viṣopameṣu viṣayeṣveṣaiva mṛtyoḥ kṛti
स्त्यक्त्वा जातिकुलाश्रमेष्वभिमतिं मुञ्चातिदूरात्क्रियाः ।
styaktvā jātikulāśrameṣvabhimatiṁ muñcātidūrātkriyāḥ ,
देहादावसति त्यजात्मधिषणां प्रज्ञां कुरुष्वात्मनि
dehādāvasati tyajātmadhiṣaṇāṁ prajñāṁ kuruṣvātmani
त्वं द्रष्टास्यमनोऽसि निर्द्वयपरं ब्रह्मासि यद्वस्तुतः ॥ ३७७ ॥
tvaṁ draṣṭāsyamano'si nirdvayaparaṁ brahmāsi yadvastutaḥ (377)

377. Cut asunder this craving for the sense-objects— which is so toxic, the very epitome of Death. Fling away all selfish actions to a great distance, giving up all superbia related to birth, caste, family, social order etc. Abide with your mind fixed firmly upon the *Ātmā*, giving up all identification with the non-Real things such as the body etc. Remember: you are merely a Witness here—thoroughly unshackled, unburdened of the mind. Remember: you are the Supreme *Brahama*—the One without a second.

लक्ष्ये ब्रह्मणि मानसं दृढतरं संस्थाप्य बाह्येन्द्रियं
lakṣye brahmaṇi mānasaṁ dṛḍhataraṁ saṁsthāpya bāhyendriyaṁ
स्वस्थाने विनिवेश्य निश्चलतनुश्चोपेक्ष्य देहस्थितिम् ।
svasthāne viniveśya niścalatanuścopekṣya dehasthitim ,
ब्रह्मात्मैक्यमुपेत्य तन्मयतया चाखण्डवृत्त्याऽनिशं
brahmātmaikyamupetya tanmayatayā cākhaṇḍavṛttyā'niśaṁ
ब्रह्मानन्दरसं पिबात्मनि मुदा शून्यैः किमन्यैर्भृशम् ॥ ३७८ ॥
brahmānandarasaṁ pibātmani mudā śūnyaiḥ kimanyairbhṛśam (378)

378. Fixing your concentration upon *Brahama*; and restraining the sense-organs to their respective centers; and with the body

held steady; and taking no thought for its maintenance; and attaining complete identity with *Brahama*—becoming one with it—always drink joyfully of the Bliss of *Brahama* within, without the least bit of break. Of what avail is anything else?—for everything else of the world is entirely hollow and bereft of joy.

अनात्मचिन्तनं त्यक्त्वा कश्मलं दुःखकारणम् ।
anātmacintanaṁ tyaktvā kaśmalaṁ duḥkhakāraṇam ,
चिन्तयात्मानमानन्दरूपं यन्मुक्तिकारणम् ॥ ३७९ ॥
cintayātmānamānandarūpaṁ yanmuktikāraṇam (379)

379. Give up all thoughts of the not-Self—which is so evil and productive of misery. It is only the state of Onlyness—where the thoughts ever dwell upon the *Ātmā*, the Bliss Absolute—which is conducive to Liberation.

एष स्वयञ्ज्योतिरशेषसाक्षी विज्ञानकोशो विलसत्यजस्रम् ।
eṣa svayañjyotiraśeṣasākṣī vijñānakośo vilasatyajasram ,
लक्ष्यं विधायैनमसद्विलक्षण मखण्डवृत्त्याऽऽत्मतयाऽनुभावय ॥ ३८० ॥
lakṣyaṁ vidhāyainamasadvilakṣaṇa makhaṇḍavṛttyā''tmatayā'nubhāvaya (380)

380. Behold, for here shines the eternal *Ātmā*, the self-effulgent witness of everything, which has the *Buddhi* for its seat. Having this *Ātmā*—which is completely distinct from the non-Real—as the only objective of contemplation, meditate upon it as your own inner self, to the exclusion of every other thought.

एतमच्छिन्नया वृत्त्या प्रत्ययान्तरशून्यया ।
etamacchinnayā vṛttyā pratyayāntaraśūnyayā ,
उल्लेखयन्विजानीयात्स्वस्वरूपतया स्फुटम् ॥ ३८१ ॥
ullekhayanvijānīyātsvasvarūpatayā sphuṭam (381)

381. Meditating ceaselessly upon the *Ātmā*—without allowing any extraneous thoughts to intervene—one must clearly and directly realize the *Ātmā* to be one's Own Real Self.

अत्रात्मत्वं दृढीकुर्वन्नहमादिषु सन्त्यजन् ।
atrātmatvaṁ dṛḍhīkurvannahamādiṣu santyajan ,
उदासीनतया तेषु तिष्ठेत्स्फुटघटादिवत् ॥ ३८२ ॥
udāsīnatayā teṣu tiṣṭhetsphuṭaghaṭādivat (382)

382. Strengthening one's identification with This (the *Ātmā*); and giving up everything other than that (body, ego etc.), one must abide having no concern for the not-Self—as if they were trifling things, like broken pots or similar useless trash.

विशुद्धमन्तःकरणं स्वरूपे निवेश्य साक्षिण्यवबोधमात्रे ।
viśuddhamantaḥkaraṇaṁ svarūpe niveśya sākṣiṇyavabodhamātre ,

शनैः शनैर्निश्चलतामुपानयन् पूर्णं स्वमेवानुविलोकयेत्ततः ॥ ३८३ ॥
śanaiḥ śanairniścalatāmupānayan pūrṇaṁ svamevānuvilokayettataḥ (383)

383. Fixing the purified mind upon the Self—which is the Witness, the Knowledge Absolute—and gradually making it quiet and subdued, one should directly Realize one's Infinite Nature as one with the Supreme-Self.

देहेन्द्रियप्राणमनोऽहमादिभिः स्वाज्ञानक्लृप्तैरखिलैरुपाधिभिः ।
dehendriyaprāṇamano'hamādibhiḥ svājñānaklṛptairakhilairupādhibhiḥ ,
विमुक्तमात्मानमखण्डरूपं पूर्णं महाकाशमिवावलोकयेत् ॥ ३८४ ॥
vimuktamātmānamakhaṇḍarūpaṁ pūrṇaṁ mahākāśamivāvalokayet (384)

384. Behold within thyself the *Ātmā*, the Self which is indivisible and infinite like the all-pervading space, which is free from all limiting adjuncts such as the body, organs, *Prānas*, *Manas* and egoism etc.,—all of which are the products of Nescience.

घटकलशकुसूलसूचिमुख्यैः गगनमुपाधिशतैर्विमुक्तमेकम् ।
ghaṭakalaśakusūlasūcimukhyaiḥ gaganamupādhiśatairvimuktamekam ,
भवति न विविधं तथैव शुद्धं परमहमादिविमुक्तमेकमेव ॥ ३८५ ॥
bhavati na vividhaṁ tathaiva śuddhaṁ paramahamādivimuktamekameva (385)

385. The space—divested of the hundreds of limiting adjuncts such as a jar, a pitcher, a silo or a needle-eye—is singular and not manifold; exactly in the same way the pristine unmanifest *Brahama*—divested of egoes, bodies etc., everything—is verily One.

ब्रह्मादिस्तम्बपर्यन्ता मृषामात्रा उपाधयः ।
brahmādistambaparyantā mṛṣāmātrā upādhayaḥ ,
ततः पूर्णं स्वमात्मानं पश्येदेकात्मना स्थितम् ॥ ३८६ ॥
tataḥ pūrṇaṁ svamātmānaṁ paśyedekātmanā sthitam (386)

386. All these limiting adjuncts—from *Brahammā* down to a clump of grass—are wholly non-Real. There is only One Reality, only one abiding principle in existence, and one should realize one's Self to be one with That Infinite *Brahama*.

यत्र भ्रान्त्या कल्पितं तद्विवेके तत्तन्मात्रं नैव तस्माद्विभिन्नम् ।
yatra bhrāntyā kalpitaṁ tadviveke tattanmātraṁ naiva tasmādvibhinnam ,
भ्रान्तेर्नाशे भाति दृष्टाहितत्त्वं रज्जुस्तद्वद्विश्वमात्मस्वरूपम् ॥ ३८७ ॥
bhrānternāśe bhāti dṛṣṭāhitattvaṁ rajjustadvadviśvamātmasvarūpam (387)

387. Through error, if something erroneous is imagined to be as a thing, then once rightly discriminated, the real thing becomes revealed as is—and is not found separate from its actuality. When the error is gone, the 'perceived-existence' of snake—

which was falsely seen in a rope—merges in the rope, and the rope continues being what it always was. Similarly the universe is in reality just the *Ātmā*—whatever else it may have been imagined to be through ignorance, delusion, error etc.

स्वयं ब्रह्मा स्वयं विष्णुः स्वयमिन्द्रः स्वयं शिवः ।
svayaṁ brahmā svayaṁ viṣṇuḥ svayamindraḥ svayaṁ śivaḥ ,
स्वयं विश्वमिदं सर्वं स्वस्मादन्यन्न किञ्चन ॥ ३८८॥
svayaṁ viśvamidaṁ sarvaṁ svasmādanyanna kiñcana (388)

388. The Self is *Brahammā*, the Self is *Vishnu*, the Self is *Indra*, the Self is *Shiva*—the Self is this here entire universe; nothing exists apart from the Self.

अन्तः स्वयं चापि बहिः स्वयं च स्वयं पुरस्तात् स्वयमेव पश्चात् ।
antaḥ svayaṁ cāpi bahiḥ svayaṁ ca svayaṁ purastāt svayameva paścāt ,
स्वयं ह्यावाच्यां स्वयमप्युदीच्यां तथोपरिष्टात्स्वयमप्यधस्तात् ॥ ३८९॥
svayaṁ hyāvācyāṁ svayamapyudīcyāṁ tathopariṣṭātsvayamapyadhastāt (389)

389. The Self is within, and the Self is without; and the Self is to the front and the Self is to the back; the Self is to the south, and the Self is to the north; and the Self is above and below and the Self is all around.

तरङ्गफेनभ्रमबुद्बुदादि सर्वं स्वरूपेण जलं यथा तथा ।
taraṅgaphenabhramabudbudādi sarvaṁ svarūpeṇa jalaṁ yathā tathā ,
चिदेव देहाद्यहमन्तमेतत् सर्वं चिदेवैकरसं विशुद्धम् ॥ ३९०॥
cideva dehādyahamantametat sarvaṁ cidevaikarasaṁ viśuddham (390)

390. The waves, and froth, and whirlpools and bubbles—are all but water at the core; and the same is true of the *Chitta* (the Absolute Consciousness), which has become all this—from the body up to the ego. Aye, everything is verily just the *Chitta*—one Singular-Consciousness, unvarying and pure.

सदेवेदं सर्वं जगदवगतं वाङ्मनसयोः
sadevedaṁ sarvaṁ jagadavagataṁ vāṅmanasayoḥ
सतोऽन्यन्नास्त्येव प्रकृतिपरसीम्नि स्थितवतः ।
sato'nyannāstyeva prakṛtiparasīmni sthitavataḥ ,
पृथक् किं मृत्स्नायाः कलशघटकुम्भाद्यवगतं
pṛthak kiṁ mṛtsnāyāḥ kalaśaghaṭakumbhādyavagataṁ
वदत्येष भ्रान्तस्त्वमहमिति मायामदिरया ॥ ३९१ ॥
vadatyeṣa bhrāntastvamahamiti māyāmadirayā (391)

391. All this universe known through words and thoughts is nothing but *Brahama*. There's nothing other than *Brahama*—which extends way beyond the farthermost ambit of the known. Are the pitcher, jug, pot, etc., ever distinct from the clay of

which they are composed? It is only the deluded soul who talks of 'you' and 'I', drunk on the wine served by the enchantress *Māyā*.

क्रियासमभिहारेण यत्र नान्यदिति श्रुतिः ।
kriyāsamabhihāreṇa yatra nānyaditi śrutiḥ ,
ब्रवीति द्वैतराहित्यं मिथ्याध्यासनिवृत्तये ॥ ३९२॥
bravīti dvaitarāhityaṁ mithyādhyāsanivṛttaye (392)

392. With many predicates, the *Shruti* declares the absence of duality in the verse, "Where one sees nothing else..." etc., in order to remove all perceived false superimpositions.

आकाशवन्निर्मलनिर्विकल्पं निःसीमनिःस्पन्दननिर्विकारम् ।
ākāśavannirmalanirvikalpaṁ niḥsīmaniḥspandananirvikāram ,
अन्तर्बहिःशून्यमनन्यमद्वयं स्वयं परं ब्रह्म किमस्ति बोध्यम् ॥ ३९३॥
antarbahiḥśūnyamananyamadvayaṁ svayaṁ paraṁ brahma kimasti bodhyam (393)

393. Like the infinite Space-Time, the Supreme *Brahama* is pristine, absolute, limitless, motionless, changeless, and void of parts, interiors, exteriors. It is the One-Existence, without-a-second. And It is one's very own Self. Other than *Brahama*, is there any thing else in existence that could possibly be the object of perception or knowingness?

वक्तव्यं किमु विद्यतेऽत्र बहुधा ब्रह्मैव जीवः स्वयं
vaktavyaṁ kimu vidyate'tra bahudhā brahmaiva jīvaḥ svayaṁ
ब्रह्मैतज्जगदाततं नु सकलं ब्रह्माद्वितीयं श्रुतिः ।
brahmaitajjagadātataṁ nu sakalaṁ brahmādvitīyaṁ śrutiḥ ,
ब्रह्मैवाहमिति प्रबुद्धमतयः सन्त्यक्तबाह्याः स्फुटं
brahmaivāhamiti prabuddhamatayaḥ santyaktabāhyāḥ sphuṭaṁ
ब्रह्मीभूय वसन्ति सन्ततचिदानन्दात्मनैतद्ध्रुवम् ॥ ३९४॥
brahmībhūya vasanti santatacidānandātmanaitaddhruvam (394)

394. Why dilate endlessly on the subject, suffice it to say: the *Jiva* is none other than *Brahama*; this whole extended universe is just only *Brahama*. The *Shrutis* point out *Brahama* to be the only existence, the One without-a-second. And it is an indubitable fact that people of enlightened consciousness—those who have given up their connection with the objective world, who have realized their identity in *Brahama*—live palpably unified within *Brahama* as Eternal Bliss and Consciousness.

जहि मलमयकोशेऽहन्धियोत्थापिताशां प्रसभमनिलकल्पे लिङ्गदेहेऽपि पश्चात् ।
jahi malamayakośe'handhiyotthāpitāśāṁ prasabhamanilakalpe liṅgadehe'pi paścāt ,
निगमगदितकीर्तिं नित्यमानन्दमूर्तिं स्वयमिति परिचीय ब्रह्मरूपेण तिष्ठ ॥ ३९५॥
nigamagaditakīrtiṁ nityamānandamūrtiṁ svayamiti paricīya brahmarūpeṇa tiṣṭha (395)

395. Destroy all hopes raised by egoism related to this gross-body—which is a collection of nauseating things; and then with great persistence do the same pertaining to the unseen subtle-body; and then realizing *Brahama*—the embodiment of eternal Bliss, whose glories the scriptures never tire of declaring to be one's own Self—ever dwell as *Brahama*.

शवाकारं यावद्भजति मनुजस्तावदशुचिः
śavākāraṁ yāvadbhajati manujastāvadaśuciḥ
परेभ्यः स्यात्क्लेशो जननमरणव्याधिनिलयः ।
parebhyaḥ syātkleśo jananamaraṇavyādhinilayaḥ ,
यदात्मानं शुद्धं कलयति शिवाकारमचलम्
yadātmānaṁ śuddhaṁ kalayati śivākāramacalam
तदा तेभ्यो मुक्तो भवति हि तदाह श्रुतिरपि ॥ ३९६ ॥
tadā tebhyo mukto bhavati hi tadāha śrutirapi (396)

396. So long as the man has even the least regard for this corpse-like body, he necessarily becomes defiled and impure and suffers at the hands of world and from birth, death, diseases etc.,—nature; but when man knows himself to be bodiless and ethereal—pure, auspicious, immovable—he assuredly becomes free from all the worldly taints. The *Shrutis* themselves testify to this.

स्वात्मन्यारोपिताशेषाभासवस्तुनिरासतः ।
svātmanyāropitāśeṣābhāsavastunirāsataḥ ,
स्वयमेव परं ब्रह्म पूर्णमद्वयमक्रियम् ॥ ३९७ ॥
svayameva paraṁ brahma pūrṇamadvayamakriyam (397)

397. When all the apparitions that are superimposed upon the Self, when all the non-Realities have been eliminated, then what remains is just the Supreme *Brahama*, all by Itself—infinite, non-dual, tranquil, motionless, bereft of activity.

समाहितायां सति चित्तवृत्तौ परात्मनि ब्रह्मणि निर्विकल्पे ।
samāhitāyāṁ sati cittavṛttau parātmani brahmaṇi nirvikalpe ,
न दृश्यते कश्चिदयं विकल्पः प्रजल्पमात्रः परिशिष्यते यतः ॥ ३९८ ॥
na dṛśyate kaścidayaṁ vikalpaḥ prajalpamātraḥ pariśiṣyate yataḥ (398)

398. When the mind-functions are all merged within the *Param-Ātmā—Brahama*, the Absolute—then this phenomenal world is perceived no more; what remains thereafter is just fluff and talk.

असत्कल्पो विकल्पोऽयं विश्वमित्येकवस्तुनि ।
asatkalpo vikalpo'yaṁ viśvamityekavastuni ,

निर्विकारे निराकारे निर्विशेषे भिदा कुतः ॥३९९॥
nirvikāre nirākāre nirviśeṣe bhidā kutaḥ (399)

399. In the sole reality *Brahama*, the construct and conception of this manifold universe is a mere apparition; how can there be any distinctions in the Reality which is Absolute, Changeless, Formless?

द्रष्टृदर्शनदृश्यादिभावशून्यैकवस्तुनि ।
draṣṭudarśanadṛśyādibhāvaśūnyaikavastuni ,
निर्विकारे निराकारे निर्विशेषे भिदा कुतः ॥४००॥
nirvikāre nirākāre nirviśeṣe bhidā kutaḥ (400)

400. In the One Reality *Brahama*—which is absolute, changeless, formless—devoid of the conceptions of seer, seeing and seen—how can there be any diversity or distinctions?

कल्पार्णव इवात्यन्तपरिपूर्णैकवस्तुनि ।
kalpārṇava ivātyantaparipūrṇaikavastuni ,
निर्विकारे निराकारे निर्विशेषे भिदा कुतः ॥४०१॥
nirvikāre nirākāre nirviśeṣe bhidā kutaḥ (401)

401. In the One Reality *Brahama*—changeless, formless, absolute, the all-pervading fullness which's like a motionless ocean that remains upon the dissolution of the universe, how can there be any diversity?

तेजसीव तमो यत्र प्रलीनं भ्रान्तिकारणम् ।
tejasīva tamo yatra pralīnaṁ bhrāntikāraṇam ,
अद्वितीये परे तत्त्वे निर्विशेषे भिदा कुतः ॥४०२॥
advitīye pare tattve nirviśeṣe bhidā kutaḥ (402)

402. In whom ignorance—the root of delusion—has become dissolved like darkness in the light, in that One Reality—the changeless formless Absolute—how can diversity endure any longer?

एकात्मके परे तत्त्वे भेदवार्ता कथं वसेत् ।
ekātmake pare tattve bhedavārtā kathaṁ vaset ,
सुषुप्तौ सुखमात्रायां भेदः केनावलोकितः ॥४०३॥
suṣuptau sukhamātrāyāṁ bhedaḥ kenāvalokitaḥ (403)

403. How can the talk of distinction and diversity apply to the Supreme-Reality which is unvarying, uniform, one? To exemplify, who has ever observed diversity in the pure blissful state of profound-sleep?

न ह्यस्ति विश्वं परतत्त्वबोधात् सदात्मनि ब्रह्मणि निर्विकल्पे ।
na hyasti viśvaṁ paratattvabodhāt sadātmani brahmaṇi nirvikalpe ,

कालत्रये नाप्यहिरीक्षितो गुणे न ह्यम्बुबिन्दुर्मृगतृष्णिकायाम् ॥४०४॥
kālatraye nāpyahirīkṣito guṇe na hyambubindurmṛgatṛṣṇikāyām (404)

404. Even before the realization of the highest Truth, the universe does not exist separate from *Brahama*—the Absolute, the quintessence of Existence. In none of the three states of time does the perceived 'snake' become actually existent within the rope, or the 'water' in the mirage.

मायामात्रमिदं द्वैतमद्वैतं परमार्थतः ।
māyāmātramidaṁ dvaitamadvaitaṁ paramārthataḥ ,
इति ब्रूते श्रुतिः साक्षात्सुषुप्तावनुभूयते ॥४०५॥
iti brūte śrutiḥ sākṣātsuṣuptāvanubhūyate (405)

405. The *Shrutis* themselves declare that the notion of duality is just an illusion, an imagination from the perspective of the Absolute Being. A hint of this non-duality is realized in the state of pristine dreamless-sleep—attested by the universal experience.

अनन्यत्वमधिष्ठानादारोप्यस्य निरीक्षितम् ।
ananyatvamadhiṣṭhānādāropyasya nirīkṣitam ,
पण्डितै रज्जुसर्पादौ विकल्पो भ्रान्तिजीवनः ॥४०६॥
paṇḍitai rajjusarpādau vikalpo bhrāntijīvanaḥ (406)

406. Something which is superimposed upon the substratum, is observed by a discriminating person to be none other than the substratum itself—just as how the 'snake' superimposed on the rope in darkness disappears, to disclose only the substratum rope upon the advent of light. The delusive superimposition lasts only so long as the error and ignorance lasts.

चित्तमूलो विकल्पोऽयं चित्ताभावे न कश्चन ।
cittamūlo vikalpo'yaṁ cittābhāve na kaścana ,
अतश्चित्तं समाधेहि प्रत्यग्रूपे परात्मनि ॥४०७॥
ataścittaṁ samādhehi pratyagrūpe parātmani (407)

407. This apparent universe has its root in the Mind; and this apparition does not endure when the Mind Dies in Meditation. Therefore dissolve the mind by meditating upon the Supreme Self—one's inmost inner essence.

किमपि सततबोधं केवलानन्दरूपं निरुपममतिवेलं नित्यमुक्तं निरीहम् ।
kimapi satatabodhaṁ kevalānandarūpaṁ nirupamamativelaṁ nityamuktaṁ nirīham ,
निरवधिगगनाभं निष्कलं निर्विकल्पं हृदि कलयति विद्वान् ब्रह्म पूर्णं समाधौ ॥४०८॥
niravadhigaganābhaṁ niṣkalaṁ nirvikalpaṁ hṛdi kalayati vidvān brahma pūrṇaṁ samādhau (408)

408. Through *Samādhi*, the wise realizes in himself that Infinite *Brahama*: which is of the nature of eternal Knowledge and absolute Bliss, which has no exemplars, which is beyond limitations, which is ever free and without activity, which is indivisible and absolute like the Space-Time.

प्रकृतिविकृतिशून्यं भावनातीतभावं समरसमसमानं मानसम्बन्धदूरम् ।
prakṛtivikṛtiśūnyaṁ bhāvanātītabhāvaṁ samarasamasamānaṁ mānasambandhadūram ,
निगमवचनसिद्धं नित्यमस्मत्प्रसिद्धं हृदि कलयति विद्वान् ब्रह्म पूर्णं समाधौ ॥४०९॥
nigamavacanasiddhaṁ nityamasmatprasiddhaṁ
hṛdi kalayati vidvān brahma pūrṇaṁ samādhau (409)

409. Through *Samādhi*, the wise directly Realizes within himself That eternal *Brahama*: which is beyond the ideas of cause and effect; the constant unvarying Oneness beyond all ideas, notions, imaginations, and beyond the notions of proofs and comparisons; which Oneness has been laid down in the Vedic dictums; which is ever familiar to us as the enduring sense of 'I'; and which is directly verifiable in *Samādhi*.

अजरममरमस्ताभाववस्तुस्वरूपं स्तिमितसलिलराशिप्रख्यमाख्याविहीनम् ।
ajaramamaramastābhāvavastusvarūpaṁ stimitasalilarāśiprakhyamākhyāvihīnam ,
शमितगुणविकारं शाश्वतं शान्तमेकं हृदि कलयति विद्वान् ब्रह्म पूर्णं समाधौ ॥४१०॥
śamitaguṇavikāraṁ śāśvataṁ śāntamekaṁ hṛdi kalayati vidvān brahma pūrṇaṁ samādhau (410)

410. Through *Samādhi*, the wise directly realizes within himself That eternal *Brahama*: which is undecaying and immortal, the only Positive Entity arrived at after Negating All Else, which has no names, which is beyond the notion of merits and demerits, which resembles a motionless ocean, which is eternal, tranquil and One.

समाहितान्तःकरणः स्वरूपे विलोकयात्मानमखण्डवैभवम् ।
samāhitāntaḥkaraṇaḥ svarūpe vilokayātmānamakhaṇḍavaibhavam ,
विच्छिन्द्धि बन्धं भवगन्धगन्धितं यत्नेन पुंस्त्वं सफलीकुरुष्व ॥४११॥
vicchinddhi bandhaṁ bhavagandhagandhitaṁ yatnena puṁstvaṁ saphalīkuruṣva (411)

411. With the mind restrained in *Samādhi*, know thyself to be the *Ātmā* of Infinite Splendor. Remaining vigilant, rent asunder all bondages which have become so persistent and strong through the repeated impressions of prior lives; and thereby attain the consummation of thy birth as a human.

सर्वोपाधिविनिर्मुक्तं सच्चिदानन्दमद्वयम् ।
sarvopādhivinirmuktaṁ saccidānandamadvayam ,
भावयात्मानमात्मस्थं न भूयः कल्पसेऽध्वने ॥४१२॥
bhāvayātmānamātmasthaṁ na bhūyaḥ kalpase'dhvane (412)

412. Meditate on the *Ātmā* within—which is the non-dual One without-a-second, the Existence-Knowledge-Bliss-Absolute, beyond limitations—and never again will you come under the sway of the waves of births and deaths.

छायेव पुंसः परिदृश्यमानमाभासरूपेण फलानुभूत्या ।
chāyeva puṁsaḥ paridṛśyamānamābhāsarūpeṇa phalānubhūtyā ,
शरीरमाराच्छववन्निरस्तं पुनर्न सन्धत्त इदं महात्मा ॥४१३॥
śarīramārācchavavannirastaṁ punarna sandhatta idaṁ mahātmā (413)

413. After the body has once been cast off to a distance like a corpse, the sage has no more attachment to it—although owing to the effects of old impressions, it is still perceived as an apparition, like a shadow following a man.

सततविमलबोधानन्दरूपं समेत्य त्यज जडमलरूपोपाधिमेतं सुदूरे ।
satatavimalabodhānandarūpaṁ sametya tyaja jaḍamalarūpopādhimetaṁ sudūre ,
अथ पुनरपि नैष स्मर्यतां वान्तवस्तु स्मरणविषयभूतं कल्पते कुत्सनाय ॥४१४॥
atha punarapi naiṣa smaryatāṁ vāntavastu smaraṇaviṣayabhūtaṁ kalpate kutsanāya (414)

414. Realizing the *Ātmā* within—eternal, pure, knowledge, bliss—set aside to a far distance this constrain of corpse-like body: bereft of consciousness and unclean by nature. Then dwell upon it no more—because something that has been vommed, excites but disgust upon being recalled.

समूलमेतत्परिदाह्य वह्नौ सदात्मनि ब्रह्मणि निर्विकल्पे ।
samūlametatparidāhya vahnau sadātmani brahmaṇi nirvikalpe ,
ततः स्वयं नित्यविशुद्धबोधानन्दात्मना तिष्ठति विद्वरिष्ठः ॥४१५॥
tataḥ svayaṁ nityaviśuddhabodhānandātmanā tiṣṭhati vidvariṣṭhaḥ (415)

415. Burning everything away—root and all—in the fiery knowledge of *Brahama*, the Eternal Absolute Self, the truly wise thenceforth dwells in solitude, always established in the *Ātmā*: which is blissful consciousness, eternal and pure.

प्रारब्धसूत्रग्रथितं शरीरं प्रयातु वा तिष्ठतु गोरिव स्रक् ।
prārabdhasūtragrathitaṁ śarīraṁ prayātu vā tiṣṭhatu goriva srak ,
न तत्पुनः पश्यति तत्त्ववेत्ताऽऽनन्दात्मनि ब्रह्मणि लीनवृत्तिः ॥४१६॥
na tatpunaḥ paśyati tattvavettā''nandātmani brahmaṇi līnavṛttiḥ (416)

416. Then that Knower of Truth no more cares whether this body—spun out by the threads of *Prārabdha*—remains standing or drops off like a garland from around the neck of a cow—being that his mind-functions ever repose in *Brahama*, the quintessence of Bliss.

अखण्डानन्दमात्मानं विज्ञाय स्वस्वरूपतः ।
akhaṇḍānandamātmānaṁ vijñāya svasvarūpataḥ ,
किमिच्छन् कस्य वा हेतोर्देहं पुष्णाति तत्त्ववित् ॥४१७॥
kimicchan kasya vā hetordehaṁ puṣṇāti tattvavit (417)

417. Having Realized the *Ātmā*—which is indivisible, infinite Bliss—as one's very own Self, for whom, and to what avail, would the knower of Truth pamper and cherish this body of clay.

संसिद्धस्य फलं त्वेतज्जीवन्मुक्तस्य योगिनः ।
saṁsiddhasya phalaṁ tvetajjīvanmuktasya yoginaḥ ,
बहिरन्तः सदानन्दरसास्वादनमात्मनि ॥४१८॥
bahirantaḥ sadānandarasāsvādanamātmani (418)

418. The Yogi who has attained perfection and is liberated-while-alive gets this as a result: a transport into the perpetual realm of Never Ending Rapture, within and without—infinite.

वैराग्यस्य फलं बोधो बोधस्योपरतिः फलम् ।
vairāgyasya phalaṁ bodho bodhasyoparatiḥ phalam ,
स्वानन्दानुभवाच्छान्तिरेषैवोपरतेः फलम् ॥४१९॥
svānandānubhavācchāntireṣaivoparateḥ phalam (419)

419. The fruit of Dispassion is: Knowledge; and the fruit of knowledge: is Withdrawal from sense-pleasures; which then leads to the Experiencing of one's Blissful Self—from whence arises Supreme Peace.

यद्युत्तरोत्तराभावः पूर्वपूर्वन्तु निष्फलम् ।
yadyuttarottarābhāvaḥ pūrvapūrvantu niṣphalam ,
निवृत्तिः परमा तृप्तिरानन्दोऽनुपमः स्वतः ॥४२०॥
nivṛttiḥ paramā tṛptirānando'nupamaḥ svataḥ (420)

420. When there is the absence of the succeeding stages, the preceding ones are but rendered ineffectual; and so with the objective world once having become severed, supreme satisfaction and matchless Bliss follow as a matter of course.

दृष्टदुःखेष्वनुद्वेगो विद्यायाः प्रस्तुतं फलम् ।
dṛṣṭaduḥkheṣvanudvego vidyāyāḥ prastutaṁ phalam ,
यत्कृतं भ्रान्तिवेलायां नाना कर्म जुगुप्सितम् ।
yatkṛtaṁ bhrāntivelāyāṁ nānā karma jugupsitam ,
पश्चान्नरो विवेकेन तत्कथं कर्तुमर्हति ॥४२१॥
paścānnaro vivekena tatkathaṁ kartumarhati (421)

421. The result of Knowledge is this: one gains Complete Impassiveness to all the worldly sorrows. How can anyone who

has committed various loathsome deeds in the state of Delusion, repeat them once possessed of Discrimination?

विद्याफलं स्यादसतो निवृत्तिः प्रवृत्तिरज्ञानफलं तदीक्षितम् ।
vidyāphalaṁ syādasato nivṛttiḥ pravṛttirajñānaphalaṁ tadīkṣitam ,
तज्ज्ञाज्ञयोर्यन्मृगतृष्णिकादौ नोचेद्विदां दृष्टफलं किमस्मात् ॥४२२॥
tajjñājñayoryanmṛgatṛṣṇikādau nocedvidāṁ dṛṣṭaphalaṁ kimasmāt (422)

422. The outcome of Knowledge should be the turning away from the non-Real—knowing that an attachment to the non-Real arising through Ignorance leads to misery. This is observed in the case of one who knows a mirage for what it is—and so doesn't chase it; and one who doesn't know a mirage—and is thereby destroyed in its futile pursuit. Otherwise what other tangible results do the knowers of *Brahama* obtain?

अज्ञानहृदयग्रन्थेर्विनाशो यद्यशेषतः ।
ajñānahṛdayagranthervināśo yadyaśeṣataḥ ,
अनिच्छोर्विषयः किं नु प्रवृत्तेः कारणं स्वतः ॥४२३॥
anicchorviṣayaḥ kiṁ nu pravṛtteḥ kāraṇaṁ svataḥ (423)

423. If the heart's Knot of Ignorance is completely undone, then what other natural causes remain which will prompt a man to selfish action (and its ensuing miseries)?—for he is no more impelled by sense-pleasures.

वासनानुदयो भोग्ये वैराग्यस्य तदावधिः ।
vāsanānudayo bhogye vairāgyasya tadāvadhiḥ ,
अहंभावोदयाभावो बोधस्य परमावधिः ।
ahaṁbhāvodayābhāvo bodhasya paramāvadhiḥ ,
लीनवृत्तैरनुत्पत्तिर्मर्यादोपरतेस्तु सा ॥४२४॥
līnavṛttairanutpattirmaryādoparatestu sā (424)

424. When the sense-objects excite no more desires—that is the culmination of Dispassion. This complete absence of impulses born of ego is arrived at through Consciousness rendered pristine (a supreme perfection that's bereft of mind and thought). The acme of self-withdrawal is reached when the thoughts that have been submerged, reappear no more.

ब्रह्माकारतया सदा स्थिततया निर्मुक्तबाह्यार्थधी-
brahmākāratayā sadā sthitatayā nirmuktabāhyārthadhī-
रन्यावेदितभोग्यभोगकलनो निद्रालुवद्बालवत् ।
ranyāveditabhogyabhogakalano nidrāluvadbālavat ,
स्वप्नालोकितलोकवज्जगदिदं पश्यन्क्वचिल्लब्धधी-
svapnālokitalokavajjagadidaṁ paśyankvacillabdhadhī-
रास्ते कश्चिदनन्तपुण्यफलभुग्धन्यः स मान्यो भुवि ॥४२५॥
rāste kaścidanantapuṇyaphalabhugdhanyaḥ sa mānyo bhuvi (425)

425. Freed from all sense of reality of the external sense-objects (due to continually remaining merged in *Brahama*); and only seeming to partake—like someone drowsy, or a little child—any sense-objects which may have been offered by another; and perceiving the world as if watching a dream, having a cognition of it only now and then—rare indeed is that holy soul. Verily that sage has come by this state as a result of fruition of endless past merits; and such a soul should be deemed most blessed on earth, and highly esteemed.

स्थितप्रज्ञो यतिरयं यः सदानन्दमश्नुते ।
sthitaprajño yatirayaṁ yaḥ sadānandamaśnute ,
ब्रह्मण्येव विलीनात्मा निर्विकारो विनिष्क्रियः ॥४२६॥
brahmaṇyeva vilīnātmā nirvikāro viniṣkriyaḥ (426)

426. Having merged his being completely in *Brahama*, he who enjoys unqualified never-ending Bliss—which has for its source no physical act or cause—he is deemed a *Sanyāsin* of steady wisdom.

ब्रह्मात्मनोः शोधितयोरेकभावावगाहिनी ।
brahmātmanoḥ śodhitayorekabhāvāvagāhinī ,
निर्विकल्पा च चिन्मात्रा वृत्तिः प्रज्ञेति कथ्यते ।
nirvikalpā ca cinmātrā vṛttiḥ prajñeti kathyate ,
सुस्थिताऽसौ भवेद्यस्य स्थितप्रज्ञः स उच्यते ॥४२७॥
susthitā'sau bhavedyasya sthitaprajñaḥ sa ucyate (427)

427. That kind of mental state which cognizes only the identity of the Self and *Brahama*, which is free from all limiting adjuncts and dualities, which concerns itself only with Pure Intelligence: that state is considered to be True Illumination. One who has this perfectly steady is called a *Sanyāsin* of steady wisdom.

यस्य स्थिता भवेत्प्रज्ञा यस्यानन्दो निरन्तरः ।
yasya sthitā bhavetprajñā yasyānando nirantaraḥ ,
प्रपञ्चो विस्मृतप्रायः स जीवन्मुक्त इष्यते ॥४२८॥
prapañco vismṛtaprāyaḥ sa jīvanmukta iṣyate (428)

428. He, whose Illumination is steady, who experiences continual Bliss, who has almost forgotten the phenomenal universe—that person is considered a *Jīvan-Mukta*: liberated-even-while-alive.

लीनधीरपि जागर्ति जाग्रद्धर्मविवर्जितः ।
līnadhīrapi jāgarti jāgraddharmavivarjitaḥ ,
बोधो निर्वासनो यस्य स जीवन्मुक्त इष्यते ॥४२९॥
bodho nirvāsano yasya sa jīvanmukta iṣyate (429)

429. One who has merged his mind in *Brahama*—but is nevertheless watchful and alert, though at the same time free from the characteristics of the waking-state—and whose awareness is free of any desire: is accepted to be a *Jīvan-Mukta*.

शान्तसंसारकलनः कलावानपि निष्कलः ।
śāntasaṁsārakalanaḥ kalāvānapi niṣkalaḥ ,
यस्य चित्तं विनिश्चिन्तं स जीवन्मुक्त इष्यते ॥४३०॥
yasya cittaṁ viniścintaṁ sa jīvanmukta iṣyate (430)

430. He, whose concerns about the phenomenal world have become completely stilled; who possesses this body comprising of parts, and yet abides as a One devoid of parts; whose mind is ever free of anxiety and fears—he is accepted to be a *Jīvan-Mukta*.

वर्तमानेऽपि देहेऽस्मिञ्छायावदनुवर्तिनि ।
vartamāne'pi dehe'smiñchāyāvadanuvartini ,
अहन्ताममताऽभावो जीवन्मुक्तस्य लक्षणम् ॥४३१॥
ahantāmamatā'bhāvo jīvanmuktasya lakṣaṇam (431)

431. The absence of the ideas of 'I' and 'mine' even with respect to the body—which is seen to follow him merely like a shadow—that is the characteristic of a *Jīvan-Mukta*: one Liberated-in-Life.

अतीताननुसन्धानं भविष्यदविचारणम् ।
atītānanusandhānaṁ bhaviṣyadavicāraṇam ,
औदासीन्यमपि प्राप्तं जीवन्मुक्तस्य लक्षणम् ॥४३२॥
audāsīnyamapi prāptaṁ jīvanmuktasya lakṣaṇam (432)

432. Not lingering over enjoyments of the past, taking no thought for the future, looking with indifference upon the present—these are the characteristics of a *Jīvan-Mukta*.

गुणदोषविशिष्टेऽस्मिन्स्वभावेन विलक्षणे ।
guṇadoṣaviśiṣṭe'sminsvabhāvena vilakṣaṇe ,
सर्वत्र समदर्शित्वं जीवन्मुक्तस्य लक्षणम् ॥४३३॥
sarvatra samadarśitvaṁ jīvanmuktasya lakṣaṇam (433)

433. Perceiving everything with impassivity and sameness—even this manifold universe which is riddled with things possessing merits and demerits and distinctively distinct from each other—that is the characteristic of a *Jīvan-Mukta*, one liberated-in-life.

इष्टानिष्टार्थसम्प्राप्तौ समदर्शितयाऽऽत्मनि ।
iṣṭāniṣṭārthasamprāptau samadarśitayā''tmani ,

उभयत्राविकारित्वं जीवन्मुक्तस्य लक्षणम् ॥४३४॥
ubhayatrāvikāritvaṁ jīvanmuktasya lakṣaṇam (434)

434. When things pleasant or painful present themselves then: to remain unruffled in either case, retaining equanimity and sameness in all circumstance—that is the characteristic of a *Jīvan-Mukta*.

ब्रह्मानन्दरसास्वादासक्तचित्ततया यतेः ।
brahmānandarasāsvādāsaktacittatayā yateḥ ,
अन्तर्बहिरविज्ञानं जीवन्मुक्तस्य लक्षणम् ॥४३५॥
antarbahiravijñānaṁ jīvanmuktasya lakṣaṇam (435)

435. Owing to the *Sanyāsin's* mind being continually immersed in tasting the bliss of *Brahama*, he entertains no distinctions of within and without: and that is the characteristic of a *Jīvan-Mukta*.

देहेन्द्रियादौ कर्तव्ये ममाहम्भाववर्जितः ।
dehendriyādau kartavye mamāhambhāvavarjitaḥ ,
औदासीन्येन यस्तिष्ठेत्स जीवन्मुक्तलक्षणः ॥४३६॥
audāsīnyena yastiṣṭhetsa jīvanmuktalakṣaṇaḥ (436)

436. Devoid of all ideas of 'I' and 'mine' with regards to the activity and functions of the body, organs, etc., he who lives unconcerned, in a spirit of detachment—he is known to be a *Jīvan-Mukta*.

विज्ञात आत्मनो यस्य ब्रह्मभावः श्रुतेर्बलात् ।
vijñāta ātmano yasya brahmabhāvaḥ śruterbalāt ,
भवबन्धविनिर्मुक्तः स जीवन्मुक्तलक्षणः ॥४३७॥
bhavabandhavinirmuktaḥ sa jīvanmuktalakṣaṇaḥ (437)

437. Guided by the *Shrutis*, he who has thusly realized his Self to be one in *Brahama* and has thereby become freed from the bondages of further transmigration—he is known as a *Jīvan-Mukta*.

देहेन्द्रियेष्वहम्भाव इदम्भावस्तदन्यके ।
dehendriyeṣvahambhāva idambhāvastadanyake ,
यस्य नो भवतः क्वापि स जीवन्मुक्त इष्यते ॥४३८॥
yasya no bhavataḥ kvāpi sa jīvanmukta iṣyate (438)

438. He who is free from the sense of 'I' with regards to the body, organs, etc., and the sense of 'other' with respect to all things else—he is accepted as a *Jīvan-Mukta*, one Liberated-in-Life.

न प्रत्यग्ब्रह्मणोर्भेदं कदापि ब्रह्मसर्गयोः ।
na pratyagbrahmaṇorbhedaṁ kadāpi brahmasargayoḥ ,
प्रज्ञया यो विजानिति स जीवन्मुक्तलक्षणः ॥४३९॥
prajñayā yo vijāniti sa jīvanmuktalakṣaṇaḥ (439)

439. Who through his own direct Realization perceives no distinction between his Self and *Brahama*—and between the universe and *Brahama*—he is known as a *Jīvan-Mukta*: Liberated even while alive.

साधुभिः पूज्यमानेऽस्मिन्पीड्यमानेऽपि दुर्जनैः ।
sādhubhiḥ pūjyamāne'sminpīḍyamāne'pi durjanaiḥ ,
समभावो भवेद्यस्य स जीवन्मुक्तलक्षणः ॥४४०॥
samabhāvo bhavedyasya sa jīvanmuktalakṣaṇaḥ (440)

440. Whether venerated by the saintly or tormented by the wicked, he who feels just the same when his body meets either treatment—he is known as a *Jīvan-Mukta*.

यत्र प्रविष्टा विषयाः परेरिता नदीप्रवाहा इव वारिराशौ ।
yatra praviṣṭā viṣayāḥ pareritā nadīpravāhā iva vārirāśau ,
लिनन्ति सन्मात्रतया न विक्रियां उत्पादयन्त्येष यतिर्विमुक्तः ॥४४१॥
linanti sanmātratayā na vikriyāṁ utpādayantyeṣa yatirvimuktaḥ (441)

441. Owing to his complete identity within the absolute existence *Brahama*, the *Sanyāsin* in whom all the sense-objects—that might come his way steered by the wish of another—get submerged like flowing rivulets merging into an ocean, producing no changes whatsoever: he indeed is liberated even while alive.

विज्ञातब्रह्मतत्त्वस्य यथापूर्वं न संसृतिः ।
vijñātabrahmatattvasya yathāpūrvaṁ na saṁsṛtiḥ ,
अस्ति चेन्न स विज्ञातब्रह्मभावो बहिर्मुखः ॥४४२॥
asti cenna sa vijñātabrahmabhāvo bahirmukhaḥ (442)

442. For one who has realized the Truth of *Brahama*, there is never anymore reaching out for the sense-objects. But if contrary is the case, then that man has Not yet realized his identity in *Brahama*—being that his senses are still outgoing in their propensities.

प्राचीनवासनावेगादसौ संसरतीति चेत् ।
prācīnavāsanāvegādasau saṁsaratīti cet ,
न सदेकत्वविज्ञानान्मन्दी भवति वासना ॥४४३॥
na sadekatvavijñānānmandī bhavati vāsanā (443)

443. If it be argued that he is still attached to the sense-objects by dint of the momentum of the past desires, then the answer is still: 'No'. Because desires unquestionably wither and fade with the onset of the Realization of oneness in *Brahama*.

अत्यन्तकामुकस्यापि वृत्तिः कुण्ठति मातरि ।
atyantakāmukasyāpi vṛttiḥ kuṇṭhati mātari ,
तथैव ब्रह्मणि ज्ञाते पूर्णानन्दे मनीषिणः ॥४४४॥
tathaiva brahmaṇi jñāte pūrṇānande manīṣiṇaḥ (444)

444. The propensities of even the most debauched person become naturally checked in the presence of his mother; similarly when *Brahama*, the Bliss-Absolute, has been truly realized, that man of realization has no more worldly inclinations—simply as a matter of course.

निदिध्यासनशीलस्य बाह्यप्रत्यय ईक्ष्यते ।
nididhyāsanaśīlasya bāhyapratyaya īkṣyate ,
ब्रवीति श्रुतिरेतस्य प्रारब्धं फलदर्शनात् ॥४४५॥
bravīti śrutiretasya prārabdhaṁ phaladarśanāt (445)

445. Yet even he who is adept at meditation is observed to still have external perceptions; and, as the *Shrutis* explain, it is the *Prārabdha* which is at work here, and this can also be inferred from the results actually observed.

सुखाद्यनुभवो यावत्तावत्प्रारब्धमिष्यते ।
sukhādyanubhavo yāvattāvatprārabdhamiṣyate ,
फलोदयः क्रियापूर्वो निष्क्रियो न हि कुत्रचित् ॥४४६॥
phalodayaḥ kriyāpūrvo niṣkriyo na hi kutracit (446)

446. *Prārabdha* work is acknowledged to have a bearing only so long as there is the perception of happiness, sorrow etc., related to that. Every result is preceded by an action; and it does not accrue independent of an originating cause.

अहं ब्रह्मेति विज्ञानात्कल्पकोटिशतार्जितम् ।
ahaṁ brahmeti vijñānātkalpakoṭiśatārjitam ,
सञ्चितं विलयं याति प्रबोधात्स्वप्नकर्मवत् ॥४४७॥
sañcitaṁ vilayaṁ yāti prabodhātsvapnakarmavat (447)

447. Through the Realization of one's identity in *Brahama*, all the accumulated actions of a hundred million cycles come to naught—just like all the actions performed in a dream are nixed upon waking up.

यत्कृतं स्वप्नवेलायां पुण्यं वा पापमुल्बणम् ।
yatkṛtaṁ svapnavelāyāṁ puṇyaṁ vā pāpamulbaṇam ,

सुप्तोत्थितस्य किन्तत्स्यात्स्वर्गाय नरकाय वा ॥४४८॥
suptotthitasya kintatsyātsvargāya narakāya vā (448)

448. Can any meritorious acts or dreadful sins—which a man fancies himself having committed in a dream—lead him to high heaven or hell?—once having awakened from his dream?

स्वमसङ्गमुदासीनं परिज्ञाय नभो यथा ।
svamasaṅgamudāsīnaṁ parijñāya nabho yathā ,
न श्लिष्यति च यत्किञ्चित्कदाचिद्भाविकर्मभिः ॥४४९॥
na śliṣyati ca yatkiñcitkadācidbhāvikarmabhiḥ (449)

449. Realizing the *Ātmā*, which is unattached and indifferent, alike the attribute-less space, the aspirant is never in the least touched by actions that would come visiting him by dint of *Prārabdha*.

न नभो घटयोगेन सुरागन्धेन लिप्यते ।
na nabho ghaṭayogena surāgandhena lipyate ,
तथात्मोपाधियोगेन तद्धर्मैर्नैव लिप्यते ॥४५०॥
tathātmopādhiyogena taddharmairnaiva lipyate (450)

450. The Space-Time is not tainted by the smell of liquor merely through the jar existing within it; similarly, the *Ātmā* is never affected by the connections of any conditioning adjuncts imagined upon it.

ज्ञानोदयात्पुरारब्धं कर्मज्ञानान्न नश्यति ।
jñānodayātpurārabdhaṁ karmajñānānna naśyati ,
अदत्वा स्वफलं लक्ष्यमुद्दिश्योत्सृष्टबाणवत् ॥४५१॥
adatvā svaphalaṁ lakṣyamuddiśyotsṛṣṭabāṇavat (451)

451. The *Karmas,* that have fashioned this body prior to the dawning of Knowledge, are not destroyed even having come by that illumining Knowledge—they still must yield their fruits; just as an arrow cannot be checked mid-flight.

व्याघ्रबुद्ध्या विनिर्मुक्तो बाणः पश्चात्तु गोमतौ ।
vyāghrabuddhyā vinirmukto bāṇaḥ paścāttu gomatau ,
न तिष्ठति छिनत्येव लक्ष्यं वेगेन निर्भरम् ॥४५२॥
na tiṣṭhati chinatyeva lakṣyaṁ vegena nirbharam (452)

452. An arrow shot with the idea that the target is a tiger, does not stop midway when the mark is perceived to be a cow; it will still pierce the target with full force.

प्रारब्धं बलवत्तरं खलु विदां भोगेन तस्य क्षयः
prārabdhaṁ balavattaraṁ khalu vidāṁ bhogena tasya kṣayaḥ
सम्यग्ज्ञानहुताशनेन विलयः प्राक्सञ्चितागामिनाम् ।
samyagjñānahutāśanena vilayaḥ prākṣañcitāgāminām ,
ब्रह्मात्मैक्यमवेक्ष्य तन्मयतया ये सर्वदा संस्थिताः
brahmātmaikyamavekṣya tanmayatayā ye sarvadā saṁsthitāḥ
तेषां तत्त्रितयं नहि क्वचिदपि ब्रह्मैव ते निर्गुणम् ॥४५३॥
teṣāṁ tattritayaṁ nahi kvacidapi brahmaiva te nirguṇam (453)

453. *Prārabdha* is certainly strong—even for a man of Realization—and becomes exhausted only through the actual experiencing of its fruits. In respect of the *Sanchita* (previously accumulated) and *Agāmi* (future) *Karmas*, they Do get destroyed in the fiery knowledge of perfect wisdom. But in truth nothing, none of these, really affects one who has realized *Brahama* and lives established in *Brahama*—and who therefore has become Transcendental.

उपाधितादात्म्यविहीनकेवलब्रह्मात्मनैवात्मनि तिष्ठतो मुनेः ।
upādhitādātmyavihīnakevalabrahmātmanaivātmani tiṣṭhato muneḥ ,
प्रारब्धसद्भावकथा न युक्ता स्वप्नार्थसम्बन्धकथेव जाग्रतः ॥४५४॥
prārabdhasadbhāvakathā na yuktā
svapnārthasambandhakatheva jāgrataḥ (454)

454. For the sage who ever abides within as *Brahama*—the One without a second, devoid of identification with the limiting adjuncts—the question of the existence of *Prārabdha* is non-meaningful (since it will never impact him in any meaningful way). For a person all questions related to the dream-objects are quite meaningless—once he has become fully awake.

न हि प्रबुद्धः प्रतिभासदेहे देहोपयोगिन्यपि च प्रपञ्चे ।
na hi prabuddhaḥ pratibhāsadehe dehopayoginyapi ca prapañce ,
करोत्यहन्तां ममतामिदन्तां किन्तु स्वयं तिष्ठति जागरेण ॥४५५॥
karotyahantāṁ mamatāmidantāṁ kintu svayaṁ tiṣṭhati jāgareṇa (455)

455. The man who has awakened from his sleep has no association of 'I' or 'mine' with regards to his former dream-body, or to the dream-objects which ministered to his dream-body in his dream-state. Because now he is quite awake and his true Self.

न तस्य मिथ्यार्थसमर्थनेच्छा न सङ्ग्रहस्तज्जगतोऽपि दृष्टः ।
na tasya mithyārthasamarthanecchā na saṅgrahastajjagato'pi dṛṣṭaḥ ,
तत्रानुवृत्तिर्यदि चेन्मृषार्थे न निद्रया मुक्त इतीष्यते ध्रुवम् ॥४५६॥
tatrānuvṛttiryadi cenmṛṣārthe na nidrayā mukta itīṣyate dhruvam (456)

456. The awakened man does not endeavor to maintain or sustain his dream-world—there being no possibility to substantiate the non-Real things seen in dreams; and if he still clings to that dreamy non-Reality, then it can be decidedly declared that he is delusional and still dreams on.

तद्वत्परे ब्रह्मणि वर्तमानः सदात्मना तिष्ठति नान्यदीक्षते ।
tadvatpare brahmaṇi vartamānaḥ sadātmanā tiṣṭhati nānyadīkṣate ,
स्मृतिर्यथा स्वप्नविलोकितार्थे तथा विदः प्राशनमोचनादौ ॥४५७॥
smṛtiryathā svapnavilokitārthe tathā vidaḥ prāśanamocanādau (457)

457. The sage who is absorbed in *Brahama,* who lives identified only with That eternal Reality—perceives nothing else besides That. And just as a person will have memory of his dreams at times, even so the man of realization may have memories of his everyday actions such as eating, releasing etc.

कर्मणा निर्मितो देहः प्रारब्धं तस्य कल्प्यताम् ।
karmaṇā nirmito dehaḥ prārabdhaṁ tasya kalpyatām ,
नानादेरात्मनो युक्तं नैवात्मा कर्मनिर्मितः ॥४५८॥
nānāderātmano yuktaṁ naivātmā karmanirmitaḥ (458)

458. The body has been fashioned by prior *Karmas*, and so *Prārabdha* may be regarded as belonging just to the body. It is absolutely unreasonable to attribute the *Prārabdha* to the *Ātmā*—for the *Ātmā* is beginning-less and is never the outcome of any *Karmas*, present or prior.

अजो नित्यः शाश्वत इति ब्रूते श्रुतिरमोघवाक् ।
ajo nityaḥ śāśvata iti brūte śrutiramoghavāk ,
तदात्मना तिष्ठतोऽस्य कुतः प्रारब्धकल्पना ॥४५९॥
tadātmanā tiṣṭhato'sya kutaḥ prārabdhakalpanā (459)

459. The *Shrutis,* whose words are infallible, declare the *Ātmā* to be "birthless, eternal and undecaying". So how can *Prārabdha* be imagined for a man who lives established only as the *Ātmā*?

प्रारब्धं सिध्यति तदा यदा देहात्मना स्थितिः ।
prārabdhaṁ sidhyati tadā yadā dehātmanā sthitiḥ ,
देहात्मभावो नैवेष्टः प्रारब्धं त्यज्यतामतः ॥४६०॥
dehātmabhāvo naiveṣṭaḥ prārabdhaṁ tyajyatāmataḥ (460)

460. *Prārabdha* can be ascribed only to the body, and so long as one lives identified with the body. But the man of realization never identifies himself with the body; and so the notion—of *Prārabdha,* as in any way affecting a self-realized sage—has simply to be thrown out the door.

शरीरस्यापि प्रारब्धकल्पना भ्रान्तिरेव हि ।
śarīrasyāpi prārabdhakalpanā bhrāntireva hi ,
अध्यस्तस्य कुतः सत्त्वमसत्यस्य कुतो जनिः ।
adhyastasya kutaḥ sattvamasatyasya kuto janiḥ ,
अजातस्य कुतो नाशः प्रारब्धमसतः कुतः ॥४६१॥
ajātasya kuto nāśaḥ prārabdhamasataḥ kutaḥ (461)

461. In fact the attributing of *Prārabdha* work even to the body is illusory for sure. How can *Prārabdha* act upon something which itself isn't Real? How can a superimposition have an existence? How can that which is non-Real have birth? How can that which cannot be born, die or suffer? How can *Prārabdha* exist for the non-Real?

ज्ञानेनाज्ञानकार्यस्य समूलस्य लयो यदि ।
jñānenājñānakāryasya samūlasya layo yadi ,
तिष्ठत्ययं कथं देह इति शङ्कावतो जडान् ॥४६२॥
tiṣṭhatyayaṁ kathaṁ deha iti śaṅkāvato jaḍān (462)

समाधातुं बाह्यदृष्ट्या प्रारब्धं वदति श्रुतिः ।
samādhātuṁ bāhyadṛṣṭyā prārabdhaṁ vadati śrutiḥ ,
न तु देहादिसत्यत्वबोधनाय विपश्चिताम् ॥४६३॥
na tu dehādisatyatvabodhanāya vipaścitām ,

462-463. "If the effects of Ignorance are destroyed to their very roots through Realization, then how does the body still continue to live?"—for fools who entertain such questions, it is only to convince them that the *Prārabdha* work is hypothesized by the *Shrutis* which unceasingly point out *Brahama* to be the only Reality; and it is done just from a relative standpoint, and not for proving the reality of the body etc., unto a man of Realization

परिपूर्णमनाद्यन्तमप्रमेयमविक्रियम् ।
paripūrṇamanādyantamaprameyamavikriyam ,
एकमेवाद्वयं ब्रह्म नेह नानास्ति किञ्चन ॥४६४॥
ekamevādvayaṁ brahma neha nānāsti kiñcana (464)

464. Know that there exists only *Brahama*, the One-without-a-second, infinite, replete, complete, transcendent and changeless, with no beginning or end—and there is no duality whatsoever in It.

सद्घनं चिद्घनं नित्यमानन्दघनमक्रियम् ।
sadghanaṁ cidghanaṁ nityamānandaghanamakriyam ,
एकमेवाद्वयं ब्रह्म नेह नानास्ति किञ्चन ॥४६५॥
ekamevādvayaṁ brahma neha nānāsti kiñcana (465)

465. In all of Existence, there exists only *Brahama*, the One without a second, the essence of Existence, Knowledge, Eternal Bliss, devoid of any activity—and there is no duality whatsoever in It.

प्रत्यगेकरसं पूर्णमनन्तं सर्वतोमुखम् ।
pratyagekarasaṁ pūrṇamanantaṁ sarvatomukham ,
एकमेवाद्वयं ब्रह्म नेह नानास्ति किञ्चन ॥४६६॥
ekamevādvayaṁ brahma neha nānāsti kiñcana (466)

466. There exists only *Brahama*, the One without a second, which is within all, which is infinite, endless, all-pervading, whole—and there is no duality whatsoever in It.

अहेयमनुपादेयमनादेयमनाश्रयम् ।
aheyamanupādeyamanādeyamanāśrayam ,
एकमेवाद्वयं ब्रह्म नेह नानास्ति किञ्चन ॥४६७॥
ekamevādvayaṁ brahma neha nānāsti kiñcana (467)

467. There exists only *Brahama*, the One without a second, which can neither be cast out nor taken up nor accepted, which is bereft of any other support—and there is no duality whatsoever in It.

निर्गुणं निष्कलं सूक्ष्मं निर्विकल्पं निरञ्जनम् ।
nirguṇaṁ niṣkalaṁ sūkṣmaṁ nirvikalpaṁ nirañjanam ,
एकमेवाद्वयं ब्रह्म नेह नानास्ति किञ्चन ॥४६८॥
ekamevādvayaṁ brahma neha nānāsti kiñcana (468)

468. There exists only *Brahama*, the One without a second, beyond attributes, without parts, subtle, absolute, taintless, and there is no duality whatsoever in It.

अनिरूप्य स्वरूपं यन्मनोवाचामगोचरम् ।
anirūpya svarūpaṁ yanmanovācāmagocaram ,
एकमेवाद्वयं ब्रह्म नेह नानास्ति किञ्चन ॥४६९॥
ekamevādvayaṁ brahma neha nānāsti kiñcana (469)

469. There exists only *Brahama*, the One without a second, beyond the range of words and thought, whose real nature is incomprehensible—and there is no duality whatsoever in It.

सत्समृद्धं स्वतःसिद्धं शुद्धं बुद्धमनीदृशम् ।
satsamṛddhaṁ svataḥsiddhaṁ śuddhaṁ buddhamanīdṛśam ,
एकमेवाद्वयं ब्रह्म नेह नानास्ति किञ्चन ॥४७०॥
ekamevādvayaṁ brahma neha nānāsti kiñcana (470)

470. There exists only *Brahama*, the One without a second, the eternal Reality, self-effulgent, self-existent, pure, intelligence,

and unlike anything finite; and there is no duality whatsoever in It.

निरस्तरागा विनिरस्तभोगाः शान्ताः सुदान्ता यतयो महान्तः ।
nirastarāgā vinirastabhogāḥ śāntāḥ sudāntā yatayo mahāntaḥ ,
विज्ञाय तत्त्वं परमेतदन्ते प्राप्ताः परां निर्वृतिमात्मयोगात् ॥ ४७१ ॥
vijñāya tattvaṁ parametadante prāptāḥ parāṁ nirvṛtimātmayogāt (471)

471. High-souled *Sanyāsins*—who have abandoned all attachments and sense-enjoyments, who are serene and self-controlled—directly Realize this Supreme Truth. And by that Self-Realization, they attain to Supreme Bliss when the body falls away.

भवानपीदं परतत्त्वमात्मनः स्वरूपमानन्दघनं विचार्य ।
bhavānapīdaṁ paratattvamātmanaḥ svarūpamānandaghanaṁ vicārya ,
विधूय मोहं स्वमनःप्रकल्पितं मुक्तः कृतार्थो भवतु प्रबुद्धः ॥ ४७२ ॥
vidhūya mohaṁ svamanaḥprakalpitaṁ muktaḥ kṛtārtho bhavatu prabuddhaḥ (472)

472. Following this Path of Discrimination, may you too become established in *Brahama*, the supreme Reality—of the nature of undiluted Bliss and identical with your true Self. Cast away all delusions created by the mind, and become illumined and liberated, and thereby attain the consummation of human life.

समाधिना साधुविनिश्चलात्मना पश्यात्मतत्त्वं स्फुटबोधचक्षुषा ।
samādhinā sādhuviniścalātmanā paśyātmatattvaṁ sphuṭabodhacakṣuṣā ,
निःसंशयं सम्यगवेक्षितश्चेच्छ्रुतः पदार्थो न पुनर्विकल्प्यते ॥ ४७३ ॥
niḥsaṁśayaṁ samyagavekṣitaśce-cchrutaḥ padārtho na punarvikalpyate (473)

473. Through that *Samādhi* in which the mind has become perfectly stilled, perceive the Reality of the Self with the eyes of clear illumination. If the meaning of the words from the *Shrutis* is perfectly and indubitably discerned, then there will no more be any doubts.

स्वस्याविद्याबन्धसम्बन्धमोक्षात्सत्यज्ञानानन्दरूपात्मलब्धौ ।
svasyāvidyābandhasambandhamokṣātsatyajñānānandarūpātmalabdhau ,
शास्त्रं युक्तिर्देशिकोक्तिः प्रमाणं चान्तःसिद्धा स्वानुभूतिः प्रमाणम् ॥ ४७४ ॥
śāstraṁ yuktirdeśikoktiḥ pramāṇaṁ cāntaḥsiddhā svānubhūtiḥ pramāṇam (474)

474. In the path of Realization of the *Ātmā*—the Existence-Knowledge-Bliss Absolute—by the breaking of one's connections with Ignorance (*Avidyā*) and its bondages, the scriptures, reasoning and the words of the Guru are the evidences; and one's own direct experiences gained through meditation are yet more corroborative proofs.

बन्धो मोक्षश्च तृप्तिश्च चिन्ताऽऽरोग्यक्षुधादयः ।
bandho mokṣaśca tṛptiśca cintā''rogyakṣudhādayaḥ ,
स्वेनैव वेद्या यज्ज्ञानं परेषामानुमानिकम् ॥ ४७५ ॥
svenaiva vedyā yajjñānaṁ pareṣāmānumānikam (475)

475. Bondage, liberation, satisfaction, anxiety, illness, hunger and similar experiencings—these are factually known only to the person personally coping with them; the knowledge of them by others is mere inference.

तटस्थिता बोधयन्ति गुरवः श्रुतयो यथा ।
taṭasthitā bodhayanti guravaḥ śrutayo yathā ,
प्रज्ञयैव तरेद्विद्वानीश्वरानुगृहीतया ॥ ४७६ ॥
prajñayaiva taredvidvānīśvarānugṛhītayā (476)

476. The Gurus and the *Shrutis* can only instruct the disciple standing from apart; it is the person actually seeking liberation who must personally strive to span the chasm of *Avidyā* (Ignorance)—by himself becoming illumined—with the added blessing of divine grace.

स्वानुभूत्या स्वयं ज्ञात्वा स्वमात्मानमखण्डितम् ।
svānubhūtyā svayaṁ jñātvā svamātmānamakhaṇḍitam ,
संसिद्धः सम्मुखं तिष्ठेन्निर्विकल्पात्मनाऽऽत्मनि ॥ ४७७ ॥
saṁsiddhaḥ sammukhaṁ tiṣṭhennirvikalpātmanā''tmani (477)

477. Through his own endeavors the seeker should know his indivisible Self in an act of direct Realization. And thus becoming perfect, he should stand face-on with the *Ātmā*, with his consciousness freed of all dualistic concepts.

वेदान्तसिद्धान्तनिरुक्तिरेषा ब्रह्मैव जीवः सकलं जगच्च ।
vedāntasiddhāntaniruktireṣā brahmaiva jīvaḥ sakalaṁ jagacca ,
अखण्डरूपस्थितिरेव मोक्षो ब्रह्माद्वितीये श्रुतयः प्रमाणम् ॥ ४७८ ॥
akhaṇḍarūpasthitireva mokṣo brahmādvitīye śrutayaḥ pramāṇam (478)

478. The ultimate verdict of all discussions in *Vedānta* is this: that the *Jiva* and the entire universe is nothing but *Brahama*, and that Liberation means abiding in *Brahama*, the indivisible Being. And of this Truth—that *Brahama*, the non-dual, the One without a second, is the only existent Reality—the proven authority are the *Shrutis* themselves.

इति गुरुवचनाच्छ्रुतिप्रमाणात् परमवगम्य सतत्त्वमात्मयुक्त्या ।
iti guruvacanācchrutipramāṇāt paramavagamya satattvamātmayuktyā ,
प्रशमितकरणः समाहितात्मा क्वचिदचलाकृतिरात्मनिष्ठतोऽभूत् ॥ ४७९ ॥
praśamitakaraṇaḥ samāhitātmā kvacidacalākṛtirātmaniṣṭhato'bhūt (479)

479. Realizing at a blessed moment the Supreme Truth—through the above instructions of the Master based on the authority of the *Shrutis*, and coupled with his own reasoning—and with his senses quiesced, and his mind concentrated, the disciple forsooth became immobile, having became perfectly established in the *Ātmā*.

किञ्चित्कालं समाधाय परे ब्रह्मणि मानसम् ।
kiñcitkālaṁ samādhāya pare brahmaṇi mānasam ,
उत्थाय परमानन्दादिदं वचनमब्रवीत् ॥४८०॥
utthāya paramānandādidaṁ vacanamabravīt (480)

480. For some time having concentrated upon the Supreme Absolute, the disciple then arose, and full of supreme Bliss spoke as follows:

शिष्य उवाच :
śiṣya uvāca :

बुद्धिर्विनष्टा गलिता प्रवृत्तिः ब्रह्मात्मनोरेकतयाऽधिगत्या ।
buddhirvinaṣṭā galitā pravṛttiḥ brahmātmanorekatayā'dhigatyā ,
इदं न जानेऽप्यनिदं न जाने किं वा कियद्वा सुखमस्त्यपारम् ॥४८१॥
idaṁ na jāne'pyanidaṁ na jāne kiṁ vā kiyadvā sukhamastyapāram (481)

481. The disciple said: Having realized the oneness of the Self and *Brahama*, my mind has vanished, its waves merged, all activities dissolved; I understand neither 'this' nor 'that'; and I cannot fathom this Bliss in which I revel—or know how boundless its extent!

वाचा वक्तुमशक्यमेव मनसा मन्तुं न वा शक्यते
vācā vaktumaśakyameva manasā mantuṁ na vā śakyate
स्वानन्दामृतपूरपूरितपरब्रह्माम्बुधेर्वैभवम् ।
svānandāmṛtapūrapūrita-parabrahmāmbudhervaibhavam ,
अम्भोराशिविशीर्णवार्षिकशिलाभावं भजन्मे मनो
ambhorāśiviśīrṇavārṣikaśilābhāvaṁ bhajanme mano
यस्यांशांशलवे विलीनमधुनाऽऽनन्दात्मना निर्वृतम् ॥४८२॥
yasyāṁśāṁśalave vilīnamadhunā''nandātmanā nirvṛtam (482)

482. The majesty of the ocean of the Supreme—replete with the swell of the nectar-like Bliss of the *Ātmā*—is impossible for the words to express in speech, or for the mind to comprehend. In an infinitesimal fraction of that blissly ocean, my mind has melted away like the hailstone. I abide satiated as the very Essence of Bliss.

क्व गतं केन वा नीतं कुत्र लीनमिदं जगत् ।
kva gataṁ kena vā nītaṁ kutra līnamidaṁ jagat ,

अधुनैव मया दृष्टं नास्ति किं महदद्भुतम् ॥४८३॥
adhunaiva mayā dṛṣṭaṁ nāsti kiṁ mahadadbhutam (483)

483. Where has the universe disappeared? By whom has it been removed? Where did it submerge? It was just here seen by me, and now it is gone! Wonder of wonders, how!!

किं हेयं किमुपादेयं किमन्यत्किं विलक्षणम् ।
kiṁ heyaṁ kimupādeyaṁ kimanyatkiṁ vilakṣaṇam ,
अखण्डानन्दपीयूषपूर्णे ब्रह्ममहार्णवे ॥४८४॥
akhaṇḍānandapīyūṣapūrṇe brahmamahārṇave (484)

484. In the ocean of *Brahama* filled with the nectar of Bliss Absolute, what is there to be eschewed? And what accepted? What is other than This? What is that which is different from It?

न किञ्चिदत्र पश्यामि न शृणोमि न वेद्म्यहम् ।
na kiñcidatra paśyāmi na śṛṇomi na vedmyaham ,
स्वात्मनैव सदानन्दरूपेणास्मि विलक्षणः ॥४८५॥
svātmanaiva sadānandarūpeṇāsmi vilakṣaṇaḥ (485)

485. Other than This, I neither see, nor hear, nor know of anything else; I simply exist as the Self: eternal Bliss, singular, bereft of any else.

नमो नमस्ते गुरवे महात्मने विमुक्तसङ्गाय सदुत्तमाय ।
namo namaste gurave mahātmane vimuktasaṅgāya saduttamāya ,
नित्याद्वयानन्दरसस्वरूपिणे भूम्ने सदाऽपारदयाम्बुधाम्ने ॥४८६॥
nityādvayānandarasasvarūpiṇe bhūmne sadā'pāradayāmbudhāmne (486)

486. O noble master, repeated salutations to thee—who art the best of noble souls, devoid of attachments, the very personification of *Brahama*, eternal Bliss, the One without a second—who art infinite, and ever the shore-less ocean of compassion;

यत्कटाक्षशशिसान्द्रचन्द्रिकापातधूतभवतापजश्रमः ।
yatkaṭākṣaśaśisāndracandrikāpātadhūtabhavatāpajaśramaḥ ,
प्राप्तवानहमखण्डवैभवानन्दमात्मपदमक्षयं क्षणात् ॥४८७॥
prāptavānahamakhaṇḍavaibhavānandamātmapadamakṣayaṁ kṣaṇāt (487)

487. —Whose gracious glance of eyes—like a cascade of moonbeams—has removed my interminable weariness brought on by the worldly afflictions, delivering me into the splendorous realm of the *Ātmā*: the unceasing Bliss of infinite majesty!

धन्योऽहं कृतकृत्योऽहं विमुक्तोऽहं भवग्रहात् ।
dhanyo'haṁ kṛtakṛtyo'haṁ vimukto'haṁ bhavagrahāt ,

नित्यानन्दस्वरूपोऽहं पूर्णोऽहं त्वदनुग्रहात् ॥४८८॥
nityānandasvarūpo'haṁ pūrṇo'haṁ tvadanugrahāt (488)

488. Blessed am I. I have reached the fulfillment of my life. I am freed of the clutches of the birth-death cycle. I am now the embodiment of eternal bliss, replete and complete—all by thy divine grace!

असङ्गोऽहमनङ्गोऽहमलिङ्गोऽहमभङ्गुरः ।
asaṅgo'hamanaṅgo'hamaliṅgo'hamabhaṅguraḥ ,
प्रशान्तोऽहमनन्तोऽहममलोऽहं चिरन्तनः ॥४८९॥
praśānto'hamananto'hamamalo'haṁ cirantanaḥ (489)

489. Unattached am I—and disembodied; I am free of the subtle-body; I am undecaying, I am serene, I am endless, I am taintless, I am ageless!

अकर्ताहमभोक्ताहमविकारोऽहमक्रियः ।
akartāhamabhoktāhamavikāro'hamakriyaḥ ,
शुद्धबोधस्वरूपोऽहं केवलोऽहं सदाशिवः ॥४९०॥
śuddhabodhasvarūpo'haṁ kevalo'haṁ sadāśivaḥ (490)

490. Not the doer, nor the experiencer am I; I am changeless—without modification, beyond activity; I am the essence of pure consciousness; I am the entirety; I am the eternal *Shiva*.

द्रष्टुः श्रोतुर्वक्तुः कर्तुर्भोक्तुर्विभिन्न एवाहम् ।
draṣṭuḥ śroturvaktuḥ karturbhokturvibhinna evāham ,
नित्यनिरन्तरनिष्क्रियनिःसीमासङ्गपूर्णबोधात्मा ॥४९१॥
nityanirantaraniṣkriyaniḥsīmāsaṅgapūrṇabodhātmā (491)

491. Verily, I am That which is other than the seer, the listener, the speaker, the doer, the experiencer. I am eternal, without parts, beyond activity, boundless, unattached, infinite: the all-pervading consciousness.

नाहमिदं नाहमदोऽप्युभयोरवभासकं परं शुद्धम् ।
nāhamidaṁ nāhamado'pyubhayoravabhāsakaṁ paraṁ śuddham ,
बाह्याभ्यन्तरशून्यं पूर्णं ब्रह्माद्वितीयमेवाहम् ॥४९२॥
bāhyābhyantaraśūnyaṁ pūrṇaṁ brahmādvitīyamevāham (492)

492. I am neither this nor that—but the Supreme, the illuminator of them all; verily I am *Brahama*, the One without a second, pure, infinite, devoid of within and without.

निरुपममनादितत्त्वं त्वमहमिदमद इति कल्पनादूरम् ।
nirupamamanāditattvaṁ tvamahamidamada iti kalpanādūram ,
नित्यानन्दैकरसं सत्यं ब्रह्माद्वितीयमेवाहम् ॥४९३॥
nityānandaikarasaṁ satyaṁ brahmādvitīyamevāham (493)

493. Verily I am *Brahama*, the One-without-a-second, the beginning-less matchless, Reality beyond all imagined distinctions such as 'you', 'I', 'this', or 'that'; I am the pristine truth, eternal-bliss embodied.

नारायणोऽहं नरकान्तकोऽहं पुरान्तकोऽहं पुरुषोऽहमीशः ।
nārāyaṇo'haṁ narakāntako'haṁ purāntako'haṁ puruṣo'hamīśaḥ ,
अखण्डबोधोऽहमशेषसाक्षी निरीश्वरोऽहं निरहं च निर्ममः ॥४९४॥
akhaṇḍabodho'hamaśeṣasākṣī nirīśvaro'haṁ nirahaṁ ca nirmamaḥ (494)

494. I am Lord *Nārāyana*, the slayer of *Naraka*; I am the Supreme Being, the Ruler, the destroyer of *Tripurasura*; I am undifferentiated consciousness, the Witness of everything; I have no ruler other than myself; devoid am I of the ideas of 'I', 'you', 'this', 'that', 'mine'.

सर्वेषु भूतेष्वहमेव संस्थितो ज्ञानात्मनाऽन्तर्बहिराश्रयः सन् ।
sarveṣu bhūteṣvahameva saṁsthito jñānātmanā'ntarbahirāśrayaḥ san ,
भोक्ता च भोग्यं स्वयमेव सर्वं यद्यत्पृथग्दृष्टमिदन्तया पुरा ॥४९५॥
bhoktā ca bhogyaṁ svayameva sarvaṁ yadyatpṛthagdṛṣṭamidantayā purā (495)

495. I alone am the Being who resides as consciousness in all beings, being their internal and external support; I myself am the experiencer, the experience, and the experienced; and I am all of that which was previously perceived by me as a distinguishable 'this' or 'that'.

मय्यखण्डसुखाम्भोधौ बहुधा विश्ववीचयः ।
mayyakhaṇḍasukhāmbhodhau bahudhā viśvavīcayaḥ ,
उत्पद्यन्ते विलीयन्ते मायामारुतविभ्रमात् ॥४९६॥
utpadyante vilīyante māyāmārutavibhramāt (496)

496. In Me, the ocean of Infinite Bliss, endless waves of the universe rise and fall with the play of the storms of My *Māyā*.

स्थुलादिभावा मयि कल्पिता भ्रमादारोपितानुस्फुरणेन लोकैः ।
sthulādibhāvā mayi kalpitā bhramādāropitānusphuraṇena lokaiḥ ,
काले यथा कल्पकवत्सरायणर्त्वादयो निष्कलनिर्विकल्पे ॥४९७॥
kāle yathā kalpakavatsarāyaṇartvādayo niṣkalanirvikalpe (497)

497. Ideas such as gross or subtle are erroneously imagined in Me by people through the manifestation of superimpositions—just as in the indivisible and Absolute Time: ages, millennia, years, half-years, seasons, etc., are imagined by the human mind.

आरोपितं नाश्रयदूषकं भवेत् कदापि मूढैरतिदोषदूषितैः ।
āropitaṁ nāśrayadūṣakaṁ bhavet kadāpi mūḍhairatidoṣadūṣitaiḥ ,

नार्द्रीकरोत्यूषरभूमिभागं मरीचिकावारि महाप्रवाहः ॥४९८॥
nārdrīkarotyūṣarabhūmibhāgaṁ marīcikāvāri mahāpravāhaḥ (498)

498. That which is perceived as superimposed upon something—due to ignorance of the deluded minds—never really taints that something. Verily the great rush of water observed by the delusional fools in a mirage, never really wets the desert tracts.

आकाशवल्लेपविदूरगोऽहं आदित्यवद्भास्यविलक्षणोऽहम् ।
ākāśavallepavidūrago'haṁ ādityavadbhāsyavilakṣaṇo'ham ,
अहार्यवन्नित्यविनिश्चलोऽहं अम्भोधिवत्पारविवर्जितोऽहम् ॥४९९॥
ahāryavannityaviniścalo'haṁ ambhodhivatpāravivarjito'ham (499)

499. Like the space-time, I am beyond all contaminations; like the sun, I am distinct from all things illumined; I am ever motionless alike the mountains, and endless like the ocean.

न मे देहेन सम्बन्धो मेघेनेव विहायसः ।
na me dehena sambandho megheneva vihāyasaḥ ,
अतः कुतो मे तद्धर्मा जाग्रत्स्वप्नसुषुप्तयः ॥५००॥
ataḥ kuto me taddharmā jāgratsvapnasuṣuptayaḥ (500)

500. I have no connections with the body—just as the sky has no connections with the clouds. So how can the states of wakefulness, dream, and deep-sleep—which are attributes of the body—ever touch me?

उपाधिरायाति स एव गच्छति स एव कर्माणि करोति भुङ्क्ते ।
upādhirāyāti sa eva gacchati sa eva karmāṇi karoti bhuṅkte ,
स एव जीर्यन् म्रियते सदाहं कुलाद्रिवन्निश्चल एव संस्थितः ॥५०१॥
sa eva jīryan mriyate sadāhaṁ kulādrivanniścala eva saṁsthitaḥ (501)

501. It is the *Upādhis* which come, and it is the *Upādhis* which go; they alone perform actions and experiences, and they alone die or grow old—whereas I, the *Ātmā,* remain always immovable alike the Kulā mountain.

न मे प्रवृत्तिर्न च मे निवृत्तिः सदैकरूपस्य निरंशकस्य ।
na me pravṛttirna ca me nivṛttiḥ sadaikarūpasya niraṁśakasya ,
एकात्मको यो निविडो निरन्तरो व्योमेव पूर्णः स कथं नु चेष्टते ॥५०२॥
ekātmako yo niviḍo nirantaro vyomeva pūrṇaḥ sa kathaṁ nu ceṣṭate (502)

502. For me, there is neither the leaning towards, nor the turning away; I am without divisions, ever the same. How can that which is One, whole, continuous, and infinite like the sky—ever strive and strain?

पुण्यानि पापानि निरिन्द्रियस्य निश्चेतसो निर्विकृतेर्निराकृतेः ।
puṇyāni pāpāni nirindriyasya niścetaso nirvikṛterniräkṛteḥ ,
कुतो ममाखण्डसुखानुभूतेः ब्रूते ह्यनन्वागतमित्यपि श्रुतिः ॥५०३॥
kuto mamākhaṇḍasukhānubhūteḥ brūte hyananvāgatamityapi śrutiḥ (503)

503. In me—who am the fulfillment of Bliss Absolute, who am without organs, without the mind, who am changeless, and formless—how can there be merits and demerits? The *Shruti* passage, 'Not touched...' etc., mention the same.

छायया स्पृष्टमुष्णं वा शीतं वा सुष्ठु दुःष्ठु वा ।
chāyayā spṛṣṭamuṣṇaṁ vā śītaṁ vā suṣṭhu duḥṣṭhu vā ,
न स्पृशत्येव यत्किञ्चित्पुरुषं तद्विलक्षणम् ॥५०४॥
na spṛśatyeva yatkiñcitpuruṣaṁ tadvilakṣaṇam (504)

504. If heat or cold, good or evil, happens to touch the shadow of a man, it does not in the least affect the man—who remains ever distinct from his shadow.

न साक्षिणं साक्ष्यधर्माः संस्पृशन्ति विलक्षणम् ।
na sākṣiṇaṁ sākṣyadharmāḥ saṁspṛśanti vilakṣaṇam ,
अविकारमुदासीनं गृहधर्माः प्रदीपवत् ॥५०५॥
avikāramudāsīnaṁ gṛhadharmāḥ pradīpavat (505)

505. Just as the properties of the room do not alter the lamp illumining it, the attributes of the thing seen, cannot directly alter the seer—being that he is distinct from them, unvarying and concern-less.

रवेर्यथा कर्मणि साक्षिभावो वह्नेर्यथा दाहनियामकत्वम् ।
raveryathā karmaṇi sākṣibhāvo vahneryathā dāhaniyāmakatvam ,
रज्जोर्यथाऽऽरोपितवस्तुसङ्गः तथैव कूटस्थचिदात्मनो मे ॥५०६॥
rajjoryathā''ropitavastusaṅgaḥ tathaiva kūṭasthacidātmano me (506)

506. Just as the sun is a mere witness of people's actions; and as the fire is aloof and burns everything without distinction; and as the rope is unrelated to any erroneous identifications that may be superimposed upon it—so too am I: the aloof Witness, the Unattached, the Unchangeable Pristine Consciousness.

कर्तापि वा कारयितापि नाहं भोक्तापि वा भोजयितापि नाहम् ।
kartāpi vā kārayitāpi nāhaṁ bhoktāpi vā bhojayitāpi nāham ,
द्रष्टापि वा दर्शयितापि नाहं सोऽहं स्वयञ्ज्योतिरनीदृगात्मा ॥५०७॥
draṣṭāpi vā darśayitāpi nāhaṁ so'haṁ svayañjyotiranīdṛgātmā (507)

507. I am not the doer, nor do I make anything do; I neither am the enjoyer nor make another the enjoyer; I neither see nor make another see—I am the self-effulgent transcendent *Ātmā*.

चलत्युपाधौ प्रतिबिम्बलौल्य मौपाधिकं मूढधियो नयन्ति ।
calatyupādhau pratibimbalaulyamaupādhikaṁ mūḍhadhiyo nayanti ,
स्वबिम्बभूतं रविवद्विनिष्क्रियं कर्तास्मि भोक्तास्मि हतोऽस्मि हेति ॥५०८॥
svabimbabhūtaṁ ravivadviniṣkriyaṁ kartāsmi bhoktāsmi hato'smi heti (508)

508. When the supervening adjunct (*Upādhi*) moves, then the Ignoramus ascribe the resulting movement of the reflection to the object itself. The sun illumining a moving object is itself devoid of the motion that shines forth. It is due to Māyā that people believe: "I am the doer", "I am the experiencer", "Alas! I am being hurt."

जले वापि स्थले वापि लुठत्वेष जडात्मकः ।
jale vāpi sthale vāpi luṭhatveṣa jaḍātmakaḥ ,
नाहं विलिप्ये तद्धर्मैर्घटधर्मैर्नभो यथा ॥५०९॥
nāhaṁ vilipye taddharmairghaṭadharmairnabho yathā (509)

509. Let it drift or drop, on land or water—I am untouched by the attributes of this cretinous jar-like body; just like the infinite all-pervading space is unaffected by the confines of the space inside a jar.

कर्तृत्वभोक्तृत्वखलत्वमत्तताजडत्वबद्धत्वविमुक्ततादयः ।
kartṛtvabhoktṛtvakhalatvamattatājaḍatvabaddhatvavimuktatādayaḥ ,
बुद्धेर्विकल्पा न तु सन्ति वस्तुतः स्वस्मिन्परे ब्रह्मणि केवलेऽद्वये ॥५१०॥
buddhervikalpā na tu santi vastutaḥ svasminpare brahmaṇi kevale'dvaye (510)

510. The transitory states of Mind (*Buddhi*)—which take on diverse modifications such as being a doer, or experiencer, or being sly, or drunk, or dull, or in joy, or in sorrow, or in bondage, or in freedom—never in reality belong to the Self, which is one with the Supreme *Brahama*, the Absolute, the one without a second.

सन्तु विकाराः प्रकृतेर्दशधा शतधा सहस्रधा वापि ।
santu vikārāḥ prakṛterdaśadhā śatadhā sahasradhā vāpi ,
किं मेऽसङ्गचितस्तैर्न घनः क्वचिदम्बरं स्पृशति ॥५११॥
kiṁ me'saṅgacitastairna ghanaḥ kvacidambaraṁ spṛśati (511)

511. Let there be changes in the *Prakriti* by the tens, hundreds, or thousands, what have I—the unattached Absolute Consciousness—to do with any of them? Can the clouds ever taint the infinite sky?

अव्यक्तादिस्थूलपर्यन्तमेतत् विश्वं यत्राभासमात्रं प्रतीतम् ।
avyaktādisthūlaparyantametat viśvaṁ yatrābhāsamātraṁ pratītam ,
व्योमप्रख्यं सूक्ष्ममाद्यन्तहीनं ब्रह्माद्वैतं यत्तदेवाहमस्मि ॥५१२॥
vyomaprakhyaṁ sūkṣmamādyantahīnaṁ brahmādvaitaṁ yattadevāhamasmi (512)

512. That which is like the Space-Time—subtle, without a beginning or end, in which the whole universe from the Undifferentiated down to the gross-body, appears merely as an apparition—I am that *Brahama*, the One without a second.

सर्वाधारं सर्ववस्तुप्रकाशं सर्वाकारं सर्वगं सर्वशून्यम् ।
sarvādhāraṁ sarvavastuprakāśaṁ sarvākāraṁ sarvagaṁ sarvaśūnyam ,
नित्यं शुद्धं निश्चलं निर्विकल्पं ब्रह्माद्वैतं यत्तदेवाहमस्मि ॥५१३॥
nityaṁ śuddhaṁ niścalaṁ nirvikalpaṁ brahmādvaitaṁ yattadevāhamasmi (513)

513. Which is the support of all, which illumines all things, which has infinite forms, is eternal, pure, motionless, absolute, omnipresent and bereft of any multiplicity—I am that *Brahama*, the One without a second.

यत्प्रत्यस्ताशेषमायाविशेषं प्रत्यग्रूपं प्रत्ययागम्यमानम् ।
yatpratyastāśeṣamāyāviśeṣaṁ pratyagrūpaṁ pratyayāgamyamānam ,
सत्यज्ञानानन्तमानन्दरूपं ब्रह्माद्वैतं यत्तदेवाहमस्मि ॥५१४॥
satyajñānānantamānandarūpaṁ brahmādvaitaṁ yattadevāhamasmi (514)

514. Which is beyond the endless differentiations of *Māyā*, which is the inmost essence of everything, which is beyond the reach of mind, which is of the nature of Truth, Knowledge, Bliss Absolute—I am that *Brahama*, the One without a second.

निष्क्रियोऽस्म्यविकारोऽस्मि निष्कलोऽस्मि निराकृतिः ।
niṣkriyo'smyavikāro'smi niṣkalo'smi nirākṛtiḥ ,
निर्विकल्पोऽस्मि नित्योऽस्मि निरालम्बोऽस्मि निर्द्वयः ॥५१५॥
nirvikalpo'smi nityo'smi nirālambo'smi nirdvayaḥ (515)

515. Void of activities, changeless, without parts, formless, absolute, eternal, self-sustained, without a need of another support, the one without a second—that One I am.

सर्वात्मकोऽहं सर्वोऽहं सर्वातीतोऽहमद्वयः ।
sarvātmako'haṁ sarvo'haṁ sarvātīto'hamadvayaḥ ,
केवलाखण्डबोधोऽहमानन्दोऽहं निरन्तरः ॥५१६॥
kevalākhaṇḍabodho'hamānando'haṁ nirantaraḥ (516)

516. I am the Universal; I am the All; I am Transcendent, the One without a second. I am the Absolute; I am Infinite Knowledge; I am Bliss; I am Eternal.

स्वाराज्यसाम्राज्यविभूतिरेषा भवत्कृपाश्रीमहिमप्रसादात् ।
svārājyasāmrājyavibhūtireṣā bhavatkṛpāśrīmahimaprasādāt ,
प्राप्ता मया श्रीगुरवे महात्मने नमो नमस्तेऽस्तु पुनर्नमोऽस्तु ॥५१७॥
prāptā mayā śrīgurave mahātmane namo namaste'stu punarnamo'stu (517)

517. This splendor of my self-effulgent sovereignty which I have gained this day is only by thy supreme grace, O noble master. Salutations to thy glory; salutations again and again to thee!

महास्वप्ने मायाकृतजनिजरामृत्युगहने
mahāsvapne māyākṛtajanijarāmṛtyugahane
भ्रमन्तं क्लिश्यन्तं बहुलतरतापैरनुदिनम् ।
bhramantaṁ kliśyantaṁ bahulataratāpairanudinam ,
अहङ्कारव्याघ्रव्यथितमिममत्यन्तकृपया
ahaṅkāravyāghravyathitamimamatyantakṛpayā
प्रबोध्य प्रस्वापात्परमवितवान्मामसि गुरो ॥५१८॥
prabodhya prasvāpātparamavitavānmāmasi guro (518)

518. Out of thy benign grace, thou hast saved me, O Master, by awakening me from this terrible nightmare—where I was living in an interminable dream, wandering lost in the birth-decay-death wilderness created by *Māyā*, where I was sorely troubled by the tiger of egoism which excruciated me day and night with a myriad afflictions.

नमस्तस्मै सदैकस्मै कस्मैचिन्महसे नमः ।
namastasmai sadaikasmai kasmaicinmahase namaḥ ,
यदेतद्विश्वरूपेण राजते गुरुराज ते ॥५१९॥
yadetadviśvarūpeṇa rājate gururāja te (519)

519. O thou King of Masters, many venerations to thee and thy unfathomable glory manifesting its splendor throughout the world. My repeated salutations to thee!

इति नतमवलोक्य शिष्यवर्यं समधिगतात्मसुखं प्रबुद्धतत्त्वम् ।
iti natamavalokya śiṣyavaryaṁ samadhigatātmasukhaṁ prabuddhatattvam ,
प्रमुदितहृदयं स देशिकेन्द्रः पुनरिदमाह वचः परं महात्मा ॥५२०॥
pramuditahṛdayaṁ sa deśikendraḥ punaridamāha vacaḥ paraṁ mahātmā (520)

520. Seeing the worthy disciple—who had realized the Truth and was replete with the Bliss of the *Ātmā*—prostrating before, the venerable master again spoke the following excellent words, glad of heart:

श्रीगुरुरुवाच :
śrīgururuvāca :

ब्रह्मप्रत्ययसन्ततिर्जगदतो ब्रह्मैव तत्सर्वतः
brahmapratyayasantatirjagadato brahmaiva tatsarvataḥ
पश्याध्यात्मदृशा प्रशान्तमनसा सर्वास्ववस्थास्वपि ।
paśyādhyātmadṛśā praśāntamanasā sarvāsvavasthāsvapi ,
रूपादन्यदवेक्षितं किमभितश्चक्षुष्मतां दृश्यते
rūpādanyadavekṣitaṁ kimabhitaścakṣuṣmatāṁ dṛśyate
तद्वद्ब्रह्मविदः सतः किमपरं बुद्धेर्विहारास्पदम् ॥५२१॥
tadvadbrahmavidaḥ sataḥ kimaparaṁ buddhervihārāspadam (521)

521. The Master said: The universe is an unbroken series of perceptions of *Brahama*; it is in every respect nothing but *Brahama*—see this with the eyes of illumination and a serene mind and under every circumstance. One who has the eyes—does he see anything else but perceptible forms all around? Similarly, what is there other than Brahama to engage the intellect of a man of realization?

कस्तां परानन्दरसानुभूतिमुत्सृज्य शून्येषु रमेत विद्वान् ।
kastāṁ parānandarasānubhūtimṛtsṛjya śūnyeṣu rameta vidvān ,
चन्द्रे महाह्लादिनि दीप्यमाने चित्रेन्दुमालोकयितुं क इच्छेत् ॥५२२॥
candre mahāhlādini dīpyamāne citrendumālokayituṁ ka icchet (522)

522. What wise person would discard the supreme Bliss of *Brahama* and revel instead in the evanescent enchantments of these petty things? When the exceedingly charming moon is shining, who would wish to gaze upon a painted moon?

असत्पदार्थानुभवेन किञ्चिन् न ह्यस्ति तृप्तिर्न च दुःखहानिः ।
asatpadārthānubhavena kiñcin na hyasti tṛptirna ca duḥkhahāniḥ ,
तदद्वयानन्दरसानुभूत्या तृप्तः सुखं तिष्ठ सदात्मनिष्ठया ॥५२३॥
tadadvayānandarasānubhūtyā tṛptaḥ sukhaṁ tiṣṭha sadātmaniṣṭhayā (523)

523. From the perception of the evanescent non-Real things, there is neither satisfaction nor the cessation of misery. So then—being satiated only in the realization of the Bliss Absolute, the One without a second—abide ever happy in the state of identity with that Reality.

स्वमेव सर्वथा पश्यन्मन्यमानः स्वमद्वयम् ।
svameva sarvathā paśyanmanyamānaḥ svamadvayam ,
स्वानन्दमनुभुञ्जानः कालं नय महामते ॥५२४॥
svānandamanubhuñjānaḥ kālaṁ naya mahāmate (524)

524. Perceiving the Self alone in every circumstance, and thinking only of the Self, the One-without-a-second—while away your time enjoying the bliss of the Self, O noble soul!

अखण्डबोधात्मनि निर्विकल्पे विकल्पनं व्योम्नि पुरप्रकल्पनम् ।
akhaṇḍabodhātmani nirvikalpe vikalpanaṁ vyomni puraprakalpanam ,
तदद्वयानन्दमयात्मना सदा शान्तिं परामेत्य भजस्व मौनम् ॥५२५॥
tadadvayānandamayātmanā sadā śāntiṁ parāmetya bhajasva maunam (525)

525. All dualistic conceptions in the *Ātmā*—which is Absolute-Knowledge-Bliss—are imaginary: like fancied castles in the air. Therefore always identifying yourself with the non-dual Bliss-

Absolute—and gaining sovereign peace thereby—remain unengaged and quiet.

तूष्णीमवस्था परमोपशान्तिः बुद्धेरसत्कल्पविकल्पहेतोः ।
tūṣṇīmavasthā paramopaśāntiḥ buddherasatkalpavikalpahetoḥ ,
ब्रह्मात्मनो ब्रह्मविदो महात्मनो यत्राद्वयानन्दसुखं निरन्तरम् ॥५२६॥
brahmātmano brahmavido mahātmano yatrādvayānandasukhaṁ nirantaram (526)

526. For one who has realized *Brahama*, the mind—which was ere the cause of manifold non-Real imagined fancies—becomes perfectly tranquil. Verily this is the state of true Quietude, in which—ever identified with *Brahama*, the One without a second—the sage enjoys uninterrupted Bliss Absolute.

नास्ति निर्वासनान्मौनात्परं सुखकृदुत्तमम् ।
nāsti nirvāsanānmaunātparaṁ sukhakṛduttamam ,
विज्ञातात्मस्वरूपस्य स्वानन्दरसपायिनः ॥५२७॥
vijñātātmasvarūpasya svānandarasapāyinaḥ (527)

527. To the man who has Realized his inner essence and savors the undiluted Bliss of the Self, there is no higher state of exhilaration than Quietude born of the state of Desirelessness.

गच्छंस्तिष्ठन्नुपविशञ्छयानो वाऽन्यथापि वा ।
gacchaṁstiṣṭhannupaviśañchayāno vā'nyathāpi vā ,
यथेच्छया वसेद्विद्वानात्मारामः सदा मुनिः ॥५२८॥
yathecchayā vasedvidvānātmārāmaḥ sadā muniḥ (528)

528. The illumined sage, whose sole pleasure is in the Self, abides ever at ease—whether going or staying put, sitting or lying, and in every other circumstance.

न देशकालासनदिग्यमादिलक्ष्याद्यपेक्षाऽप्रतिबद्धवृत्तेः ।
na deśakālāsanadigyamādilakṣyādyapekṣā'pratibaddhavṛtteḥ ,
संसिद्धतत्त्वस्य महात्मनोऽस्ति स्ववेदने का नियमाद्यवस्था ॥५२९॥
saṁsiddhatattvasya mahātmano'sti svavedane kā niyamādyavasthā (529)

529. The sage who has realized the Truth perfectly—and consequently whose mind-functions encounter no obstructions—no longer depends on the conditions of place, time, posture, bearings, moral disciplines, objects of meditation and so forth. What rules and regulations can there be for realizing one's inmost essence?

घटोऽयमिति विज्ञातुं नियमः कोऽन्ववेक्षते ।
ghaṭo'yamiti vijñātuṁ niyamaḥ ko'nvavekṣate ,
विना प्रमाणसुष्ठुत्वं यस्मिन्सति पदार्थधीः ॥५३०॥
vinā pramāṇasuṣṭhutvaṁ yasminsati padārthadhīḥ (530)

530. To know that this is a Jar, what regulations need one follow except that the means of knowledge be free of defects?—which alone ensures a proper cognition of the object.

अयमात्मा नित्यसिद्धः प्रमाणे सति भासते ।
ayamātmā nityasiddhaḥ pramāṇe sati bhāsate ,
न देशं नापि वा कालं न शुद्धिं वाप्यपेक्षते ॥५३१॥
na deśaṁ nāpi vā kālaṁ na śuddhiṁ vāpyapekṣate (531)

531. So this *Ātmā*—which is the eternal Absolute Truth—manifests itself as soon as the right means of knowledge become present; it does not depend upon the place, or time, or purity and so forth conditions.

देवदत्तोऽहमित्येतद्विज्ञानं निरपेक्षकम् ।
devadatto'hamityetadvijñānaṁ nirapekṣakam ,
तद्वद्ब्रह्मविदोऽप्यस्य ब्रह्माहमिति वेदनम् ॥५३२॥
tadvadbrahmavido'pyasya brahmāhamiti vedanam (532)

532. To a person named Devadatta, the knowledge, "I am Devadatta", is independent of the circumstance; similar is the case here. Unto the knower of *Brahama,* the realization "I am *Brahama*" is simply unconditional.

भानुनेव जगत्सर्वं भासते यस्य तेजसा ।
bhānuneva jagatsarvaṁ bhāsate yasya tejasā ,
अनात्मकमसत्तुच्छं किं नु तस्यावभासकम् ॥५३३॥
anātmakamasattucchaṁ kiṁ nu tasyāvabhāsakam (533)

533. Whose very sun-like effulgence causes even the non-Real, shadowy, insubstantial universe to appear to be substantial—who can illumine That Supreme Reality? Who or what indeed can manifest that Being - from whom are all beings and things?

वेदशास्त्रपुराणानि भूतानि सकलान्यपि ।
vedaśāstrapurāṇāni bhūtāni sakalānyapi ,
येनार्थवन्ति तं किन्नु विज्ञातारं प्रकाशयेत् ॥५३४॥
yenārthavanti taṁ kinnu vijñātāraṁ prakāśayet (534)

534. Who or what indeed can illumine that eternal Being by which the *Vedas* and *Purānas* and all scriptures, and all beings, and all things are endowed with any meaning at all?

एष स्वयञ्ज्योतिरनन्तशक्तिः आत्माऽप्रमेयः सकलानुभूतिः ।
eṣa svayañjyotiranantaśaktiḥ ātmā'prameyaḥ sakalānubhūtiḥ ,
यमेव विज्ञाय विमुक्तबन्धो जयत्ययं ब्रह्मविदुत्तमोत्तमः ॥५३५॥
yameva vijñāya vimuktabandho jayatyayaṁ brahmaviduttamottamaḥ (535)

535. Here is the self-effulgent *Ātmā* of limitless power, beyond the range of conditioned knowledge—and yet the common experience of everybody—realizing which alone the incomparable knower of *Brahama* lives his life full of glory and freed of bondages.

न खिद्यते नो विषयैः प्रमोदते न सज्जते नापि विरज्यते च ।
na khidyate no viṣayaiḥ pramodate na sajjate nāpi virajyate ca ,
स्वस्मिन्सदा क्रीडति नन्दति स्वयं निरन्तरानन्दरसेन तृप्तः ॥५३६॥
svasminsadā krīḍati nandati svayaṁ nirantarānandarasena tṛptaḥ (536)

536. Satisfied in the perennial undiluted Bliss of *Brahama*, the sage is neither grieved nor elated by the presence or absence of any sense-object. Neither attached nor averse to anything, he always disports just within the *Ātmā*—taking delight therein alone.

क्षुधां देहव्यथां त्यक्त्वा बालः क्रीडति वस्तुनिः ।
kṣudhāṁ dehavyathāṁ tyaktvā bālaḥ krīḍati vastuniḥ ,
तथैव विद्वान् रमते निर्ममो निरहं सुखी ॥५३७॥
tathaiva vidvān ramate nirmamo nirahaṁ sukhī (537)

537. Forgetting his hunger and bodily pains just as a child plays with his toys, in the same way the man of realization always revels in the Bliss of the within *Ātmā*, and abides he ever joyful, forgetful of the ideas of 'I' and 'mine'.

चिन्ताशून्यमदैन्यभैक्षमशनं पानं सरिद्वारिषु
cintāśūnyamadainyabhaikṣamaśanaṁ pānaṁ saridvāriṣu
स्वातन्त्र्येण निरङ्कुशा स्थितिरभीर्निद्रा श्मशाने वने ।
svātantryeṇa niraṅkuśā sthitirabhīrnidrā śmaśāne vane ,
वस्त्रं क्षालनशोषणादिरहितं दिग्वास्तु शय्या मही
vastraṁ kṣālanaśoṣaṇādirahitaṁ digvāstu śayyā mahī
सञ्चारो निगमान्तवीथिषु विदां क्रीडा परे ब्रह्मणि ॥५३८॥
sañcāro nigamāntavīthiṣu vidāṁ krīḍā pare brahmaṇi (538)

538. Such men of realization have their fill without any anxiety for meal, or the humiliation of begging; and they drink of the waters of the streams; and they live sovereign and free; and they sleep without fear in the forests and cremation grounds; and the earth is their only bed; and their robe is perhaps some bark of a tree, or the sky which requires no washing and drying; and they ever wander on the footpaths of Vedānta; and their only pastime is to revel in Bliss: the Bliss of the Supreme *Brahama*.

विमानमालम्ब्य शरीरमेतद् भुनक्त्यशेषान्विषयानुपस्थितान् ।
vimānamālambya śarīrametad bhunaktyaśeṣānviṣayānupasthitān ,
परेच्छया बालवदात्मवेत्ता योऽव्यक्तलिङ्गोऽननुषक्तबाह्यः ॥५३९॥
parecchayā bālavadātmavettā yo'vyaktaliṅgo'nanuṣaktabāhyaḥ (539)

539. The Knower of *Ātmā*—who wears no outward marks and is unattached to external things—recumbs within the body without really identifying with it; and he receives all sense-objects—which may come his way through the will of outside—just like a child.

दिगम्बरो वापि च साम्बरो वा त्वगम्बरो वापि चिदम्बरस्थः ।
digambaro vāpi ca sāmbaro vā tvagambaro vāpi cidambarasthaḥ ,
उन्मत्तवद्वापि च बालवद्वा पिशाचवद्वापि चरत्यवन्याम् ॥५४०॥
unmattavadvāpi ca bālavadvā piśācavadvāpi caratyavanyām (540)

540. Established in the supernal sphere of Absolute Consciousness, he may roam about in the world—sometimes like one inebriated, or sometimes like a child, or at times like a ghoul having no other clothes on his person except the quarters, or perhaps wearing some cloth or an animal skin at other times.

कामान्निष्कामरूपी संश्चरत्येकचरो मुनिः ।
kāmānniṣkāmarūpī saṁścaratyekacaro muniḥ ,
स्वात्मनैव सदा तुष्टः स्वयं सर्वात्मना स्थितः ॥५४१॥
svātmanaiva sadā tuṣṭaḥ svayaṁ sarvātmanā sthitaḥ (541)

541. Favoring solitude, the sage may appear to partake of the sense-objects, but at his essence he is the very embodiment of desirelessness, always satisfied within his Self—which he knows to be the Self of all.

क्वचिन्मूढो विद्वान् क्वचिदपि महाराजविभवः
kvacinmūḍho vidvān kvacidapi mahārājavibhavaḥ
क्वचिद्भ्रान्तः सौम्यः क्वचिदजगराचारकलितः ।
kvacidbhrāntaḥ saumyaḥ kvacidajagarācārakalitaḥ ,
क्वचित्पात्रीभूतः क्वचिदवमतः क्वाप्यविदितः
kvacitpātrībhūtaḥ kvacidavamataḥ kvāpyaviditaḥ
चरत्येवं प्राज्ञः सततपरमानन्दसुखितः ॥५४२॥
caratyevaṁ prājñaḥ satataparamānandasukhitaḥ (542)

542. Sometimes a fool, sometimes a sage, sometimes possessed of a regal visage; sometimes wandering about, sometimes behaving like a motionless python of benignant poise; sometimes respected, sometimes insulted, sometimes unknown—thus abides the man of realization, ever replete with Bliss Supreme.

निर्धनोऽपि सदा तुष्टोऽप्यसहायो महाबलः ।
nirdhano'pi sadā tuṣṭo'pyasahāyo mahābalaḥ ,
नित्यतृप्तोऽप्यभुञ्जानोऽप्यसमः समदर्शनः ॥५४३॥
nityatṛpto'pyabhuñjāno'pyasamaḥ samadarśanaḥ (543)

543. Though without any riches, yet ever content; though without any help, yet full of strength; though not enjoying the sense-objects, yet eternally satisfied; though himself without an exemplar, yet he looks upon all with an equal eye.

अपि कुर्वन्नकुर्वाणश्चाभोक्ता फलभोग्यपि ।
api kurvannakurvāṇaścābhoktā phalabhogyapi ,
शरीर्यप्यशरीर्येष परिच्छिन्नोऽपि सर्वगः ॥५४४॥
śarīryapyaśarīryeṣa paricchinno'pi sarvagaḥ (544)

544. Though doing, yet inactive; though experiencing the fruits of past *Karmas*, yet untouched by them; although possessed of body, yet without its affiliations; though limited, yet omnipresent he abides.

अशरीरं सदा सन्तमिमं ब्रह्मविदं क्वचित् ।
aśarīraṁ sadā santamimaṁ brahmavidaṁ kvacit ,
प्रियाप्रिये न स्पृशतस्तथैव च शुभाशुभे ॥५४५॥
priyāpriye na spṛśatastathaiva ca śubhāśubhe (545)

545. Neither pleasure nor pain, nor any good or evil, ever touches the Knower of *Brahama*—who always abides bereft of the body-idea.

स्थूलादिसम्बन्धवतोऽभिमानिनः सुखं च दुःखं च शुभाशुभे च ।
sthūlādisambandhavato'bhimāninaḥ sukhaṁ ca duḥkhaṁ ca śubhāśubhe ca ,
विध्वस्तबन्धस्य सदात्मनो मुनेः कुतः शुभं वाऽप्यशुभं फलं वा ॥५४६॥
vidhvastabandhasya sadātmano muneḥ kutaḥ śubhaṁ vā'pyaśubhaṁ phalaṁ vā (546)

546. Pleasure, sorrow, good, evil—these affect only one who is connected with the gross-body etc., and identifies himself with those; how can good, or evil, or their effects, affect the sage who has severed all bondages and remains identified just with the Supreme Reality?

तमसा ग्रस्तवद्भानादग्रस्तोऽपि रविर्जनैः ।
tamasā grastavadbhānādagrasto'pi ravirjanaiḥ ,
ग्रस्त इत्युच्यते भ्रान्त्यां ह्यज्ञात्वा वस्तुलक्षणम् ॥५४७॥
grasta ityucyate bhrāntyāṁ hyajñātvā vastulakṣaṇam (547)

तद्वद्देहादिबन्धेभ्यो विमुक्तं ब्रह्मवित्तमम् ।
tadvaddehādibandhebhyo vimuktaṁ brahmavittamam ,
पश्यन्ति देहिवन्मूढाः शरीराभासदर्शनात् ॥५४८॥
paśyanti dehivanmūḍhāḥ śarīrābhāsadarśanāt (548)

547-548. During an eclipse, the sun is said to be swallowed by *Rahu*, but it isn't actually so; it's only the ignoramus—not knowing the reality—who are found saying that the sun is so swallowed on account of their delusional mind. Similarly ignorant people may look upon the perfect knower of *Brahama*—who is in reality completely oblivious of the body etc., and their bondages—and treat him as being possessed of a body, seeing but just the mere appearance of it.

अहिर्निर्ल्वयनीं वायं मुक्त्वा देहं तु तिष्ठति ।
ahirnirlvayanīṁ vāyaṁ muktvā dehaṁ tu tiṣṭhati ,
इतस्ततश्चाल्यमानो यत्किञ्चित्प्राणवायुना ॥५४९॥
itastataścālyamāno yatkiñcitprāṇavāyunā (549)

549. In truth, the knower of *Brahama* abides discarding the body: just like a snake its slough; and his body simply moves willy-nilly hither thither, through the force of the *Prānas*.

स्रोतसा नीयते दारु यथा निम्नोन्नतस्थलम् ।
strotasā nīyate dāru yathā nimnonnatasthalam ,
दैवेन नीयते देहो यथाकालोपभुक्तिषु ॥५५०॥
daivena nīyate deho yathākālopabhuktiṣu (550)

550. As a piece of wood is borne by the currents to high grounds or low, even so is his body carried by the momenta of his past *Karmas* and their diverse fruits—as and when they choose to present themselves in due course.

प्रारब्धकर्मपरिकल्पितवासनाभिः संसारिवच्चरति भुक्तिषु मुक्तदेहः ।
prārabdhakarmaparikalpitavāsanābhiḥ saṁsārivaccarati bhuktiṣu muktadehaḥ ,
सिद्धः स्वयं वसति साक्षिवदत्र तूष्णीं चक्रस्य मूलमिव कल्पविकल्पशून्यः ॥५५१॥
siddhaḥ svayaṁ vasati sākṣivadatra tūṣṇīṁ
cakrasya mūlamiva kalpavikalpaśūnyaḥ (551)

551. Through the impetus begotten of *Prārabdha*, the man of Realization—who truly lives bereft of the body-idea—seems to move amidst sense-enjoyments just like those subject to transmigration; he himself however lives unmoved within the body, alike the pivot of a potter's wheel. He abides merely as a Witness, free of all mental oscillations, just recumbent within the body.

नैवेन्द्रियाणि विषयेषु नियुङ्क्त एष नैवापयुङ्क्त उपदर्शनलक्षणस्थः ।
naivendriyāṇi viṣayeṣu niyuṅkta eṣa naivāpayuṅkta upadarśanalakṣaṇasthaḥ ,
नैव क्रियाफलमपीषदवेक्षते स स्वानन्दसान्द्ररसपानसुमत्तचित्तः ॥५५२॥
naiva kriyāphalamapīṣadavekṣate sa svānandasāndrarasapānasumattacittaḥ (552)

552. He neither directs the sense-organs to their objects nor forcibly tears them away—staying like an unconcerned spectator who has chanced upon them; and he has not the least regard for the fruits of actions—his mind being thoroughly inebriated with drinking the undiluted elixir of the Bliss of *Ātmā*.

लक्ष्यालक्ष्यगतिं त्यक्त्वा यस्तिष्ठेत्केवलात्मना ।
lakṣyālakṣyagatiṁ tyaktvā yastiṣṭhetkevalātmanā ,
शिव एव स्वयं साक्षादयं ब्रह्मविदुत्तमः ॥५५३॥
śiva eva svayaṁ sākṣādayaṁ brahmaviduttamaḥ (553)

553. He who—giving up all considerations of the suitability or unsuitability of the circumstances in which the worldly waves may have tossed him for the moment—lives abiding only as the Absolute *Ātmā*, is verily *Shiva* Himself; and he is regarded as the highest amongst the Knowers of *Brahama*.

जीवन्नेव सदा मुक्तः कृतार्थो ब्रह्मवित्तमः ।
jīvanneva sadā muktaḥ kṛtārtho brahmavittamaḥ ,
उपाधिनाशाद्ब्रह्मैव सन् ब्रह्माप्येति निर्द्वयम् ॥५५४॥
upādhināśādbrahmaiva san brahmāpyeti nirdvayam (554)

554. The perfect knower of *Brahama* becomes eternally free even while living in the body and thereby attains the fulfillment of life. Through the destruction of impositions—which had ere kept him separated—he truly becomes one in *Brahama*, the One without a second—which he had been all along, but for the superimpositions of the mind.

शैलूषो वेषसद्भावाभावयोश्च यथा पुमान् ।
śailūṣo veṣasadbhāvābhāvayośca yathā pumān ,
तथैव ब्रह्मविच्छ्रेष्ठः सदा ब्रह्मैव नापरः ॥५५५॥
tathaiva brahmavicchreṣṭhaḥ sadā brahmaiva nāparaḥ (555)

555. For his theatrical role, an actor may don one costume or another, or perhaps none at all, but in all circumstance he always remains the person he actually is; similarly the perfect knower of *Braham*, is first and foremost *Brahama*, and always *Brahama*.

यत्र क्वापि विशीर्णं सत्पर्णमिव तरोर्वपुः पततात् ।
yatra kvāpi viśīrṇaṁ satparṇamiva tarorvapuḥ patatāt ,
ब्रह्मीभूतस्य यतेः प्रागेव तच्चिदग्निना दग्धम् ॥५५६॥
brahmībhūtasya yateḥ prāgeva taccidagninā dagdham (556)

556. Let the body of the *Sanyāsin* who has realized his complete identity in *Brahama,* wither and fall anywhere, like a leaf from a tree—it matters little to him; for the *Sanyāsin* has already burnt the body in the fiery kiln of wisdom a long time ago.

सदात्मनि ब्रह्मणि तिष्ठतो मुनेः पूर्णाऽद्वयानन्दमयात्मना सदा ।
sadātmani brahmaṇi tiṣṭhato muneḥ pūrṇā'dvayānandamayātmanā sadā ,
न देशकालाद्युचितप्रतीक्षा त्वङ्मांसविट्पिण्डविसर्जनाय ॥५५७॥
na deśakālādyucitapratīkṣā tvaṅmāṁsaviṭpiṇḍavisarjanāya (557)

557. The sage who always abides established in the eternal Reality *Brahama*—the One without a second, of the nature of Infinite Bliss—does not depend upon the customary considerations of place, time, etc., for giving up this bundle of bones, flesh, skin.

देहस्य मोक्षो नो मोक्षो न दण्डस्य कमण्डलोः ।
dehasya mokṣo no mokṣo na daṇḍasya kamaṇḍaloḥ ,
अविद्याहृदयग्रन्थिमोक्षो मोक्षो यतस्ततः ॥५५८॥
avidyāhṛdayagranthimokṣo mokṣo yatastataḥ (558)

558. The giving up of the body is not necessary Liberation, nor is Liberation in the acceptance of the symbolic staff, or the *Kamandalu* bowl. True Liberation comprises of destroying bondages; it lies in undoing all the knots of the Mind: the Mind which had become ghastly gnarled through Ignorance.

कुल्यायामथ नद्यां वा शिवक्षेत्रेऽपि चत्वरे ।
kulyāyāmatha nadyāṁ vā śivakṣetre'pi catvare ,
पर्णं पतति चेत्तेन तरोः किं नु शुभाशुभम् ॥५५९॥
parṇaṁ patati cettena taroḥ kiṁ nu śubhāśubham (559)

559. If a tree leaf falls in a small stream, or a sacred river, or a place consecrated to Lord Shiva, or simply by the roadside—of what good or evil consequence is that to the tree?

पत्रस्य पुष्पस्य फलस्य नाशवद्देहेन्द्रियप्राणधियां विनाशः ।
patrasya puṣpasya phalasya nāśavaddehendriyaprāṇadhiyāṁ vināśaḥ ,
नैवात्मनः स्वस्य सदात्मकस्यानन्दाकृतेर्वृक्षवदस्ति चैषः ॥५६०॥
naivātmanaḥ svasya sadātmakasyānandākṛtervṛkṣavadasti caiṣaḥ (560)

560. Similar to a leaf, or flower, or fruit falling from a tree, the falling of the body, organs, *Prānas, Buddhi* is just like that to the *Ātmā*—it doesn't affect the *Ātmā* in the least. The *Ātmā*—the Reality, the Embodiment of Bliss, which is one's true Self—always endures unaffected, similar to the Tree in the example.

प्रज्ञानघन इत्यात्मलक्षणं सत्यसूचकम् ।
prajñānaghana ityātmalakṣaṇaṁ satyasūcakam ,
अनूद्यौपाधिकस्यैव कथयन्ति विनाशनम् ॥५६१॥
anūdyaupādhikasyaiva kathayanti vināśanam (561)

561. The *Shrutis* indicate the true nature of the *Ātmā* with the words, "The Embodiment of Consciousness..." etc. The Scriptures establish the enduring Reality of the *Ātmā* and talk of only the adjuncts meeting their end, and never the *Ātmā*.

अविनाशी वा अरेऽयमात्मेति श्रुतिरात्मनः ।
avināśī vā are'yamātmeti śrutirātmanaḥ ,
प्रब्रवीत्यविनाशित्वं विनश्यत्सु विकारिषु ॥५६२॥
prabravītyavināśitvaṁ vinaśyatsu vikāriṣu (562)

562. The Shruti passage, "Verily is this *Ātmā* immortal, my dear...", speaks of the Immortality of the *Ātmā*—amidst all else which is perishable and subject to change.

पाषाणवृक्षतृणधान्यकडङ्कराद्या दग्धा भवन्ति हि मृदेव यथा तथैव ।
pāṣāṇavṛkṣatṛṇadhānyakaḍaṅkarādyā dagdhā bhavanti hi mṛdeva yathā tathaiva ,
देहेन्द्रियासुमन आदि समस्तदृश्यं ज्ञानाग्निदग्धमुपयाति परात्मभावम् ॥५६३॥
dehendriyāsumana ādi samastadṛśyaṁ jñānāgnidagdhamupayāti parātmabhāvam (563)

563. As stone, tree, grass, paddy, husk, etc., when burnt, are all reduced just to the dust and ash, even so the entire objective universe—comprising of body, organs, *Prānas*, *Manas* etc., of all beings and things—when burnt in the fiery wisdom of Realization, stand reduced to just *Brahama*, the Supreme Self.

विलक्षणं यथा ध्वान्तं लीयते भानुतेजसि ।
vilakṣaṇaṁ yathā dhvāntaṁ līyate bhānutejasi ,
तथैव सकलं दृश्यं ब्रह्मणि प्रविलीयते ॥५६४॥
tathaiva sakalaṁ dṛśyaṁ brahmaṇi pravilīyate (564)

564. Just as darkness—which is completely distinct from the light—vanishes in the sun's radiance, even so this entire objective universe vanishes in *Brahama* with the Dawning of the Light of Knowledge.

घटे नष्टे यथा व्योम व्योमैव भवति स्फुटम् ।
ghaṭe naṣṭe yathā vyoma vyomaiva bhavati sphuṭam ,
तथैवोपाधिविलये ब्रह्मैव ब्रह्मवित्स्वयम् ॥५६५॥
tathaivopādhivilaye brahmaiva brahmavitsvayam (565)

565. When a jar is broken, the space enclosed by it becomes the endless Space; even so the knower of *Brahama* verily becomes

the limitless *Brahama*—upon the superimposing adjuncts having become destroyed.

क्षीरं क्षीरे यथा क्षिप्तं तैलं तैले जलं जले ।
kṣīraṁ kṣīre yathā kṣiptaṁ tailaṁ taile jalaṁ jale ,
संयुक्तमेकतां याति तथाऽऽत्मन्यात्मविन्मुनिः ॥५६६॥
saṁyuktamekatāṁ yāti tathā''tmanyātmavinmuniḥ (566)

566. Just as the milk poured into milk, and the oil into oil, and water in water—become united and one with the Entire, even so the sage who has realized the *Ātmā*, becomes One with the *Param-Ātmā*.

एवं विदेहकैवल्यं सन्मात्रत्वमखण्डितम् ।
evaṁ videhakaivalyaṁ sanmātratvamakhaṇḍitam ,
ब्रह्मभावं प्रपद्यैष यतिर्नावर्तते पुनः ॥५६७॥
brahmabhāvaṁ prapadyaiṣa yatirnāvartate punaḥ (567)

567. Experiencing the utmost Solitude and Onlyness—which comes from disembodiedness—and becoming eternally identified with *Brahama*, the Absolute Reality, the sage suffers no more transmigration.

सदात्मैकत्वविज्ञानदग्धाविद्यादिवर्ष्मणः ।
sadātmaikatvavijñānadagdhāvidyādivarṣmaṇaḥ ,
अमुष्य ब्रह्मभूतत्वाद् ब्रह्मणः कुत उद्भवः ॥५६८॥
amuṣya brahmabhūtatvād brahmaṇaḥ kuta udbhavaḥ (568)

568. With all his bodies (sheaths)—from the gross to subtle that had been comprised in Nescience—having been burned away in the Knowledge of Realization—that of the Oneness of the *Jiva* and *Brahama*—the Yogi verily becomes *Brahama* himself. And does *Brahama* ever have any birth or death?

मायाक्लृप्तौ बन्धमोक्षौ न स्तः स्वात्मनि वस्तुतः ।
māyāklṛptau bandhamokṣau na staḥ svātmani vastutaḥ ,
यथा रज्जौ निष्क्रियायां सर्पाभासविनिर्गमौ ॥५६९॥
yathā rajjau niṣkriyāyāṁ sarpābhāsavinirgamau (569)

569. Bondage and Liberation—which are conjured up by *Māyā*—never really exist in the *Ātmā*: one's Self. It is similar to how the appearance and disappearance of the snake does not really exist in the rope, which remains unchanged throughout the apparent transformation—that became conceptualized in delusion and later removed with enlightenment.

आवृतेः सदसत्त्वाभ्यां वक्तव्ये बन्धमोक्षणे ।
āvṛteḥ sadasattvābhyāṁ vaktavye bandhamokṣaṇe ,
नावृतिर्ब्रह्मणः काचिदन्याभावादनावृतम् ।
nāvṛtirbrahmaṇaḥ kācidanyābhāvādanāvṛtam ,
यद्यस्त्यद्वैतहानिः स्याद् द्वैतं नो सहते श्रुतिः ॥५७०॥
yadyastyadvaitahāniḥ syād dvaitaṁ no sahate śrutiḥ (570)

570. Bondage and Liberation may be talked of when there is the presence or absence of some binding fetters or coverings veils; but there can be no impositions upon *Brahama*—being that there exists nothing else other than *Brahama*. And if nothing else exists, then what can bind? If besides *Brahama*, something else also exists, then the non-duality of *Brahama* is negated, and the *Shrutis* would stand falsified—because nowhere do they allow for duality.

बन्धश्च मोक्षश्च मृषैव मूढा बुद्धेर्गुणं वस्तुनि कल्पयन्ति ।
bandhañca mokṣañca mṛṣaiva mūḍhā buddherguṇaṁ vastuni kalpayanti ,
दृगावृतिं मेघकृतां यथा रवौ यतोऽद्वयाऽसङ्गचिदेतदक्षरम् ॥५७१॥
dṛgāvṛtiṁ meghakṛtāṁ yathā ravau yato'dvayā'saṅgacidetadakṣaram (571)

571. If the sun is obscured due to an intervening cloud, then a simpleton may falsely impute the 'dimming of sun' to be some characteristic of the sun itself. Similarly, Bondage and Liberation—the attributes of *Buddhi*—are falsely assumed upon *Brahama* by the unwitting. In truth, *Brahama* is non-dual Absolute Consciousness, completely unattached, ever free.

अस्तीति प्रत्ययो यश्च यश्च नास्तीति वस्तुनि ।
astīti pratyayo yaśca yaśca nāstīti vastuni ,
बुद्धेरेव गुणावेतौ न तु नित्यस्य वस्तुनः ॥५७२॥
buddhereva guṇāvetau na tu nityasya vastunaḥ (572)

572. The idea that bondage exists, and the idea that it does not—these are attributes imagined merely from the perspective of the Mind, and that too when considered in comparison to the Supreme who is absolute and free; but from the perspective of the Supreme Absolute Himself, these notions never actually belong to Him.

अतस्तौ मायया क्लृप्तौ बन्धमोक्षौ न चात्मनि ।
atastau māyayā klṛptau bandhamokṣau na cātmani ,
निष्कले निष्क्रिये शान्ते निरवद्ये निरञ्जने ।
niṣkale niṣkriye śānte niravadye nirañjane ,
अद्वितीये परे तत्त्वे व्योमवत्कल्पना कुतः ॥५७३॥
advitīye pare tattve vyomavatkalpanā kutaḥ (573)

573. So then, Bondages and Liberation are created merely by *Māyā*, and they have a bearing only in the realm of *Māyā*, and they are not any realities which pertain to the *Ātmā*. Can there be any limitation in regards to the Supreme Absolute—which is without parts, without activity, calm, unimpeachable, taintless, and the One-without-a-second? Nay; just as there are none with regards to the infinite Space-Time.

न निरोधो न चोत्पत्तिर्न बद्धो न च साधकः ।
na nirodho na cotpattirna baddho na ca sādhakaḥ ,
न मुमुक्षुर्न वै मुक्त इत्येषा परमार्थता ॥५७४॥
na mumukṣurna vai mukta ityeṣā paramārthatā (574)

574. Truth be told: there is neither death nor birth; neither a bound soul nor a struggling soul; neither a seeker after liberation nor a liberated man. Verily this is the ultimate Truth from the highest perspective—from the standpoint of *Brahama* Himself.

सकलनिगमचूडास्वान्तसिद्धान्तरूपं परमिदमतिगुह्यं दर्शितं ते मयाद्य ।
sakalanigamacūḍāsvāntasiddhāntarūpaṁ paramidamatiguhyaṁ darśitaṁ te mayādya ,
अपगतकलिदोषं कामनिर्मुक्तबुद्धिं स्वसुतवदसकृत्त्वां भावयित्वा मुमुक्षुम् ॥५७५॥
apagatakalidoṣaṁ kāmanirmuktabuddhiṁ svasutavadasakṛttvāṁ bhāvayitvā mumukṣum (575)

575. Knowing you to be aspiring for liberation, and finding in you a fitting recipient—purged of the taints of *Kali-Yuga* and with a mind free of desires—I have revealed to you this day, repeatedly and in several different ways, and as lovingly as one does to one's own child—this most excellent of profound secrets: **the Fiery Crest-Jewel of Wisdom** of the *Vedānta* philosophy, the very pinnacle of Vedic knowledge.

इति श्रुत्वा गुरोर्वाक्यं प्रश्रयेण कृतानतिः ।
iti śrutvā gurorvākyaṁ praśrayeṇa kṛtānatiḥ ,
स तेन समनुज्ञातो ययौ निर्मुक्तबन्धनः ॥५७६॥
sa tena samanujñāto yayau nirmuktabandhanaḥ (576)

576. Hearing the words of the Master, the seeker prostrated before him with reverence, and then taking his permissions went his own way—a freed soul.

गुरुरेव सदानन्दसिन्धौ निर्मग्नमानसः ।
gurureva sadānandasindhau nirmagnamānasaḥ ,
पावयन्वसुधां सर्वां विचचार निरन्तरः ॥५७७॥
pāvayanvasudhāṁ sarvāṁ vicacāra nirantaraḥ (577)

577. And the Master—with his mind ever immersed in the ocean of eternal absolute Bliss—continued to wander about, sanctifying the whole world with his presence as before.

इत्याचार्यस्य शिष्यस्य संवादेनात्मलक्षणम् ।
ityācāryasya śiṣyasya saṁvādenātmalakṣaṇam ,
निरूपितं मुमुक्षूणां सुखबोधोपपत्तये ॥५७८॥
nirūpitaṁ mumukṣūṇāṁ sukhabodhopapattaye (578)

578. Thus by the way of a dialogue between the master and disciple, the Nature of the *Ātmā* has been delineated here—for easy comprehension of those seekers who are aspiring for Liberation.

हितमिदमुपदेशमाद्रियन्तां विहितनिरस्तसमस्तचित्तदोषाः ।
hitamidamupadeśamādriyantāṁ vihitanirastasamastacittadoṣāḥ ,
भवसुखविरताः प्रशान्तचित्ताः श्रुतिरसिका यतयो मुमुक्षवो ये ॥५७९॥
bhavasukhaviratāḥ praśāntacittāḥ śrutirasikā yatayo mumukṣavo ye (579)

579. May those *Sanyāsins* who are aspiring for Freedom, who have purged themselves of all the taints of the mind by the observances of prescribed disciplines, who are averse to the worldly pleasures and are of serene minds and who take delight in the *Shrutis*—take joy in this salutary teaching.

संसाराध्वनि तापभानुकिरणप्रोद्भूतदाहव्यथा-
saṁsārādhvani tāpabhānukiraṇaprodbhūtadāhavyathā-
खिन्नानां जलकाङ्क्षया मरुभुवि भ्रान्त्या परिभ्राम्यताम् ।
khinnānāṁ jalakāṅkṣayā marubhuvi bhrāntyā paribhrāmyatām ,
अत्यासन्नसुधाम्बुधिं सुखकरं ब्रह्माद्वयं दर्शय-
atyāsannasudhāmbudhiṁ sukhakaraṁ brahmādvayaṁ darśaya-
त्येषा शङ्करभारती विजयते निर्वाणसन्दायिनी ॥५८०॥
tyeṣā śaṅkarabhāratī vijayate nirvāṇasandāyinī (580)

580. Those who are afflicted by the incinerating pains of the scorching sun-flames of the three-fold worldly miseries, those who are wandering about deluded in this desolate desert in search of life-giving water—for them, here is the triumphant message of *Shankara* which points out the soothing Ocean of Nectar known as *Brahama*, the One without a second, within easy reach, and to lead them out to Liberation.

॥ इति शङ्कराचार्यविरचितं विवेकचूडामणिः ॥
iti śaṅkarācāryaviracitaṁ vivekacūḍāmaṇiḥ
Composed by Shankarāchārya, this was the Text of Vivekachūdāmani
[the Fiery Crest-Jewel of Wisdom]

ॐ तत्सत् — aum tat-sat
AUM, That One [Alone Is] Real

www.ingramcontent.com/pod-product-compliance
Lightning Source LLC
Chambersburg PA
CBHW030333100526
44592CB00010B/679
* 9 7 8 1 9 4 5 7 3 9 7 9 8 *